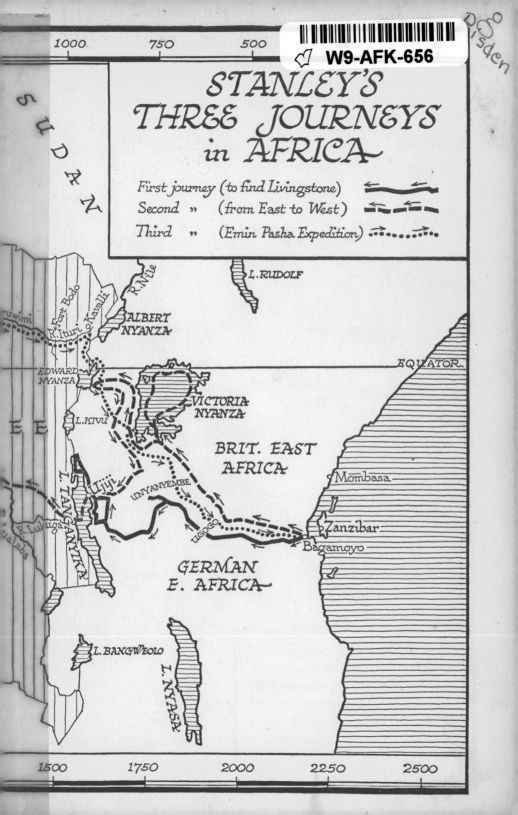

STANLEY'S THREE JOURNEYS in AFRICA

First journey (to find Livingstone)
Second " (from East to West)
Third " (Emin Pasha Expedition)

BULA MATARI

TRANSLATED FROM THE GERMAN BY
EDEN AND CEDAR PAUL

HENRY M. STANLEY

JACOB WASSERMANN

BULA MATARI

STANLEY
CONQUEROR OF A CONTINENT

TRANSLATED FROM THE GERMAN BY
EDEN AND CEDAR PAUL

LIVERIGHT·INC·PUBLISHERS
NEW YORK

CONTENTS

ILLUSTRATIONS

INTRODUCTION BY THE AUTHOR

A GOOD while ago, some of my friends asked me what I was working at. When I told them that I wanted to write a life of Henry Morton Stanley and had, with this end in view, been studying the subject for several years, they were very much surprised. What, they inquired, could interest me in a man whose doings had been of little moment in his lifetime and would leave no conspicuous traces in history—a man whose name had already lapsed into oblivion? I dissented from these opinions. Stanley's name, I rejoined, was haunted by that melody of fame which arouses responses in the unconscious; it was characterised by the rhythms which derive from a mention by millions upon millions of tongues; and what they styled "oblivion" was no more than a passing forgetfulness. Of course, they conceded, they might be mistaken in their judgment of the man and his work; but it seemed to them that neither the man nor the work had been unique, representative, exemplary. What, then, distinguished Stanley, asked one of them, from the numberless worthy pioneers who had explored the African continent during the latter half of the nineteenth century; men as brave and self-sacrificing as he, but less pretentious, and equipped with far higher scientific qualifications? Why give him the preference over a Nachtigal or a Schweinfurth, a Rohlfs or a Livingstone, a Baker or a Casati (to say nothing of a hundred others)? "Granted that Stanley is your hobby," said this critic somewhat mockingly, "at least you will agree that the features in him that have attracted you need not necessarily convince us of the man's importance!"

My answer was that I did not feel called upon to justify my undertaking. Certainly this particular explorer had a fascination for me, and there was, presumably, some deep-lying cause for the feeling he aroused. Maybe purely psychological issues were at work; something in his character, in his type, perhaps in the epoch. "Still," I added, "youthful impressions have undoubtedly played their part in the matter. Stanley's triumphs were gained when I was an adolescent; the whole world was talking of him then; he was the hero of the lads of my generation; his name was a trumpet-call; his mere existence stirred us as a child is stirred by a fairy-tale."

"So be it, at that date," intervened another of my friends; "but now the romance has been dispelled. His picture is but one among many others, faded and dusty, hung in an out-of-the-way part of the gallery, which no one ever visits. To us, at any rate, Stanley is an empty name. What is he to you? A geographer? A discoverer? An adventurer? Explain to us the lure."

An awkward question! How can we account for the lure which the destiny of one among thousands exerts upon our minds? Why should this career have been a revelation to the man's contemporaries; and why has the lapse of half a century thrown such a light upon his image that it is neither rendered deceptive by proximity, nor yet caricatured by remoteness? It was hard to explain, but I wanted to explain; so I spoke of the re-markable incidents of his life; of his exceptional talents; his colossal energy; his superhuman tenacity; his rare faculty for command, which was extraordinary in a man risen from the ranks; above all, of his amazing in-tuition, made manifest in all his foolhardy schemes, and guiding him, as a sleep-walker is guided, through mani-fold perils. There has always been something anachro-nistic, for me, about H. M. Stanley. To speak of him merely as a traveller or an explorer is deceptive; we do him more justice when we regard him as the founder of a colony; in truth he was a belated condottiere or con-quistador. During the sixteenth century he would have made history in quite another fashion than was possible to one born into a lukewarm and jejune era. His kinship with the great navigators and land-stormers who flour-ished between 1500 and 1700 is conspicuous. The mod-ern scientist devoted to the service of what is called civilisation (he was fond of the word) was in him con-tinually overridden by the man of action and the con-queror.

"Agreed, agreed!" exclaimed the youngest of those present at this friendly though perplexing discussion. "I do not dispute the soundness of what you have been say-ing; and all the same I doubt whether you have adduced a sufficient reason for entering upon so arduous a task. You spoke of a deep-lying cause, but I think the cause is superficial, or not deep enough to warrant the undertak-ing. There must have been some definite idea at work, a conceptual theme; for the existence of something of the kind is characteristic of your literary undertakings. They invariably have, so to say, a focus on which the light-rays are concentrated."

"Yes," I answered, "you are right; and, even while you were speaking, the 'focus' of my *Stanley* became plainer to me. Let me try to formulate my aim. Such men as he are, through and through, men of action. Their lives are, in each instance, one long concatenation of deeds. Take Stanley, for example. Scarcely is one action completed, than he is in the throes of beginning the next; and every link is fired by the same passion, animated by the same presence of mind, instinct with the same reso-lution. When the moment comes for reflection, his thoughts are relevant to actions and not to other thoughts. As substitutes for what religious folk sometimes call 'collection' and for spiritual contemplation, Stanley has the traditional pietism of the British puritans, the primi-tive faith of a mind extraordinarily simple and straight-forward, though subject to interesting transformations under the pricks of destiny.

"Now I want, in the first place, to show that the urge towards activity (ostensibly so practical, so fruit-ful, so mundane, and so utilitarian) can, when unduly intensified, lead to a positive frenzy in which the doer is really 'beside himself'; with the result that his actions do not merely lack the much-vaunted foundation of reality, but unavoidably and automatically culminate in the realm of the preposterous. Next I wish, as a logical inference from the foregoing, to demonstrate the mys-terious tragedy of this, as of all activity, so that what are called action and the life of action are destructive to the whole being of the doer unless he finds some inward

xii

counterpoise to action. Activity in and by itself, however broad in scope, can never establish for any one that stable mental equilibrium which alone can make existence bearable. Thus the more a man becomes immersed in unbalanced activities, the more does he lose the faculty for such action as is really worth while. Cannot we study the phenomenon of action dying at the root, of a puzzling loss of the true essence of personality, in the men of action who have been most renowned in history —in Alexander, in Attila, in Cæsar, in Napoleon, in Cromwell? At some particular moment in their career, we note that, of a sudden, for reasons that at first elude us, madness and destruction overwhelm them? Do we not know that a merchant, a manufacturer, a civil servant, who has for decades been engaged in the same daily round, will inexplicably break down when the day of retirement comes and inactivity is forced upon him?

"I am sure you will not suspect me of advocating quietism. My concern is with the balance between doing and being, or rather with the impossibility of achieving this balance in the contemporary world; and in that sense Stanley's figure has become symbolical for me. The adventurous elements intrude into life from without. Haphazard, as it were, are Stanley's varying fortunes and extraordinary achievements: his glimpses of unfamiliar and stupendous landscapes; the warmth and colour of exotic wanderings and travel through a wilderness where, before him, no European had set foot and which had been closed to civilised man since the first days of creation; the tribal extravagances and the uncanny religious rites of the Dark Continent. Doubtless such things were new and strange to Stanley; but new

xiii

and strange had been the experiences of Columbus and of many another of those who forced their way beyond the boundaries of the then known world. What made things so different for Stanley from what they were for the men engaged in conquest and discovery when the Middle Ages were over and the New Times were in the article of birth, was that Stanley's mind had been formed in a European or (if you will) European-American community; in a community which never allows its sons even for an hour to follow the promptings of the heart without reserve, which keeps them in bondage by invisible ties, dictates their resolves, inoculates them with laws and moral regulations, prescribes for them standards of social behaviour, allows them only just so much time and just so much money as it thinks proper, and will promptly outlaw them and destroy them if they disobey an injunction or overstep a mark.

"Stanley, therefore, was not a free spirit; he was not a bred-in-the-bone condottiere; he could not disregard the instructions of the man who had commissioned him, nor shake off the authority of the land where he had been born and the country in which he had been nationalised; he was a salaried employee quite as much as if he had been sitting at a desk editing a newspaper. Europe-America was his chief, was the 'limited company' to which he was accountable. One feels that he drags a lengthening chain. Five thousand miles from London and ten thousand from New York it clanks along after him at every footstep through the African forest, where, even in the boundless wild, he is but a subordinate. By temperament he was a man to found empires; and indeed he came near to establishing the Congo State with Henry M. Stanley as its undisputed ruler. Certainly this was his dream—and, instead, he had to pen books, to compile popularly written accounts of his travels. This was the new feature about the man: that the explorer and empire-builder was, first, last, and all the time, a reporter and a journalist. This made his work scintillating, enigmatical, and, from a certain outlook, magnificent. It gave him the stamp of an improviser, an adventurer, without parallel among the men who were in other respects of the same kidney.

"For the like reason his fate was so tragical, overshadowed by the doom of measureless activity. Again and again I was impressed by this conviction. I was seized with the longing to wrest his figure from the past, in which it was already mouldering, to cleanse it from the dust which clung to it and hid it from the world. Likely enough, however, I might have hesitated much longer before setting my hand to the task, had it not been for a strange experience which powerfully influenced my imagination and overcame my inhibitions. I do not know whether I shall be able to make the circumstances clear to you. For several weeks I had been much occupied in the study of the legends of the saints, and among them I came across the story of the life of St. Elizabeth of Hungary. I read how, after the death of her husband, the Landgrave of Thuringia, she was at length enabled to realise the Franciscan ideal of unconditional poverty. Breaking with her family, abandoning her children, stripped to the skin, on an ice-cold night in winter, she left the fortress where she had been living and took shelter among the barrels and lumber in a lean-to behind a wayside tavern. She had wantoned in charity and benevolence; had, to the great annoyance of her relatives, given away all her possessions, money, clothing, trinkets, stores of provisions; had gone in these matters to greater lengths than had any member of the ruling caste before her. The craving for unbalanced, unmeasured activity had taken possession of her, had become an end in itself, followed its own laws, a force which drove instead of being guided by her will. The image of the gently nurtured young princess, whom immoderate activity had plunged into the abyss of unmitigated suffering, haunted me. Always I pictured her among the dirty barrels in the shed behind that miserable pot-house; and, immense though the distance may seem to you from the vision of St. Elizabeth to the vision of Stanley, the remoteness exists only in the objective world. In my own mind it was traversed in the brief instant needed for a shudder. . . ."

BULA MATARI

*

STANLEY

CONQUEROR OF A

CONTINENT

CHAPTER ONE

CHILDHOOD AND YOUTH

STANLEY'S account of his childhood, given with a wealth
of bitter detail in the *Autobiography* whose later parts
are fragmentary, reads like one of Dickens's novels.
Nor is this surprising, since his youth belonged to the
early Victorian period which brought forth *David Cop-
perfield* and *Oliver Twist*. Within a particular epoch, individuals have on the average a destiny characteristic
of that epoch. Unless such books were historical monuments, they would never become, so to say, "exhibits"
bearing witness to the typical features of the era to
which they belong. Moreover, an author so outstanding
as Charles Dickens influences the style of the views of
his contemporaries and his successors.

John Rowlands (the original name of the man who
became famous as "Henry Morton Stanley") was born
in North Wales sometime between 1840 and 1842. To
his Welsh origin may perhaps be ascribed his imper-
turbability, his tenacity, his ruggedness, his peasant

3

toughness of fibre. Since he occasionally speaks of his "dishonourable" birth, we may assume him to have been an illegitimate child. Anyhow, he knew nothing of his father, and saw his mother only two or three times. Left, for good or for evil, to the care of unloving relatives, he grew up like one of the lower animals: no home life, never a kindly word, none to give him help and sustenance. When he was six years old, he was sent to the St. Asaph Union Workhouse, one of those notorious institutions pilloried for all time in the pages of *Oliver Twist*.

"It is a fearful fate, that of a British outcast," writes Stanley in this connexion, "because the punishment afflicts the mind and breaks the heart. It is worse than that which overtakes the felonious convict, because it appears so unmerited, and so contrary from that which the poor have a right to expect from a Christian and civilised people. . . . It took me some time to learn the unimportance of tears in a workhouse."

James Francis, to whose tender mercies the little boy was now entrusted, had been a working miner until he met with an accident which cost him his left hand. Being a man of some education, he was appointed Master of St. Asaph Union Workhouse, where he remained for many years, acting also as instructor to the children committed to the institution. "Soured by misfortune, brutal of temper, and callous of heart," he became more and more savage, more and more relentless in his cuffings and slappings, or in "deliberate punishment with the birch, ruler, or cane, which, with cool malice, he inflicted." At last it was discovered that he had lost his reason, and he died in a madhouse. The reader will have no difficulty in imagining what children had to suffer at the hands of this remorseless lunatic. It would be superfluous to multiply instances of brutality, and I will content myself with quoting the story of one affair which left a scar upon young Rowland's imagination:

"When I reached my eleventh year, the king of the school for beauty and amiability was a boy of about my own age named Willie Roberts. Some of us believed that he belonged to a very superior class to our own. His coal-black hair curled in profusion over a delicately moulded face of milky whiteness. His eyes were soft and limpid, and he walked with a carriage which tempted imitation. Beyond these indications of him I remember little, for just then I fell ill with some childish malady which necessitated my removal to the infirmary, where I lay for weeks. But as I was becoming convalescent I was startled by a rumour that he had suddenly died.

"When I heard that his body was in the dead-house I felt stricken with a sense of irreparable loss. As the infirmary opened upon the courtyard which contained our morgue, some of the boys suggested that it might be possible to view him, and, prompted by a fearful curiosity to know what death was like, we availed ourselves of a

5

favourable opportunity, and entered the house with quaking hearts. The body lay on a black bier, and, covered with a sheet, appeared uncommonly long for a boy. One of the boldest drew the cloth aside, and at the sight of the waxen face with its awful fixity we started back, gazing at it as if spellbound. There was something grand in its superb disregard of the chill and gloom of the building, and in the holy calm of the features. It was the face of our dear Willie, with whom we had played, and yet not the same, for an inexplicable aloofness had come over it. We yearned to cry out to him to wake, but dared not, for the solemnity of his countenance was appalling.

"Presently the sheet was drawn farther away, and we then saw what one of us had insinuated might be seen. The body was livid, and showed scores of dark weals. One glance was enough, and, hastily covering it, we withdrew, with minds confirmed in the opinion that signs of violence would appear after death as testimonies against him who was guilty of it. After what we had seen, it would have been difficult for any one to have removed from our minds the impression that Francis was accountable for Willie's death."

The moral energy of John Rowlands's temperament is manifested by the way in which, during this period of suffering, he strove for religious conviction; and we shall see that, in adult life, piety was one of his most conspicuous traits. In apparently desperate situations, of which there was no lack in his career, it was his ability to lift his eyes reverently towards the Divine Being in whom he believed that saved him from despair. This must never be forgotten. It is one of the primary elements of a character whose elasticity and persistent readiness for action at all times and in all places would otherwise be hard to understand.

"I now conceived God to be a very real personage, as active to-day as in Biblical periods in His supervision of mundane concerns. I fancied God's Presence visible in very small events, but, to obtain the Divine interposition in one's favour, it was necessary to earnestly solicit it, and to be worthy of it by perfect sinlessness. . . . I made a grand effort to free myself from my vanity and pride. I compelled myself for a season to make the sacrifices demanded of me. . . . I rose at midnight to wrestle in secret with my wicked self, and, while my school-fellows reposed, I was on my knees, laying my heart bare before Him who knows all things. . . . I believed in the immediate presence of Angels who were deputed to attend us for our protection; that the emissaries of the Evil One ranged about during the darkness of the night, seeking to wreak their spite against those averse to them; and I believed that the frightful dreams from which we sometimes suffered were due to their machinations."

We should err were we to suppose that the man who penned these reminiscences at the age of fifty must have touched them up, even unconsciously. They ring true as youthful endeavours to escape from the miseries of workhouse life and a forlorn situation. Besides, they are the appropriate expression of national characteristics; embodying, indeed, the relationships of an individual to the Divine Powers, yet not simply as an individual, but as member of a community having an unalterable attitude in such matters. "It would be impossible to reveal myself, according to the general promise involved in the title of this book, if I were to be silent regarding my religious convictions. Were I to remain silent, the true key to the actions of my life would be missing." These words cannot be misunderstood, even by those who may doubt whether they are an exhaustive statement of the truth; and it matters not whether they express a protective coloration of the writer's personality, or proceed from its inmost core.

Here is a touching avowal:

"I must have been twelve ere I knew that a mother was indispensable to every child. To most boys of twelve such a simple fact must have been obvious, but, as my grandsire and nurse had sufficed for my earliest wants, the necessity for a mother had not been manifest to me. Now that I was told my mother had entered the house with two children, my first feeling was one of exultation that I also had a mother, and a half-brother and a half-sister, and the next was one of curiosity to know what they were like, and whether their arrival portended a change in my condition.

8

"Francis came up to me during the dinner-hour, when all the inmates were assembled, and, pointing out a tall woman with an oval face, and a great coil of dark hair behind her head, asked me if I recognised her.

" 'No, sir,' I replied.

" 'What, do you not know your own mother?'

"I started, with a burning face, and directed a shy glance at her, and perceived that she was regarding me with a look of cool, critical scrutiny. I had expected to feel a gush of tenderness towards her, but her expression was so chilling that the valves of my heart closed as with a snap."

From this admirable pen-portrait in miniature, a human soul—that of the artist—looks forth.

At length life in St. Asaph Union Workhouse became insupportable. Matters were brought to a head, when Stanley was fifteen, by an act of rebellion, a hammer-and-tongs conflict between himself and James Francis, in which he laid the tyrant out, and had no resource but to flee from the inferno where he had spent nearly ten years of childhood. He made his way to Pfynnon Benno, a village where he had relatives. At Brynford, not far away, a cousin named Moses Owen was master at the National School. Owen agreed to engage him as pupil-teacher, his pupils being boys of his own age whom he had to instruct in history and geography, conning the lessons beforehand during the night hours. Cousin Moses, however, had a difficult temper.

9

After nine months young John Rowlands could not put up with it any longer, and went to Tremeirchion to stay with his Aunt Mary, Moses Owen's mother. She was willing to house him in return for his doing chores on the farm, but "was an exacting mistress and an unsympathetic relative, though, in every other sense, she was an estimable woman." She unbent only on Sundays. "What I lacked most to make my youth complete in joy was affection." Mary Owen was proud; "they were all exceedingly proud in Tremeirchion."

As farm-hand, John had to mind the sheep on Craig Fawr, and, alone on the mountain with his charges, he would let his imagination draw fanciful pictures of the destiny awaiting him. These were his happiest hours. After a while, however, another aunt appeared on the scene, visiting Tremeirchion from Liverpool, and declared herself able to find the youth a promising situation in Liverpool. He was loth to quit the Welsh hills, as if foreseeing that he was now to set out upon lifelong wanderings, a breathless hunt for happiness and success.

Success was by no means the immediate outcome of the remove to Liverpool. The man who was to give him employment proved a humbug; and his relatives, though kindly, were impecunious. He spent weeks tramping the streets in search of a job, and at length secured one at a haberdasher's on a wage of five shillings a week, his duties to last from seven in the morning till nine at night, and to consist of shop-sweeping, lamp-trimming, window-

10

polishing, etc. The heavy shutters proving too much for his strength, he was laid up after two months, and his place was promptly filled by an older and heftier youth. After a week in bed, he had to resume the hunt for work. His search led him to the docks, where the water-side boys taught him the difference between a first-class clipper and an ordinary emigrant packet, and how to distinguish between a vessel turned out from a Boston shipyard and one of British build.

Near the docks he got engaged at a butcher's stall. The proprietor was a pleasant-looking man, but John Rowlands was under the immediate supervision of the foreman, "a hard, sinister-faced Scotsman," one of those sadistic slave-drivers who are common in all petty-bourgeois occupations. This man made his life a burden to him. His daily task was the carrying of baskets of fresh meat to the vessels in the docks, and while he was thus engaged something happened to turn him into a new course. One day he was sent to the packet-ship "Windermere" with a basket of provisions and a note to the captain. While the latter was reading it, the youth gazed admiringly at the rich furniture of the cabin, the gilded mirrors, and the glittering cornices. Aware of his interest, the master mariner asked him whether he would like to sail as cabin-boy on the "Windermere," offering five dollars a month and an outfit. Why should he hesitate? Did not this open up a chance of realising the shepherd lad's dreams? His home surroundings in Liv-

11

erpool were extremely unattractive. He had, indeed, to overcome a certain feeling of affection for his native land and family. "If my discontent had not been so great . . . I had clung to them like a limpet to a rock," he writes picturesquely in his autobiography. His aunt and his uncle tried to dissuade him. "But there rose up before me a great bulk of wretchedness, my slavish dependence upon relatives who could scarcely support themselves, my unfortunate employment, my cousin Teddy's exasperating insolence, my beggar's wardrobe, and daily diet of contumely." He determined to accept the captain's offer and sailed three days later.

He had soon good reason to regret his decision. Not even at the workhouse had he been so badly treated as on the "Windermere." Thrashings and hunger, hunger and thrashings. "Seize that scrubbing-broom, you —— joskin! Lay hold of it, I say, and scrub, you —— son of a sea-cook. Scrub like ——! Scrub until you drop! Sweat, you —— swab. Dig into the deck, you —— —— white-livered lime-juicer." Such were the adjurations of the mate, and the foremast hands were little kinder. All the horrors made familiar to readers of the old sea-literature and the new, from Marryat to Jack London and Traven's *Totenschiff*, were repeated or anticipated on the "Windermere." There was no further question of Rowlands being cabin-boy. Lured on board by the splendours of the cabin furnishings, he was to be ordinary ship-boy and common drudge, the plan being to treat

12

him so roughly that he would desert at the first port, leaving behind his outfit and the promised five dollars a month in wages. He did, in fact, vanish into the purlieus of the town five days after the vessel reached New Orleans. Since he had not run away instantly, the policy of hazing him was continued in harbour until it had the desired effect.

This first Atlantic voyage remained one of his gloomiest memories. The proletarian relationship towards his environment, as revealed to him by his experiences in the American ship, is characterised in the following remarkable passage: "From this date began, I think, the noting of a strange coincidence, which has since been so common with me that I accept it as a rule. When I pray for a man, it happens that at that moment he is cursing me; when I praise, I am slandered; if I command, I am reviled; if I feel affectionate or sympathetic towards one, it is my fate to be detested or scorned by him. I first noticed this curious coincidence on board the 'Windermere.' I bore no grudge and thought no evil of any person ... extolled the courage, strength, and energy of my shipmates ... but invariably they damned my eyes, my face, my heart, my soul, my person, my nationality. . . . It was a new idea that came across my mind. My memory clung to it as a novelty, and at every instance of the coincidence I became more and more confirmed that it was a rule, as applied to me. . . . In the

13

meantime, my mind was becoming as impervious to such troubles as a swan's back to a shower of rain."

Although the underlying assumption of naivety may, in the foregoing citation, seem a trifle overdrawn, this particular attitude of a man towards his fellows could hardly be expressed in more striking terms. It is the attitude of a man of action who will be lost if he does not learn how to mistrust. Measureless confidence at the outset must be a step on the way towards defensiveness and reserve. Such an avowal as the one I have quoted is only possible to a person endowed with genuine simplicity—and a childlike, a countrified simplicity was eminently characteristic of H. M. Stanley.

There is a touch of comedy (quite involuntary comedy) in his account of his visit to a brothel in the company of the other ship-boy, Harry, a lad of his own age, but more sophisticated. This was during the few days at New Orleans, before he had made up his mind to desert. Bear in mind that the memoirs were written by a man of fifty, who had become world-famous. "Now when I stepped on the levee, frisky as a lamb, I was about as good as a religious observance of the Commandments can make one. To me those were the principal boundary-stones that separated the region of right from that of wrong. Between the greater landmarks, there were many well-known minor indexes; but there were some which were almost undiscoverable to one so young and untravelled as I was. Only the angelically im-

14

maculate could tread along the limits of right and wrong without a misstep. After dinner we sauntered through a few streets, in a state of sweet content, and, by and by, entered another house, the proprietress of which was extremely gracious. Harry whispered something to her, and we were shown to a room called a parlour. Presently, there bounced in four gay young ladies, in such scant clothing that I was speechless with amazement. My ignorance of their profession was profound, and I was willing enough to be enlightened; but when they proceeded to take liberties with my person, they seemed to me to be so appallingly wicked that I shook them off and fled out of the house. Harry followed me, and, with all the arts he could use, tried to induce me to return; but I would as soon have jumped into the gruel-coloured Mississippi as have looked into the eyes of those giggling wantons again. My disgust was so great that I never, in after years, could overcome my repugnance to females of that character."

There is no reason for scepticism as to his account of this matter, even if he be always a little inclined to depict himself and his doings as worthy of constituting a model for others. Although he was not entirely free from bumptiousness (in part the expression of his Welsh blood, and in part the outcome of his sufferings in youth), he invariably did his utmost to live up to his convictions of what was right. His description of his life in New Orleans contains a charming account of his

15

acquaintanceship with a girl masquerading as a boy. He spent several days and nights with her, sharing a bed. Surprised to notice that she never undressed, and becoming aware of various other peculiarities, he at length put two and two together and realised the true sex of his stable-companion. Like himself she had run away from England as a "ship-boy," like himself she had deserted on reaching America; and he had chummed up with her out of sympathy. The evening after their explanation, Alice Heaton, who had hitherto been "Dick" to him, had vanished from his ken, and he never saw or heard of her again. At the time of the chance meeting the boy and the girl were both about fifteen. The affair is told with such delicacy that the reader is left with no doubt in his mind as to the faithfulness of the narration. It is a trifling detail in the story of one who was to do great things, but it inspires absolute confidence as to its truth.

In no other era than during the middle of the nineteenth century could a young man's life-history have developed along the lines followed by that of John Rowlands. Every turn in his fortunes, the nature of the successive incidents, social relationships, modes of intercourse, wage-earning occupations, sentimental ties formed under stress of a peculiar moral code, the bourgeois complexion of the individual mind and of society at large—all, all without exception, bears the imprint of the age. As we look back, much of what

16

Stanley has to tell is charged with a romantic flavour. This is not exclusively the outcome of that distance in time which, in space, lends blueness to the hills; and yet the effect is analogous, for all worldly happenings, which to those subject to them seem merely anecdotal, tend to assume a romantic air when they have become part of the mighty current of history. Thus the circumstances under which young John Rowlands, the homeless runaway, was engaged as store-clerk in the employ of the firm of Speake and McCreary, wholesale and commission merchants, and in which he was subsequently adopted as son by the wealthy merchant Henry Stanley, read as if taken from a novel by Rider Haggard or Ouïda. Yet they are none the less true for that, their strange aroma being given to them by the style of the epoch to which they belong—a style which is often more faithfully reflected by writers of moderate ability than by the great masters of the literary world.

The first conversation between John and the elder Stanley is typical. The former found the latter seated in front of Speake and McCreary's place, deep in the morning paper. John accosted Stanley, inquired for a job, gave a sketch of his recent adventures.

"As you are the first gentleman I have seen, I thought I would apply to you for work, or ask you for advice as to how to get it."

"So," he ejaculated, tilting his chair back again. "You are friendless in a strange land, eh, and want

17

work to begin making your fortune, eh? Well, what
work can you do? Can you read? What book is that
in your pocket?"

"It is my Bible, a present from our bishop. Oh,
yes, sir, I can read."

"Let me see your Bible. . . . Can you write
well?"

"Yes, sir, a good round-hand, as I have been told."

"Then let me see you mark that coffee-sack, with
the same address you see on the one near it. There is
the marking-pot and brush."

In a few minutes, John had addressed twenty sacks;
and Mr. Stanley, equally charmed by such readiness and
dexterity, and by the Bible bearing a personal inscription from an English bishop, was not slow to recommend
this alert and well-behaved youngster to his friend
Speake. Bible and coffee-sack; there you have the United
States of America in a nutshell—or at any rate the
United States of those days shortly before the Civil
War.

Mr. Stanley was a broker who dealt between
planters up-river and merchants in New Orleans, and
traded through a brother with Havana and other West
Indian ports. He was married to a woman much younger
than himself, who took a fancy to John Rowlands, so
that even before the adoption (which came after Mrs.
Stanley's untimely death) John was regarded as almost
one of the family. The kindliness with which he was now

18

universally treated ministered to his self-confidence. He grew aware of developing capacities which he felt called upon to foster. Hitherto he had suffered from the anxiety that gnaws at the heart of the despised and rejected; now he was freed from this incubus. "The view of the sky," he writes, "was as freely mine as another's. These American rights did not depend on depth of pocket, or stature of a man, but every baby had as much claim to them as the proudest merchant."

America was still, to a great extent, the country which European idealists believed it to be; it was still the Promised Land of German revolutionary refugees. Had Stanley never left Britain, it seems likely enough that he would have been stifled in that insular atmosphere. Reflecting upon how near he came to lacking the fortitude needed in order to disregard his Liverpool relatives' advice and to ship aboard the "Windermere," he pens some remarkable words upon the importance of being able to say "No!" on occasions. "In my opinion the courage to deliver a proper 'No' ought to be cultivated as soon as a child's intelligence is sufficiently advanced. The few times I have been able to say it have been productive of immense benefit to me, though, to my shame be it said, I yearned to say 'Yes.' " A striking avowal, this; for Stanley's career often brought him into situations where there could be no compromise between Yes and No. Like many men who rise from the ranks, he was endowed with an exceptional faculty for

19

self-education; and his piety, too, though not perhaps the most decisive factor in his make-up, went far beyond mere lip-service and respect for tradition.

He describes his patron's young wife as "the first lady I ever conversed with." It would seem that she must have stirred his ambition to become a man of culture, for, with the passion natural to him in all his undertakings, he now rushed into the world of books, devouring Gibbon's *Decline and Fall,* Spenser's *Faery Queen,* Pope's *Homer,* Milton's *Paradise Lost,* Plutarch's *Lives,* etc., etc. His enthusiasm for intellectual development gave him a lift in the social world. The South before the War of Secession was like the Latin countries of Europe in its light-heartedness and cheerfulness. Since there were such multitudes of Negro slaves, almost every White was one of the lords of the earth; and, as if in preparation for the coming struggle, all the Whites formed, so to say, one great family. This solidarity was manifested, as a private instance of a public principle, in John Rowlands's personal relationships with the Stanleys. Mr. Stanley had to depart on a long journey, and the youth continued to visit Mrs. Stanley on Sundays. When the latter was taken suddenly and desperately ill, Rowlands, wishing to give the overworked maidservant help in the housework and the nursing, asked for a few days' leave of absence; and, this being refused, he impulsively threw up his job. Though that did not avail to save Mrs. Stanley's life, the quixotic action was really the main reason why Mr. Stanley subsequently adopted him. As John watched by the deathbed of the woman he had so much admired, he slowly came to understand (again and again in the autobiography we encounter these original reflections) "how even the most timid woman could smilingly welcome Death, and willingly yield to his cold embrace. I had hitherto had a strong belief that those who died had only been conquered through a sheer want of will on their part ('All men think all men mortal but themselves'), and that the monster, with its horrors of cold, damp earth, and worms, needed only to be defied to be defeated of its prey." It may be true enough that for each one of us it is naught but his own strength which enables him to cling to life.

Since Mr. Stanley was away, and might not be back for months, John Rowlands had to seek work wherever he could find it. But work was hard to come by. "I descended to odd jobs, such as the sawing of wood, and building of wood-piles for private families." For a month he was sick-nurse to the captain of a brig in the harbour. The money thus earned enabled him to take passage by steamboat to St. Louis, and he went thither full of hope, expecting to find Mr. Stanley. "All men must pass through the bondage of necessity before they emerge into life and liberty." But luck was against him. On reaching St. Louis he was dumbfounded to learn that Mr. Stanley had returned to New Orleans a week be-

fore. He had hardly a cent left in his pocket, and was
not slow to decide that his only resource was to make
his way south once more. The Mississippi drew him like
a magnet, and he offered to work his way down the river
on one of the flat-boats or scows laden with timber from
the primeval forest. He was to be general help, had to
peel potatoes, stir mush, carry water, wash tin pans,
scour the plates, and sometimes lend his strength at pull-
ing one of the tremendously long oars.

After his return to New Orleans there followed an
idyl, perhaps the only idyl in the life of Henry Morton
Stanley, the only considerable period in which he was
happy and free from care. I might pass the matter over
in silence, were it not for the light thrown by this idyl
on the development of his character. Had it not been
for the tenderness and love shown him at this juncture
by his adoptive father, whose name he now assumed, I
doubt whether Stanley would ever have acquired the
spiritual self-command, the inward consolidation, which
were essential to the playing of the part destiny had
assigned him. When the tale is told, indeed, when the
battle is lost and won, what we call a man's "mission"
or "vocation" seems guided by a flawless logic. In his
earliest dreams, John Rowlands had often pictured to
himself what a happy boy he would be if he only had
a father or a mother. "Now, as an answer from the
Invisible, came this astounding revelation of His power."
The older man pledged himself to take charge of the

younger man's future. "Before I could quite grasp all that this declaration meant for me, he had risen, taken me by the hand, and folded me in a gentle embrace. My senses seemed to whirl about for a few half-minutes; and finally I broke down, sobbing from extreme emotion. It was the only tender action I had ever known, and, what no amount of cruelty could have forced from me, tears poured in a torrent under the influence of the simple embrace."

Next come some practical details. "Most of the day was spent in equipping me for the new position I was to assume. I was sumptuously furnished with stylish suits ... toilet articles to which I was an utter stranger, such as toothbrushes and nailbrushes, and long white shirts, resembling girls' frocks, for nightdresses. It had never entered my head before that teeth should be brushed, or that a nailbrush was indispensable, or that a nightdress contributed to health and comfort!"

Like all those whose rise from unculture to culture has been sudden and quasi-miraculous (Kaspar Hauser, for instance), young Stanley had an amazing memory. Having scanned a column of figures once, he could repeat the whole series without fail. "My memory was frequently of great use to my father as an auxiliary to his memorandum-book of shipments, purchases, and sales." Mr. Stanley took young Henry with him on his business journeys, for the youth's powers of observation were to be trained. The conversations between the adoptive father and the adopted son, as recorded by the latter, show clearly that the elder Stanley was a man of taste and of wide education. In many respects, both as regards substance and form, they recall the conversations in Goethe's *Wanderjahre*. Even if we feel that caution necessitates pruning them of a good deal that may have been editorial adornment on the part of the writer of the *Autobiography*, enough will remain to justify the reverence felt by the disciple for one who had enabled him to find himself, and had launched him on a voyage of spiritual discovery. Such silent leaders, whom no one remembers when their work has been done, abound everywhere; and there has never been a great achievement but would, if traced to its primal sources, be found to spring from unknown names.

Yet there is a mystery enwrapping this relationship between the Stanleys. According to all that the younger man reports, his adoptive father must have been well-to-do. In a land and a climate where cholera, malaria, and other deadly diseases were rife, Mr. Stanley's business journeys involved perpetual risk. Yet he took no steps to safeguard the future of the youth who was henceforward called by his name. During the autumn of 1860, being about to sail for the West Indies, he arranged for Henry Morton (approaching twenty years of age) to stay for a while at a friend's plantation in Arkansas. This friend, Major Ingham, and young Stanley bade farewell to him on the Havana steamer. Father and son never saw

24

each other again, and from the day of parting Henry Morton Stanley was as poor and uncared for as John Rowlands had been before the romantic adoption. The only difference was that he now knew from personal experience what it could signify not to be poverty-stricken and fatherless. We are told that Mr. Stanley died suddenly in 1861, and that Henry Morton heard of his death long after. We get the impression that before the parting there must have been an estrangement, which the autobiographer shrouds in silence.

CHAPTER TWO

THE YEARS OF PREPARATION

———————

FOR a little while, Stanley felled timber on Major Ingham's estate, but a broil with the overseer (a rough fellow of the Legree type) led him to quit. Then, at Cypress Bend in Arkansas, he worked in the employment of a storekeeper named Altschul, of German-Jewish extraction. He was still there when the Civil War broke out, and the war-fever, sedulously disseminated by Southern propagandists and the local Press, spread even into the wilderness. It is the same old story; was the same across the Atlantic in the eighteen-sixties as here in Europe during 1914; was doubtless the same when the Hellenes took up arms against the Persians. In this matter, mankind seems unchangeable. Since landing in America, Stanley had found politics "repulsively dry," but now a friend of his own age, Dan Goree, explained the situation to him. Dan's father owned about one hundred and twenty slaves, worth from $500 to $1200 a head, and to deprive him (as the Abolitionists designed)

26

of property he had bought with hard cash would be pure robbery. That was why all the [White] people of the South were rising against the Northerners, and they would fight, to the last man. If Dan knew that the Northerners were at that time prepared to compensate the slave-owners should the slaves be liberated, he kept the information to himself, and Stanley was only to learn the fact after he had become a prisoner of war. Then, naturally, since he had a strong sense of justice, his views as to the relations between North and South underwent a radical change. But at this time, in the Southern atmosphere, the Southern outlook seemed reasonable to him. The general sentiment was bellicose. While the men, who would bear the heat and burden of the day, were not lacking in pugnacity, the women were in a raging fever, declaring themselves ready, should their men-folk prove backward, to go to the front and slaughter the Yankees. "In a land where the women are worshipped by the men, such language made men war-mad." Stanley was looked at askance, because he showed no great eagerness to volunteer. "About this time, I received a parcel which I half-suspected, as the address was written in a feminine hand, to be a token of some lady's regard; but on opening it, I discovered it to be a chemise and petticoat, such as a negro lady's-maid might wear. I hastily hid it from view, and retired to the back room, that my burning cheeks might not betray me to some onlooker. In the afternoon, Dr. Goree called, and was excessively cordial and kind. He asked me if I did not intend to join the valiant children of Arkansas to fight, and I answered 'Yes.' "

It was still a primitive sort of warfare, with an extremely inefficient commissariat (so that the men often went hungry), a pseudo-romantic camp life, actions fought without proper leadership under the guidance of zealous subordinates by soldiers armed at best with obsolete flintlocks. "The ammunition was rolled in cartridge-paper, which contained powder, a round ball, and three buckshot. When we had loaded, we had to tear the paper with our teeth, empty a little powder into the pan, lock it, empty the rest of the powder into the barrel, press paper and ball into the muzzle, and ram home." The general under whom Stanley served, Burgevine by name, was in later years commander of the mercenaries in the Imperial Chinese Army levied to suppress the Taiping rebellion. Dismissed by the Imperialists, he sought the service of the Taipings. He had conceived the idea of dethroning the Son of Heaven and becoming autocrat of the Middle Kingdom himself. He went so far as to try to tempt Gordon to join him as his accomplice. That was one of the reasons why Gordon left China, made his way to Egypt, and thus (through the instrumentality of Emin Pasha) came to play a part in Stanley's life-story. How marvellously entangled is the web of destiny! Under the searchlight of history this often becomes plain enough where men of note are

28

concerned, but it remains hidden from our eyes in the case of those who never rise to fame.

The years that ensued until Stanley reached the age of twenty-five were marked by a succession of hardships and privations. He writes: "Looking back upon the various incidents of these six years, though they appear disjointed enough, I can dimly see a connexion, and how one incident led to another, until the curious and somewhat involved design of my life, and its purpose, was consummated. But this enlistment was, as I conceive it, the first of many blunders; and it precipitated me into a veritable furnace, from which my mind would have quickly recoiled, had I but known what the process of hardening was to be. . . . I had to learn that what was unlawful to a civilian was lawful to a soldier. The 'Thou shalt not' of the Decalogue was now translated 'Thou shalt.' Thou shalt kill, lie, steal, blaspheme, covet, and hate; for, by whatsoever fine name they were disguised, every one practised these arts, from the President down to the private in the rear rank. . . . My only consolation, during this curious 'volte-face' in morality, was that I was an instrument in the strong, forceful grip of circumstance, and could no more free myself than I could fly. . . . The poetry of the military profession had departed under many pains."

An extremely modern outlook on war, this; and, indeed, the inborn humanism of the man is one of the most agreeable discoveries we make in the study of his hard-bitten character. Here is one of his descriptions of disciplinary punishment after the Prussian model: "I had seen unfortunate culprits horsed on triangular fence-rails, and jerked up by vicious bearers, to increase their pains; others, straddled ignominiously on poles; or fettered with ball and chain; or tied up with the painful buck and gag; or hoisted up by the thumbs; while no one was free of fatigue duty, or exempt from fagging to some one or other, the livelong day." Official supplies being short, he was initiated into the mysteries of foraging, "which, in army vocabulary, meant not only to steal from the enemy, but to exploit Secessionist sympathisers, and obtain for love or money some trifle to make life more enjoyable." To ingratiate himself with his comrades, he tried to outdo even the most expert of them at this art, and made a successful night raid upon a farm in order to secure the materials for a hearty Christmas dinner. "Secretly, I was persuaded that it was as wrong to rob a poor Unionist as a Secessionist; but the word 'foraging,' which, by general consent, was bestowed on such deeds, mollified my scruples."

We have the impression, often enough, that we are reading the utterances of some champion of pacifism, of a disciple of Tolstoy or Romain Rolland, although these thoughts were conceived many decades before the officially organised slaughter which is called war came to be stigmatised by such great teachers as no less criminal than private murder. Consider what Stanley writes of the battle of Shiloh (towards the end of which he was taken prisoner by the Northerners): "It was the first Field of Glory I had seen in my May of life, and the first time that Glory sickened me with its repulsive aspect, and made me suspect it was all a glittering lie. ... My thoughts reverted to the time when these festering bodies were idolised objects of their mothers' passionate love, their fathers standing by, half-fearing to touch the fragile little things, and the wings of civil law outspread to protect parents and children in their family loves, their coming and going followed with pride and praise, and the blessing of the Almighty overshadowing all. Then, as they were nearing manhood, through some strange warp of Society, men in authority summoned them from school and shop, field and farm, to meet in the woods on a Sunday morning for mutual butchery with the deadliest instruments yet invented, Civil Law, Religion, and Morality complaisantly standing aside, while ninety thousand young men, who had been preached and moralised to for years, were let loose to engage in the carnival of slaughter." If, in this matter, the Stanley of fifty is accurately recording the sentiments of the Stanley of twenty (and I believe that he is), the part he played in the battle of Shiloh cannot but remind us of that famous scene in the opening of Stendhal's *Chartreuse de Parme,* wherein the young hero, his mind in a maze, is wandering hither and thither over the battlefield of Waterloo.

Dirt, vermin, pestilence, horrors piled upon horrors, were what awaited him at Camp Douglas, the prison-pen near Chicago. The miseries of those interned there were unspeakable—as are all such miseries which give the lie direct to the pretences of Christian civilisation. The barns in which the men were housed swarmed with lice; dysentery and typhus began to rage; the sick prayed for death to relieve their sufferings. In the light of our own recent experiences, it is not without grim reflections that we read what Stanley wrote in 1894 of the scenes he had witnessed more than three decades earlier: "Just as the thirties were stupider and crueller than the fifties, and the fifties more bloody than the seventies, in the mercantile marine service, so a war in the nineties will be much more civilised than the Civil War of the sixties. Those who have survived that war, and have seen brotherly love re-established, and reconciliation completed, when they think of Andersonville, Libby, Camp Douglas, and other prisons, and of the bloodshed in 2261 battles and skirmishes, must in this present peaceful year needs think that a moral epidemic raged, to have made men so intensely hate then what they profess to love now." But for him these hardships were an indispensable schooling; they steeled his nerves, and developed his capacity for swift decisions in threatening situations.

32

At Camp Douglas, ere long, he was faced with an urgent moral dilemma. He was offered discharge from prison if he would enlist in the Union army. He hesitated a while, though feeling from moment to moment that another week in those plague-stricken surroundings would cost him his reason or his life. In the end his meditations turned him towards accepting the conditions of release. It was true that every American friend of his was a Southerner; his adoptive father had been a Southerner, which made him blind through gratitude. "I had a secret scorn for people who could kill one another for the sake of African slaves. There were no blackies in Wales, and why a sooty-faced nigger from a distant land should be an element of disturbance between white brothers was a puzzle to me. . . . Had the Southerners invaded Africa and made captives of the blacks, I might have seen some justice in decent and pious people declaiming against the barbarity. . . . But as I had seen the Negro in the South, he was a half-savage, who had been exported by his own countrymen, and sold in open market, agreeably to time-honoured custom. . . . So far as I knew of the matter, it was only the accident of a presidential election which had involved the North and the South in a civil war. . . ." He hung in the wind for a while, until at length, with several other prisoners, he decided to accept the terms of release, enrolled himself in the U. S. artillery service,

33

and, on June 4, 1862, was once more free to breathe fresh air.

His term with the Federals was of brief duration. He was already sickening with dysentery and malarial fever, and was sent to hospital immediately on arrival at Harpers Ferry. On June 22nd he was discharged as unfit for military service.

He had no further obligations to either army—but he had not a penny in his pocket. "A pair of blue military trousers clothed my nethers, a dark serge coat covered my back, and a mongrel hat my head. I knew not where to go; the seeds of disease were still in me, and I could not walk three hundred yards without stopping to gasp for breath." Fortunately, it was summer, and, though death seemed imminent, it did not kill him to lie at night under the stars. He thought only of food and shelter. "Hagerstown is but twenty-four miles from Harpers Ferry; but it took me a week to reach a farmhouse not quite half-way." There he got permission to shake down on some hay in an outhouse. "My lips were scaled with the fever, eyes swimming, face flushed red, under the layer of a week's dirt." Such a Lazarus could not be hunted away from the door. In Stanley's memory the farmer was enshrined as a Good Samaritan. Kindness, milk diet, then more generous food, aided by his own vitality, led to a rapid recovery. "Early in July I was able to assist in the last part of the harvest and to join in the harvest supper." He stayed with this friendly farmer till the middle of August, well fed and cared for, "and when I left him he insisted on driving me to Hagerstown, and paying my railway fare to Baltimore."

With these words the *Autobiography* closes. From that point in his life's journey until his great voyages of discovery begin, we have nothing available but a fragmentary journal and occasional sketches wherewith to trace his course. Thus there is a wide space over which something akin to darkness prevails. All that we are able to discern is unceasing restlessness, perpetual activity, a desperate struggle against the disfavour of fortune, and an indefeasible conviction that he will prevail. In every phase we get the impression of a man who is imperturbably and almost fanatically following his star; and this impression is all the stronger when (as here) details are lacking, and we are sure of nothing but the main trend.

In the autumn of the year 1862 he was "harvesting in Maryland." Then, for a time, he was one of the hands on an oyster schooner. Next his heart turned with longing towards his own kin—for he obviously had strong family feeling, which survived all rebuffs. At times he was animated by a veritable craving for the affection of his relatives, were it but the lukewarm affection shown him by his uncles and his aunts and his cousins, which had so often disappointed him in the past and was to disappoint him once again. Herein we cannot but see further testimony to the childlike piety and simplicity

35

which were his fundamental characteristics. What he should have foreseen, happened. When, in November, 1862, he reached Liverpool and made his way to Denbigh, where his mother lived, it was only to be told— arriving impecunious, shabbily clothed, and in poor health—that he was a disgrace to them in the eyes of their neighbours; and that the sooner they saw the last of him, the better pleased they would be.

During 1863 and 1864 he served in various ships, voyaging to the West Indies, Spain, and Italy. He was wrecked off Barcelona, and swam ashore naked. This adventure is condensed into a two-line passage in his diary. At Brooklyn, late in 1863, we have another laconic entry: "Boarding with Judge X. Judge drunk; tried to kill his wife with hatchet; attempted three times. —I held him down all night. Next morning, exhausted; lighted cigar in parlour; wife came down—insulted and raved at me for smoking in her house." The shortest of short stories! One might call it "Thumbnail Sketch of Manners and Customs, in Forty-Two Words."

In August, 1864, he enlisted in the U. S. Navy, on the receiving ship "North Carolina," was then assigned to the "Minnesota," and afterwards to the "Moses H. Stuyvesant," where he served in the capacity of ship's writer. It seems obvious that he only undertook this war service because he could earn better pay under better conditions than on merchant ships. In December, 1864, he was present when General Butler assailed Fort Fisher

from the sea, exploding beneath its walls a vessel laden
with powder. Next year he was on hand when another
expedition, under General Terry, attacked the same fort.
After a bombardment by the fleet, two thousand sailors
and marines were landed, but were repelled by a murderous fire. Fort Fisher was now taken, however, by a
simultaneous onslaught from the landward side. Stanley
described both these attacks in letters which were welcomed by the newspapers. It was his début as reporter.

We do not know under what conditions he finally
became a salaried reporter, nor for what newspaper, but
obviously the letters he had composed describing his
experiences as ship's writer in the Federal Navy paved
the way for this career, having made him one of the
familiars of the pen. In those days the newspaper reporter of the modern type was a rare figure. Newspapers
had not then become the leading power in the State.
Stanley was so isolated both spiritually and socially,
was so lonely a being, that he had no "pull" in journalistic circles. We can only suppose, therefore, that the impulse to become a reporter, one who describes the happenings of the day for public information, must have
come from the awakening of a dormant gift. He was by
nature a man of actualities; his eyes were peculiarly
fitted for the observation of the real in its dramatic manifestations; he always glimpsed the decisive features of
any happening, its popular superficies as one might say;
and he saw whatever was calculated to stimulate the folk

37

imagination. If there be any classicist of the newspaper world, it is Henry M. Stanley. He, if any writer, has given journalistic impressionism world-wide historical significance.

When, in April, 1865, the war came to an end, Stanley left the Navy, and had done with sea life for ever. Wanderings by land now had their turn, wanderings that led him far afield: St. Joseph, Missouri, across the plains, Indiana, Salt Lake City, Denver, Black Hawk, Omaha; such are the fugitive entries in his diary. He only felt at rest when he was in motion, impelled by an overflowing youthful energy and an innate love of novelty and adventure. In his later years he told how, during these days, his exuberant vigour was such, that when a horse stood in his path his impulse was, not to go round, but to jump over it. At Omaha he struck up acquaintance with the members of a theatrical troupe, and, at a benefit supper, got drunk for the first and only time in his life.

With W. H. Cook, in May, 1866, he started for Denver. "We bought some planking and tools, and, in a few hours, constructed a flat-bottomed boat. Having furnished it with provisions and arms against the Indians, towards evening we floated down the Platte River." Here we have the germ of Stanley's Congo voyage! "After twice upsetting, and many adventures and narrow escapes, we reached the Missouri River." From Omaha they travelled to Boston, where, in July,

38

1866, they took passage in a sailing-ship for Smyrna. They had planned to go far into Asia. Apparently the means for this harum-scarum adventure must have been obtained by Stanley out of his journalistic earnings, but we may presume that now likewise he was (in part, at any rate) to act as newspaper correspondent.

Ill-luck, however, dogged the heels of the expedition. In a fit of mischief, the American lad they had brought with them as attendant set fire to some brushwood. The flames spread, and threatened to set a near-by village ablaze. The inhabitants were in the mood to lynch these unwelcome travellers, and were appeased with difficulty. Then, in the wilds of the interior, they engaged a treacherous guide, who brought down on them a horde of Turcomans. The bandits flogged them, robbed them of the money they had with them ($1200) and their letter of credit, and made off with the travelling kit. The ill-used Americans were thereupon arraigned as malefactors, hustled from place to place for five days, and were saved from imminent death by the intervention of a benevolent old man. Through the friendly offices of a Mr. Peloso, agent of the Imperial Ottoman Bank, they were delivered from prison and sent to the Turkish capital. There the American minister and the American consul-general gave them ungrudging assistance. The bandits were arrested, tried, found guilty, and punished; and the Turkish Government refunded the stolen money.

"That," writes Dorothy Stanley in her capacity as editor of her husband's *Autobiography* and journals, "was the end of the Stanley-Cook exploration of Asia. The explorer's first quest had met a staggering set-back. But 'repulse is interpreted according to the man's nature' as Morley puts it; 'one of the differences between the first-rate man and the fifth-rate lies in the vigour with which the first-rate man recovers from this reaction, crushes it down, and flings himself once more into the breach.'"

Two years after the Civil War, the flooding of the North American continent with immigrants began. A stream of settlers poured unceasingly across the Western prairies. The Union Pacific Railroad was being pushed onward at the rate of four miles a day. The Powder River military road was being constructed to Montana, passing through the best hunting-grounds of the Sioux. Forts had to be erected along it, for the Indians were in a ferment, and there were attacks on the white settlers. In March, 1867, a force was dispatched under General Hancock, and the expectation was that there would be sharp fighting, so Stanley accompanied the expedition as correspondent of the *Missouri Democrat*. Hancock was an exception among leaders of expeditionary forces. He was a man of pacific temper, and freely imparted to Stanley the humane plans which, in the end, he was unable wholly to realise. What he hoped was to make the tribes parley, to detach the reconcilables from the irreconcilables, and to enter into treaties with the former. In actual fact, the hostile Sioux and Cheyennes were detached from their allies, the Kiowas, Arapahoes, and Comanches; but when some of the more bellicose chiefs stole away from the conference, and began outrages on the settlers, Hancock had no alternative but to retaliate by destroying their villages. The plains seethed with menace and occasional outbreaks, and a widespread Indian war seemed imminent.

In July, therefore, Congress sent a Peace Commission, headed by General Sherman, with a staff of distinguished officers, two chief Indian Commissioners, and Senator Henderson of Missouri. This body of negotiators, which was animated by the same conciliatory spirit as General Hancock, travelled far and wide over the plains for two thousand miles. They met the principal tribes in council, and made a series of treaties which, in conjunction with the distribution of presents, and with the mood aroused in the Indians by addresses that were frank, friendly, and truthful, brought about a general pacification.

Congress, when proceeding with so much caution and consideration, was plainly aware that the Indians were defending ancient rights. A humanitarian outlook, the heritage of the eighteenth century, induced the representatives of the American people to make the fullest possible allowance for the interests of both sides. But

41

these were in sharp conflict. For the Red Indians, it was, in the last resort, a life-or-death consideration. As far as the Whites were concerned, however, it was also a vital problem, being that of room for expansion. It was not, for either party, so much a question of right as of necessity; and therefore, to speak plainly, a question of power. Looked at as a struggle between two rival powers, the preponderance of one of them was manifestly overwhelming. To begin with, Stanley (who accompanied the Peace Commission) sympathised strongly with the children of the wild, since they were being bereft of their homes and their hunting-grounds. He was greatly impressed by the pathos and the dignity of the Indian braves.

White Bear, chief of the Kiowas, said at the conference: "I love the land and the buffalo, and will not part with them. . . . I don't want any of those medicine houses built in the country; I want the papooses brought up exactly as I am. . . . I have heard that you intend to settle us on a reservation near the mountains. I don't want to settle there. I love to roam over the wide prairie, and, when I do it, I feel free and happy; but when we settle down, we grow pale and die."

Commissioner Taylor replied: "Your Great Father at Washington . . . has sent us to see you in order that we may receive from your own lips how you stand. We want to hear your grievances and complaints. My friends, speak fully, speak freely, and speak the whole truth. If you have been wronged, we wish to have you righted; and if you have done wrong, you will make it right. . . . War is bad, peace is good. We must choose the good and not the bad. Therefore we are to bury the tomahawk and live together like brothers of one family."

Another Indian chief rejoined: "The Great Father in Washington has made roads stretching east and west. Those roads are the cause of all our troubles. . . . The country across the River Platte belongs to the Whites; the country north of the river belongs to us. When we see game there, we want to hunt it. Have the roads stopped just where they are, or turn them in some other direction. We can then live peacefully together."

A third chief: "Ever since I was born I have eaten wild meat. My father and grandfather ate wild meat before me. We cannot give up quickly the customs of our forefathers."

Sherman: "We need these roads. . . . The roads will be built, and you must not interfere with them. . . . The Indians are permitted to hunt the buffalo as usual. . . . If we find that the road hurts you, we will pay compensation. . . . You also ask of us presents, more especially powder and lead to hunt buffalo. We will give you some presents, because you have come here to see us. But we will not give you much till we come to a satisfactory agreement. . . . We propose to help you as long as you need help. . . . You can own herds of cattle and horses; you can have cornfields. . . . But if you don't choose your

43

homes now, it will be too late next year. . . . The white
men are collecting in all directions . . . building towns.
. . . You can see for yourselves how travel across the
country has increased so much that the slow ox-wagon
will no longer serve the purposes of the white man. We
build iron roads, and you can no more stop the loco-
motive than you can stop the sun or the moon."

At that time the Indian problem was a focus of
unrest in the States, just as the Negro problem is to-day.
As previously said, Stanley to begin with leaned towards
the side of the oppressed Redskins, though he regarded
the Southern Negroes as of little account. For him the
Indian was a fine creature, wise and self-controlled, fatalist and strong. But in the end he swung over to the other
side, justifying his change of front by arguments which
are not entirely convincing. Twenty-eight years later he
wrote that the Whites had done no more than follow the
laws of their being, and had as much right to the plains
as the Indians. Indeed, it would not be difficult to prove
that they had a better right. "The mounds in the Mississippi valley, the temple ruins of Central America, and
the silent cities of Arizona prove that there once existed
in America semi-civilised millions. But the Pilgrim
Fathers found no such people when they landed in America in 1629; they found only war-bred savages, who
were devoted to internecine strife, descendants, probably, of those nomads who had dispossessed the true
aborigines." Now the tables were turned. Why should

44

the Redskins complain? All it was incumbent upon the
United States Government to do was to protect them
from being exploited by unscrupulous Whites. In the
main, however, they had themselves to blame for their
troubles. "It was in their nature to destroy their own
families, tribes, and each other." They suffered from
"the thousand and one accidents of savage life, the
ravages of infectious disease . . . the neglect of the sick,
the lack of means and knowledge to arrest illness . . .
the insanitary condition of their camps . . . the brutal
treatment and heavy labour to which they subjected the
squaws . . . and the natural sterility of their women con-
sequent upon privation . . . and breeding-in."

This grave indictment must not be regarded as
penned by an ordinary private individual. It voices the
opinions of one who (having formed them as an outcome of what he saw as correspondent with Hancock's
expeditionary force and as a newspaper reporter present
at the sittings of the Peace Commission) was able to
give them wide currency, and thus to influence public
opinion—for sixty years ago (as now) readers of the
American Press were as suggestible and gullible as little
children. Stanley, being both masterful and ambitious,
could not have been slow to realise the scope of the
powers his new occupation had put into his hands. It
seems probable that he was one of the principal initia-
tors of the scheme to establish Indian reservations, a
politically sound one, from the Whites' outlook, seeing

45

that its enforcement did so much to hasten the decay and disappearance of the Redskins! At any rate, he enthusiastically advocated the plan, not only in the columns of the *Chicago Tribune*, but also in those of the *New York Herald*, for which he had at length begun to write. This much is certain, that during the months he spent with the Peace Commission he acquired very definite ideas of how to deal with savages. The quiet tone of assured superiority in which Sherman, Henderson, and Taylor addressed the Indian delegates, and the alternations between treating the latter, sometimes as children, and sometimes as distinguished warriors, could not fail to make an ineradicable impression upon the mind of a born psychologist like Stanley. Many years later, in Africa, he used the experience now gained, and developed by him as a virtuoso. If many of his great schemes were frustrated, that was not his fault, but the fault of his European associates.

At this date he was earning round about $90 a week by his journalistic activities. Since he lived thriftily, he was able, before long, to put by $3000, which was soon to prove of considerable use to him. Hearing that a British expedition was to be sent to Abyssinia, he severed his connexion with various provincial papers, and went to New York. There he called on James Gordon Bennett, the young editor-proprietor of the *New York Herald*. The following conversation took place:

"Oh, you are the correspondent who has been following Hancock and Sherman lately. I must say your letters and telegrams have kept us very well informed. I wish I could offer you something permanent."

"You are very kind to say so, and I am emboldened to ask you if I could not offer myself to you for the Abyssinian expedition."

"I do not think this Abyssinian expedition is of sufficient interest to Americans, but on what terms would you go?"

Stanley stated his terms, and Bennett said:

"Have you ever been abroad before?"

"Oh, yes, I have travelled in the East, and have been to Europe several times."

"Well, how would you like to do this on trial? Pay your own expenses to Abyssinia, and if your letters are up to the standard, and your intelligence is early and exclusive, you shall be well paid by the letter, or at the rate by which we engage our European specials, and you will be placed on the permanent list."

"Very well, sir, I am at your service."

"When do you intend to start?"

"The day after to-morrow."

"Good! Consider it arranged."

Stanley had gained his end, was in a fair way to becoming one of the regular correspondents of the *New York Herald*.

The then ruler of Abyssinia, the "Negus" as he was

officially styled, Theodore by name, was notorious in his day. The son of a shopkeeper, he had secured advancement by his military skill. The first great step to power was achieved by working upon the religious sentiments of his fellow-countrymen, for he announced himself as the Messiah destined to drive the Mohammedans out of Palestine, secured thereby many adherents, and ultimately succeeded in establishing himself as emperor. It was very important to him to win the support of the British consul, a man named Cameron, possessed of considerable ability, and disposed to stimulate the Negus's ambition. Cameron induced Theodore to write a letter to Queen Victoria, offering the latter a formal alliance. No answer was vouchsafed to this missive, and Theodore's wounded vanity made him mistrustful of his friend Cameron. He threatened the lives of the British missionaries. His megalomania growing, he came to regard himself as mightier than any European potentate. All white men in Magdala who failed to do him reverence were imprisoned and tortured. Cameron suffered this fate, and some of the missionaries' native servants were put to death. The consul managed to send news to England. Thereupon the British government categorically demanded the release of prisoners of British nationality, and, since the Negus proved obdurate, declared war on Abyssinia. The proposed campaign was, however, unpopular in England. The opposition made much of the dangers to which white soldiers would be exposed

in the African climate and, bowing to the pressure of
public opinion, the Government decided that the punitive expedition should consist mainly of troops from
Hindustan, under the command of Sir Robert Napier
(afterwards Lord Napier of Magdala).

Having landed at Zula in the Red Sea, Stanley,
accompanied by his Arab servant, made his way to the
camp at Koomaylee, fourteen miles inland, whence the
march on the capital was to begin. The details of this
march to Magdala, four hundred miles distant and ten
thousand feet above sea-level, cannot be considered here.
Enough to say that it was not war-making in the modern
style, resembling rather one of those ancient thrusts
forward into the unknown such as are described by
Herodotus and Xenophon. The little army (only six
thousand men, over and above those who had to maintain communications) encountered no serious resistance.
The physical hardships of the advance through the
mountainous land, with difficulties of transport and supply, cost more lives than were sacrificed in the few
engagements by which Theodore (who completely under-
estimated the strength of his enemy) tried to check the
invasion. When he at length began to realise his peril,
inflamed with a tyrant's wrath he threatened to slaughter
his prisoners. Then, seized with panic, and hoping to
propitiate Sir Robert Napier, he sent to the British camp
all the Europeans he had been keeping under duress.
Finally, when Magdala was being bombarded and the

49

invaders were entering the town through a breach in the walls, he shot himself with a revolver—the weapon being found clutched in his hand, and bearing (a dramatic touch) a silver plate with an inscription to the effect that it had been presented by Queen Victoria to "Emperor Theodorus" in 1854 "as a slight token of her gratitude for his kindness to her servant Plowden," who had been Cameron's predecessor as consul. The victory was overwhelming. Stanley describes the looting of the treasure tents, and mentions something that was very characteristic of Theodore's pinchbeck majesty: "The ground was strewn with an abundance of seemingly costly things. . . . If all that glittered among these tons of treasure were gold, the English government need not have entertained much concern about the cost of the expedition. But . . . though there were a very considerable number of wares manufactured out of the precious metal, the major part of them were gilt." Assuredly this scene would have appealed to Bernard Shaw's sardonic humour!

If the looters were chagrined to find that all which glitters is not gold, one must admit that Stanley, too, in his rôle of war correspondent, had some reason to be disappointed by the contrast between semblance and substance in the matter of his Abyssinian adventure. He had seen no fighting worthy of the name. But he had gained one thing that stayed with him through life: the image of Africa—its stupendous novelty, its formidable loneliness, the unexpected grandeur of its landscape, the clarity and charm of its colouring, the illimitable distances that produced a feeling of voluptuous anxiety; and, last but not least, the dreamlike transparency of the African light, which seems to permeate stones and wood and water, to transform the air into a new and rapturous element, and which I myself always remember as tinged with the unreality of experience on some other planet than our own. How are we to account for Stanley's perpetual return to this magic realm, his renewed and ever again renewed attempts to solve its enigmas, except by the supposition that (however specious the pretexts on which these African journeys were undertaken) he was really under an obsession, was moved by a libido, for which "exploratory impulse" is far too tame a phrase? Beyond question, some mysterious influence was at work, an influence which remained a puzzle to himself, though the attentive observer can trace it in every line he wrote about Africa, and can discern its operations plainly through all his subsequent career.

As newspaper correspondent he soon scored a remarkable success, which he owed in part to luck and in part to his own foresight and indefatigability. On the way out, he had made private arrangements with the chief of the telegraph office at Suez about transmitting his dispatches. During the return march from Magdala, he could not get permission to send an advance courier

51

with his news; his letters and telegrams, he was told, must go in the bag which carried the official and the other Press bulletins. In the Red Sea the steamer was aground for four days; and when the vessel at length reached Suez, it was quarantined for another five days. Money and ingenuity can work wonders, however, especially money in the East. Stanley drafted a long telegram and got it smuggled ashore to his friend in the telegraph service, who promptly sent it off. Next day the cable between Alexandria and Malta broke, and weeks elapsed before communications were re-established. (Remember that this was not only forty years before the days of wireless, but that the Suez Canal was not yet finished.) Stanley's message to the *New York Herald*, re-cabled across the Atlantic, was the first news of the taking of Magdala and the defeat and suicide of Theodore, to reach London. Surprise, incredulity, denunciations of the *Herald* and its "imposture"—then conviction and acceptance. Stanley had won his place in the front rank of the world's newspaper correspondents, through his realisation that what is now called a "scoop" depends (first of all) upon getting ahead of rivals. He found the sport stimulating.

It need hardly be said that he secured the coveted position on the permanent staff of the *New York Herald*. Bennett sent him to Crete, to describe the insurrection there, but Stanley considered it of trifling importance, although the European Press was raising a great hubbub about the affair. Thereafter the diary (we are in the late summer and early autumn of 1868) dilates upon a personal experience, which must not be omitted, but can only be given in brief. Upon the Island of Syra, Stanley made the acquaintance of a venerable Greek named Evangelides, who was keen on marrying off the young Anglo-American, at first to his own daughter, and then—since this girl did not take Henry Morton's fancy —to another Greek maiden, a friend's daughter, endowed with both beauty and charm. For a while Stanley toyed with the notion, fell in love more or less with the fair Virginia, and at length, in dread of committing the irremediable folly, incontinently took to his heels. Nothing could be more disastrous, he felt, than the loss of his independence. In this episode the great explorer, self-depicted, cuts an irresistibly comic figure—a modern Paris determined to escape the lures of a most attractive but not very intelligent Helen.

A few days later he was instructed to go to Athens to witness a royal baptism and to describe the temples and ruins of the Greek capital; then to Smyrna, Rhodes, Beyrout, and Alexandria. His reports to the newspaper were beginning to show the concise and energetic style of his later years, for he was perfecting himself in his profession. Words came easily to his pen, images flowed inexhaustibly through his mind; but he was far from being a penny-a-liner who thinks only of filling as many columns as possible. He was a man who had something to say about the things which he saw with discerning and unflinching eyes. Even the most venial, the most complaisant, of falsehoods was repugnant to him, partly from pride, partly from a spiritual shame, and partly from a sense of moral dignity which was native and not acquired—was no less constitutional than were his vertiginous tempo, his incredible energy, his lightning-flash judgments of men and things, and his heroic self-denial. "I am only my own master in so far as I can master my wishes and my passions," he said on one occasion.

Although in general he was of a good-natured disposition, he had a contempt for his globe-trotting fellow-countrymen. They seemed to him insipid, talkative, insufferable. Whenever, on his travels, he encountered civilised human beings, he was sickened by their triviality and malice. On a journey to Suez he found himself in the same coupé with two handsome young Englishmen, perhaps a year or so younger than himself (then twenty-seven). "They were inexperienced and shy.... I had provided myself with a basket of oranges and a capacious cooler. They had not.... When ... the fine sand came flying stinging hot against the face, they were obliged to unbutton and mop themselves, and they looked exceedingly uncomfortable. I conquered my reserve, and spoke, offering them oranges, water, sandwiches, etc. Their shyness vanished. They ate and laughed and enjoyed themselves, and I with them.... Being entertainer, as it were, I did my best for the

54

sake of good-fellowship, talking of Goshen, Pithom, Rameses, Moses' Wells, and what not. We came at last to Suez; and, being known at the hotel, I was at once served with a room. While I was washing, I heard voices. I looked up; my room was separated from the next by an eight-foot partition. In the other room were my young friends of the journey, and they were speaking of me. Old is the saying that 'listeners hear no good of themselves'; but, had I been a leper or a pariah, I could not have been more foully and slanderously abused." Such experiences made him mistrustful, and ever more inclined to shun the haunts of civilisation.

Returning to London, he received orders to go to Spain, where he spent six months, and learned Spanish so quickly that within three months he could make a speech in Spanish, and became occasional correspondent to a Spanish newspaper. (This gift for languages enabled him, later, to master Arabic, and to converse in from sixteen to eighteen Central African dialects.) The insurrection of September, 1868, which had driven Isabella from the throne, had led to the establishment of a provisional government under a regency, General Prim acting as Minister for War. In the summer of 1869, when Stanley was in the country, there were Carlist disturbances. He hurried from Madrid in search of the rebellious Carlists, who were said to have risen at Santa Cruz de Campezo. Being too late, for the insurrectionists had fled to the mountains, he returned to the capital.

Then came the news that several battalions and regiments had been dispatched towards Saragossa. "Naturally I wanted to know what was going on there . . . so one hour later, at 8.30 p.m., I took the train, and reached Saragossa next morning at six." There was a tumult, in defiance of an order to give up arms. Barricades in the streets! Stanley watched the street-fighting from a point of vantage.

"As the bullets flattened themselves with a dull thud against the balcony where I stood, I sought the shelter of the roof, and, behind a friendly cornice, I observed the desperate fighting."

Next he set out for Valencia, "from whence came reports of fierce cannonading." He was told he could not go, the trains did not run, miles of railway had been destroyed.

"Can I telegraph?"

"No."

"Why not?"

"By order of the Minister for War, no telegrams are allowed to pass."

Well, then, he would go to Alicante, and thence by sea to Valencia. He would get there if he had to circumnavigate Spain. "I exclude all words like 'fail' and 'can't' from my vocabulary."

Here we have the invincible journalist, and such, amid multifarious transmogrifications, he remained throughout life. Now and again he would ride all night,

56

in order to reach betimes some remote place where fighting had been reported. He could sleep when he had made his observations and penned his letters and telegrams.

"It is only by railway celerity that I can live. Away from work ... I ... feel as though the world were sliding from under my feet. ... I feel myself so much the master of my own future, that I can well understand Cæsar's saying to the sailors, 'Nay, be not afraid, for you carry Cæsar and his fortunes!' "

From these turbulent scenes in Spain, he was summoned by wire to Paris, to see James Gordon Bennett.

CHAPTER THREE

FAVOURING FORTUNE

———————

At three o'clock in the afternoon of October 16, 1869, Stanley left Madrid, and reached Paris on the night of the 17th.

"I went straight to the Grand Hotel, and knocked at the door of Mr. Bennett's room. Entering, I found him in bed." The following conversation ensued.

"Who are you?"

"My name is Stanley."

"Ah, yes, sit down. I have important business on hand for you. Where do you think Livingstone is?"

"I really do not know, sir."

"Do you think he is alive?"

"He may be, and he may not be."

"Well, I think he is alive, and that he can be found, and I am going to send you to find him."

"What, do you really think I can find Dr. Livingstone? Do you mean me to go to Central Africa?"

"Yes; I mean that you shall go, and find him wher-

58

ever you may hear that he is, and to get what news you can of him. Perhaps the old man may be in want. Take enough with you to help him should he require it. Of course you will act according to your own plans, and do what you think best—but find Livingstone!"

Stanley could not but wonder at the cool instruction that he was to set out for the unknown heart of Africa in search of a man whom all the world believed to be dead.

"Have you seriously considered the great expense you are likely to incur on account of this little journey?"

"What will it cost?"

"Burton and Speke's expedition to Central Africa cost five thousand pounds."

"Well, draw a thousand pounds now, and when you have got through that, draw another thousand; and when that is spent, draw another thousand; and when you have finished that, draw another thousand; and so on. But find Livingstone."

"After that, I have nothing more to say. Do you mean me to go straight on to Africa and begin the search for Dr. Livingstone?"

"No!" Such was the astounding answer of the newspaper proprietor, who was prepared for lavish expenditure, but wanted his money's worth and to kill as many birds as possible with one stone. "I wish you to go to the inauguration of the Suez Canal first, and then proceed up the Nile. I hear Baker is about to start for

Upper Egypt. Find out what you can about his expedition, and, as you go up, describe, as well as possible, whatever is interesting for tourists; and then write up a guide—a practical one—for Lower Egypt, tell us about whatever is worth seeing and how to see it. Then you might as well go to Jerusalem; I hear Captain Warren is making some interesting discoveries there. Then visit Constantinople and find out about that trouble between the Khedive and the Sultan. Then—let me see—you might as well visit the Crimea and those old battle-grounds. Then go across the Caucasus to the Caspian Sea, I hear there is a Russian expedition bound for Khiva. Thence you may get through Persia to India; you could write an interesting letter from Persepolis. Bagdad will be close on your way to India; suppose you go there and write up something about the Euphrates Valley Railway. Then, when you have come to India, you can go after Livingstone. Probably you will hear by that time that Livingstone is on his way to Zanzibar; but if not, go into the interior and find him, if alive. Get what news of his discoveries you can; and if you find that he is dead, bring all possible proofs of his being dead. That is all. Good night, and God be with you."

A programme to stagger even a Stanley!

He was so much preoccupied by his talk with Bennett that he found it very hard to keep his own counsel when, later that night, he saw Edward King, a journalist from New England, whose quarters he shared in Paris.

He would have liked to exchange opinions with King upon the probable results of his intended journey, but dared not mention his true goal—for King's newspaper might have been inclined to enter into competition with the *New York Herald*. All he could disclose to his friend was the mission to report upon the formal opening of the Suez Canal.

In lapidary style he recounts how he fulfilled his employer's preliminary commissions: "I went up the Nile, and saw Mr. Higginbotham, chief engineer in Baker's expedition, at Philae, and was the means of preventing a duel between him and a mad young Frenchman, who wanted to fight Mr. Higginbotham with pistols, because that gentleman resented the idea of being taken for an Egyptian, through wearing a fez cap. I had a talk with Captain Warren at Jerusalem, and descended one of the pits with a sergeant of engineers to see the marks of the Tyrian workmen on the foundation-stones of the Temple of Solomon. I visited the mosques of Stamboul with the Minister Resident of the United States and the American Consul-General. I travelled over the Crimean battlegrounds with Kingslake's glorious book in my hand. I dined with the widow of General Liprandi at Odessa. I saw the Arabian traveller Palgrave at Trebizond, and Baron Nicolay, the Civil Governor of the Caucasus, at Tiflis. I lived with the Russian Ambassador while at Teheran, and wherever I went through Persia I received the most hospitable welcome from the gentle-

men of the Indo-European Company; and, following
the examples of many illustrious men, I wrote my name
upon one of the Persepolitan monuments. In the month
of August, 1870, I arrived in India. On October 12th I
sailed on the barque 'Polly' from Bombay to Mauritius.
As the 'Polly' was a slow sailer, the passage lasted thirty-
seven days. On board this barque was William Lawrence
Farquhar—hailing from Leith, Scotland—in the capacity of first mate. He was an excellent navigator, and,
thinking he might be useful to me, I engaged him, his
wages to begin from the date we should leave Zanzibar
for Bagamoyo. As there was no opportunity of getting
to Zanzibar direct, I took ship to Seychelles. Three or
four days after arriving at Mahé, one of the Seychelles
group, I was fortunate enough to get a passage for myself, William Lawrence Farquhar, and Selim—a Christian Arab boy from Jerusalem, who was to act as
interpreter—on board an American whaling-vessel
bound for Zanzibar, at which port we arrived on January 6, 1871."

Thence Stanley set forth on the search for Livingstone, which (characteristically) he describes as "an
Icarian flight of journalism." With a tang of bitterness,
he adds (in the preface to *How I Found Livingstone*):
"Some, even, have called it quixotic; but this is a word
I can now refute, as will be seen before the reader ar-
rives at the 'Finis.'" Stanley erred in repudiating the
epithet. There was as much of the Don Quixote in him

as in all great explorers and discoverers, though he
knew it not.

David Livingstone, the "River-Seeker," as the natives called him, was in character and general aspect the
precise opposite of Henry Morton Stanley. It was one of
the jests of history (unless you prefer to regard it as a
dispensation of Providence) that these men, so different,
should encounter each other in the remotest wild, each
of them in a signal moment of his career: Stanley to be
made famous by the search and its outcome, Livingstone
when his life-work was done and death was near at hand;
Stanley an iron-willed man of action, Livingstone a
dreamer; Stanley a conquistador and a newspaper reporter (a combination never before seen in the world),
Livingstone a doctor and a missionary; Stanley eager
to make all his doings instantly known to the world,
Livingstone detesting nothing so much as he detested
publicity, one whose main desire was to hide himself
in the wilderness until the final release from his self-
imposed tasks, and who would fain have kept his discoveries to himself. If we were to search for a pre-
eminent specimen of those rare beings whose temperament and whose nobility of mind make them shun the
limelight, despise fame, and loathe self-advertisement,
assuredly, having remembered Livingstone, we should
be content. The meeting between him and Stanley was
trebly instructive, for it was a meeting not only of two

men, but of two outlooks on life and of two epochs.

Livingstone was of Scottish descent. His great-grandfather fell at Culloden, fighting for the old line of kings. His grandfather had been a farmer in Ulva, one of the Hebrid Isles, and there his father was born. Later, to better his condition, the grandfather removed to Blantyre Works, getting employment for himself and most of his sons at Menteith and Company's cotton mills. David's father, however, was a tea-dealer in a small way of business, being "too conscientious ever to become rich." Young David studied medicine and qualified as a doctor; he also joined the London Missionary Society and took orders. Thus as priest and medical practitioner he was doubly fitted for missionary work, and it seemed to him his high calling to combine religious and scientific activities. In the year 1840, when he was twenty-seven years of age, he embarked for South Africa, reaching Cape Town after a voyage of three months, and he spent a long time in Bechuanaland. Nine years later, accompanied by his wife and children, he crossed the Kalahari desert to Lake Ngami, in 1851 reached the upper waters of the Zambesi, and spent from 1853 to 1856 in wanderings hither and thither to Loanda and back to Quilimane, discovering on the way the Victoria Falls. For six years, from 1858 to 1864, he explored the region between the Zambesi, on the one hand, and Lake Nyassa and Lake Shirwa, on the other, went up the Rovuma, visited Lake Tanganyika, explored the

Luapula river and the lakes it connects, Moero and
Bangweolo. His family had long since been sent back
to the homeland.

These names tell us little. In actual fact, Livingstone was not so much busied with exploration as with
converting the heathen. He was a missionary by heartfelt conviction, a sincere Christian, and a most estimable
man. Even the tribes and the individuals that took no
interest in the religion to which he wished to convert
them, regarded him with veneration, and treated his
visits as festal occasions. He loved the blacks. Few
Europeans have been more intimately acquainted than
he became with their customs, their rites, their character,
and their institutions. He was, perhaps, unique in this
respect, for his knowledge was derived, not from superficial observation, but from daily life in the company of
those whom he delighted to study. That was why they
came to regard him as so notable a figure, as a veritable
saint, as one whose teaching brought consolation, one
who was able to settle disputes and was a terror to slave-
traders. His books are full of insight into the intimate
life of his protégés; he studied the diseases to which they
were liable, their relations with animals and plants, with
weather and the seasons. A judicious equanimity was
characteristic alike of his behaviour and of his literary
style. An extract will best convey to my readers an idea
of the latter.

"The Bechuanas are universally much attached to

65

children. A little child toddling near a party of men while they are eating is sure to get a handful of the food. This love of children may arise, in great measure, from the patriarchal system under which they dwell. Every little stranger forms an increase of property to the whole community, and is duly reported to the chief— boys being more welcome than girls. The parents take the name of the child, and often address their children as Ma (mother), or Ra (father). Our eldest boy being named Robert, Mrs. Livingstone was, after his birth, always addressed as Ma-Robert, instead of Mary, her Christian name. I have examined several cases in which a grandmother has taken upon herself to suckle a grand-child. Masina of Kuruman had no children after the birth of her daughter Sina, and had no milk after Sina was weaned, an event which is usually deferred till the child is two or three years old. Sina married when she was seventeen or eighteen, and had twins; Masina, after at least fifteen years' interval since she last suckled a child, took possession of one of them, applied it to her breast, and milk flowed, so that she was able to nurse the child entirely. Masina was at this time at least forty years of age. I have witnessed several other cases analogous to this. A grandmother of forty, or even less (for they be-come withered at an early age), when left at home with a young child, applies it to her own shrivelled breast, and milk soon flows. In some cases, as in that of Ma-bogosine, the chief wife of Mahure, who was about

66

thirty-five years of age, the child was not entirely dependent on the grandmother's breast, as the mother suckled it too. I had witnessed the production of milk so frequently by the simple application of the lips of the child that I was not therefore surprised when told by the Portuguese in Eastern Africa of a native doctor who, by applying a poultice of the pounded larvæ of hornets to the breast of a woman, aided by the attempts of the child, could bring back the milk."

Consider, again, the description of the death of Sebituane, a Bechuana chief with whom Livingstone had been connected by ties of close friendship: "He was much pleased with the proof of confidence we had shown in bringing our children. . . . Poor Sebituane had fallen sick of an inflammation of the lungs, which originated in and extended from an old wound. . . . I saw his danger, but, being a stranger, I feared to treat him medically, lest, in the event of his death, I should be blamed by his people. I mentioned this to one of his doctors, who said, 'Your fear is prudent and wise; this people would blame you.' . . . On the Sunday afternoon in which he died, when our usual religious service was over, I visited him with my little boy Robert. 'Come nearer,' said Sebituane, 'and see if I am any longer a man; I am done.' He was thus sensible of the dangerous nature of his disease, so I ventured to assent, and added a single sentence regarding hope after death. 'Why do you speak of death?' said one of a relay of fresh doc-

67

tors; 'Sebituane will never die.' If I had persisted, the impression would have been produced that by speaking about it I wished him to die. . . . His last words were, 'Take Robert to Maunku' (one of his wives) 'and tell her to give him some milk.' I had never felt so much grieved by the loss of a black man before. . . . The deep, dark question of what is to become of such as he must, however, be left where we find it, believing that, assuredly, 'the Judge of all the earth will do right.' "

Livingstone had left the island of Zanzibar in March, 1866. On April 7th he had set out from Mikindiny Bay upon a fresh journey into the interior, and since then he had been lost to sight. No letters from him reached home; his family was much concerned at his silence; the general public, or a great part of it, was disturbed about his fate. Every one knew that he was strongly disinclined to advertise himself, to posture before the footlights; but, when full allowance had been made for his peculiar temperament, it was hard to explain why his movements were wrapped in such persistent obscurity. There seemed good reason for dreading lest disaster should have befallen him, and the newspapers were continually asking, "What has become of David Livingstone?" It was natural enough, therefore, that James Gordon Bennett, the keenest newspaper man of the day, should commission Stanley to find him.

When Bennett's emissary returned, there was no

longer any doubt where Livingstone had been, and that
the explorer had found it physically impossible to send
news home. The surface explanation of the affair is
plausible enough. He had become obsessed with the idea
of discovering the sources of the Nile. Such was the reason he gave to Stanley and to the world, and both Stanley
and the world believed him. To the geographers of the
mid-Victorian era, the sources of the Nile were what the
Poles, North and South, became at the turn of the century—the supreme goal. They exercised a lure beyond
compare; represented an enigma clamouring for solu-
tion. The impulse which animated the would-be discoverers was in part that of all who try to excel in some
modern sport, who long to establish a "record"; but in
part it was more primitive, more ancient, being a desire
to lighten the darkness of the unknown. Livingstone
spoke also to Stanley of another motive, which Stanley
seems to have, without further question, accepted as
genuinely operative. The latter was often asked: "Why
did not Livingstone come back of his own accord when
he found his energies waning, age creeping on him and
fettering him in its strong bonds, his means so reduced
that he was unable to accomplish anything, even if youth
would have been restored to him?" Stanley's answer
was that Livingstone's return to home and kindred was
prevented by an over-scrupulous fidelity to a promise
made to his friend Sir Roderick Murchison, the famous
geologist, to the effect that he would set the matter of

69

the watershed north and west of Lake Tanganyika at rest. But a vow of this sort is hardly to be taken seriously. A man who clings to it under such disastrous conditions as those which afflicted Livingstone must, if he be not insane, have some other, hidden reason. Fables of the kind may become constituents of what is termed history, but they have no bearing upon the realities of life. We must look, then, for the hidden cause to which I have alluded.

Let us consider, first, the plain problem of the sources of the Nile. The puzzle was, I repeat, that of the watershed north and west of Lake Tanganyika. Strive as Livingstone might to solve it, misfortune dogged him. Dauntlessly he urged his steps forward over the high plateau between Nyassa and Tanganyika, but steadily evil, in various guises, haunted him. His Indian escort malingered and halted, faint-hearted, on the road, until they were dismissed. Then his Johanna escort played the same trick and deserted him, after which his porters, under various pretences, absconded. A canoe capsized on Lake Bangweolo, thus depriving him of his medicine-chest, leaving him a prey to malarial fever and other illness and bereft of the goods needed for barter.

The watershed, when he reached it, grew to be a tougher problem than he had conceived it. On the northern slope a countless multitude of streams poured northward into an enormously wide valley. United they formed a river of such volume and current that he

paused in wonder. So remote from all known rivers—
Nile, Niger, Congo—and yet so large. No one bitten by
the explorer's urge could refrain from the attempt to
trace its course. In Cazembe the natives told him of other
lakes and rivers without end, all trending northward.
For months he travelled north and west until his supplies were totally exhausted. Hearing of a caravan
bound eastward, he wrote a letter to Zanzibar, asking
for goods to be sent to him at Ujiji, on the eastern shore
of Lake Tanganyika. Meanwhile he had got mere sub-
sistence, on loan from an Arab trader, and had therefore to march whithersoever the Arab went. In 1869 he
reached Ujiji. No answer yet, but a draft on Zanzibar
enabled him to purchase some bags of beads and a few
bales of cloth, trade goods with which to strike westward
once more in search of the great river, the Lualaba, discovered two years before, far to the south.

Livingstone was now in his fifty-seventh year, tooth-
less, ill-clad, a constant victim to disease, meagre and
gaunt from famine; when he was within a hundred miles
of the river he became affected with ulcers of a virulent
type, which incapacitated him for months. His few followers were demoralised. They refused to stay with a
man who seemed bent on self-destruction and was so
blind as to be unable to see that he was marching to his
doom. But in the ninth month he was restored to health,
and a small body of men came to his relief—in answer
to the letter sent to Zanzibar in 1867. Their business,

71

they said, was to convey him to the coast, but he persuaded them to accompany him westward. At length he reached the Lualaba once more, to be faced with an insoluble puzzle. The river, at a point thirteen hundred miles from its source, was deep, two thousand yards wide, and still flowing northward. But, according to his instruments, it was only two thousand feet above sealevel, the same height as the river which was beyond question the Nile, seven hundred miles farther north still. How, then, could this river be (as he had hitherto believed) the Nile? He wanted to follow the great stream downward in canoes, but his men mutinied, and he had no option but to return to Ujiji. Reaching it on or about November 1, 1871, he found that his caravan had been disbanded and the goods sold by the man left in charge, so that his condition was more forlorn than ever. The sea, nine hundred miles away, was as inaccessible as the moon, for a bandit chief named Mirambo was ravaging the eastward regions. Then, like an angel from heaven, unexpected and inexplicable, Stanley appeared upon the scene.

Such are the manifest facts of the case, facts which are indubitable. I feel no doubt as regards the fearful privations, the fatigues and hardships of the countless marches, the torment of failure in attempt after attempt, the bodily sufferings and sickness of the ageing white man in the heart of Africa; but what I find it hard to believe, when I picture this medical missionary and ex-

72

plorer as known to us from his own account, from Stanley's, and from other descriptions, is his alleged obsession with the discovery of the sources of the Nile. Can that really have been his master passion? I know it would not have stimulated me to endure so much! As a ruling passion, the desire to know where the Nile takes its rise is, as the term implies, a passion, an affect; and what are we to think of David Livingstone if his supreme affect, his crowning aim, was merely to achieve a geographical discovery which any steadfast man with strong nerves could achieve as well as he, and would certainly achieve in due course even if Livingstone should fail? Are we to suppose that he, the converter of the heathen, the priest, the saint, when he forsook his family, cut himself off from his country, renounced intellectual consolations and all the comforts of life, was really under the spell of so secular, so mundane, an impulse? He was the River-Seeker? So be it. The nickname is expressive, calling up the image of a bewitchment which appears to have seized every one to whom this uncanny region, this Dark Continent, uttered its call. Stanley, as we shall learn, was a signal instance among those who listened to the Sirens' song.

But David Livingstone, inspired with a strong religious faith, must have been immune to the witchery; for his soul's sake he would have sublimated such an impulse, have subordinated it to his apostolic mission. He did so, we can be sure, and without too much effort, for

73

in truth his ruling passion was not that of the explorer, but that of the missionary. He wanted, above all, to initiate the African natives into the truths and the mysteries of Christianity, to make them participators in its sacraments. More than this, he wanted to sacrifice himself for the cause; to take up his cross; and in that sacred cause to suffer poverty and loneliness like the hermits and the saints of old. Such was his ideal, and in the end he realised it to the full, accommodating himself only by degrees to his mission, not attaining to complete understanding of the nature of his task of self-renunciation until those crowning years when he was utterly alone in the wilderness. Thus did he attain to sainthood, in that he forwent the rewards which the world is sometimes willing to bestow upon those who renounce it, in that his self-sacrifice remained his own carefully guarded secret. For me, at any rate, that is the key to his behaviour, which has always been a puzzle to the psychologists of the civilized world.

Unavowed self-sacrifice! We find it again and again in the lives of the saints. Think, for example, of the legend of St. Alexius, who, meanly clad, departed on a pilgrimage to the confines of the then known world. At length, returning as a mendicant, he took up his abode beneath the steps of his father's palace, and dwelt there unrecognised for seventeen years, nourished contemptuously on scraps thrown to him as if he had been a pariah dog. He died without disclosing his identity, but there-

74

upon heavenly voices revealed his greatness and his lineage. It seems to me unquestionable that Livingstone had deliberately conceived such an ideal of self-martyrdom; that his misguided search for the sources of the Nile and the absurd pledge he had given to Sir Roderick Murchison were but pretexts—a mask behind which a man devoted to the religious life concealed his true purposes from the secular European world. That accounts for what would otherwise remain inexplicable in his conduct. He was a man of God wrapped in inscrutable silence! It accounts, likewise, for Stanley's bewilderment during the months he spent with Livingstone. What Stanley now encountered without fully recognising it, encountered perhaps for the first time in his life, was greatness—and greatness makes those who contemplate it feel small.

Having reached Zanzibar, Stanley began inquiries forthwith. His task was harder than that of a detective who has, in a great city, to find an individual "wanted" by the police; harder even than that of one looking for a fountain-pen which has been dropped haphazard on Mont Blanc. Where was Livingstone? Where was some one who knew about him, had heard from him? No one had any news. It was said, indeed, that two years earlier the missionary had been reported as travelling westward from Lake Tanganyika. One informant insisted categorically that he was dead. Another professed to have information that Livingstone had wedded a chief's daughter and settled down in an inaccessible region. Stanley persisted. God alone knows how many persons he interrogated, how many Arab sheiks, merchants, caravan-leaders he visited, always ferreting out news. He was shrewd; the Welsh are born fishers of men; his journalistic aptitudes and training had given him a flair; he knew how to make people talk.

Especially helpful were the American consul, Captain Webb, and the British consul, Dr. John Kirk (afterwards Sir John Kirk). The latter had personally known the lost missionary; was mentioned in the newspapers as "the former companion of Dr. Livingstone." Stanley, introduced to Kirk by Webb, spent an evening with the former. Kirk related anecdotes of jungle life, experiences while shooting big game, incidents of his travels with Livingstone.

"Ah, yes, Dr. Kirk," said Stanley, with assumed indifference, "about Livingstone—where is he, do you think, now?"

"Well, really, you know," replied Kirk, "that is very difficult to answer. He may be dead; there is nothing positive on which we can base sufficient reliance. Of one thing I am sure: nobody has heard anything definite of him for over two years. I should fancy, though, he must be alive. We are continually sending something up for him. . . . I really think the old man should come home now; he is growing old . . . and if he died, the world would lose the benefit of his discoveries. He keeps neither notes nor journals; it is very seldom he takes observations. He simply makes . . . a dot, or something, on a map, which nobody could understand but himself."

"What kind of a man is he to get on with, Doctor?"

"Well, I think he is a very difficult man to deal with. Personally, I have never had a quarrel with him, but I have seen him in hot water with fellows so often, and that is the principal reason, I think, why he hates to have anybody with him."

(Ten chances to one that the world will describe a man's most salient characteristic as the very opposite of what it really is.)

"I am told Livingstone is a very modest man," said Stanley. "How about that?"

"Oh, he knows the value of his own discoveries; no man better. He is not quite an angel," replied Kirk, with a laugh.

"Supposing I met him in my travels—I might possibly stumble across him, if he travels anywhere in the direction I am going—how would he conduct himself towards me?"

"To tell you the truth, I do not think he would like it very well. I know if Burton, or Grant, or Baker, or any of those fellows were going after him, Livingstone would put a hundred miles of swamp in a very short time between himself and them."

Stanley was damped. He thought it inadvisable to

question Kirk further, for he did not wish this gentleman nor Captain Webb (as yet) to know his true purpose—being still afraid of rival journalists. He gave out that he intended to ascend the Rufiji to its source. Although Captain Webb, being U.S. consul, was friendly and helpful enough to the correspondent of the *New York Herald,* as Henry M. Stanley's card proclaimed himself to be, it was not a matter to arouse much enthusiasm. Stanley was, indeed, surprised that any one could believe that a newspaper should send a "special" to discover the sources of so insignificant a river as the Rufiji.

Dr. Kirk's information was disconcerting. Suppose that the British consul was right, and that Livingstone, for some inexplicable reason, did not want to be found! The hitherto self-confident newspaper man began to regard his mission in a new light. Perhaps, after all, he was not engaged upon a rescue expedition. Maybe the man for whose sake he was about to risk his own life had deliberately hidden himself in the wilds. An absurd possibility this, but one which had to be reckoned with. Still, it could not, in the end, influence Stanley's actions. His instructions were: "Find Livingstone!" and find Livingstone he would, if the explorer were still above ground.

Fifteen months had elapsed since Stanley had received his marching orders from James Gordon Bennett. During that time no news of Livingstone had come to hand in Zanzibar. The explorer had given no sign of life. But neither had Bennett! There was no letter confirming the verbal order to go in search of the traveller, no remittance. Eighty dollars was all the money the special correspondent had left in his possession, which would certainly not suffice to equip a caravan and hire porters for a march into the interior. It would barely be enough to carry him to the mainland, only twenty-five miles away. He had to take his host, Captain Webb, into his full confidence, and to explain the real purpose of the expedition. Through Webb's backing he was able to draw upon Bennett for enough cash to provide the necessary equipment and hire his staff. This last consisted of two white men (a recently discharged third mate, an American named Shaw, had been engaged in addition to Farquhar), thirty-one armed natives, termed "soldiers," and one hundred and fifty-three porters. There were also twenty-seven pack-animals and two saddle-horses. Besides being, like their leader, new to African travel, both Farquhar and Shaw were, unfortunately, confirmed topers.

For the inexperienced commander of the expedition, various practical problems concerning the outfit had been difficult to solve. Materials were needed for barter. How much cloth? How many beads? How much wire? The Europeans at Zanzibar could not advise him upon these points, and he had to seek information from the Arab ivory-traders. He learned what quantities of

79

linen and cotton cloth would represent a day's food for
the caravan; was told which kinds to get for the various
districts he would pass through, and what were the local
peculiarities of taste in respect of the colours and shapes
of glass beads. Black beads were the favourites in
Ugogo; egg beads in Ujiji and Uguhha; white beads in
Ufipa; and so on. As to wire, thickness and quality were
of moment; and of this commodity Stanley took with
him three hundred and fifty pounds of thick brass wire.
"Commodity"; but, in truth, money. "While beads stand
for copper coins in Africa, and cloth for silver, wire is
reckoned as gold in the countries beyond Lake Tanganyika"—and that was the region where he expected
to get tidings of Livingstone.

He had, then, a goal, though certainly a vague one.
It was necessary for him to take note of the extent of the
diverse regions through which he would pass on his way
thither, for thus only could he decide how to stock his
caravan with the requisite amounts of the different articles of barter—the "currency" of the respective locali-
ties. He cudgelled his brains with the names of them,
twisted his tongue round the unfamiliar vocables:
Mukunguru, Ghulabio, Sungomazzi, Kadunduguru, and
what not. Captain Webb's capacious storeroom was almost filled with the cloth, the beads, and the wire; but
much had still to be obtained: provisions, cooking uten-
sils, boats, rope, twine, tents, canvas, tar, needles, tools,
ammunition, guns, hatchets, medicines, bedding, pres-

ents for chiefs—everything had to be thought of. He had
a weary time of it chaffering with the native dealers,
and watching to see that his own light-fingered men did
not rob him of his stores. The whole "business" of the
explorer had to be learned from A to Z, remembering
that an oversight or error before the start might become
a matter of life or death in the wilds. He was getting to
grips with realities, was growing aware that "adventure"
when retold in books became invested with a sheen like
the patina which covers the surface of old bronze. The
enterprise upon which he was engaged had lost the
flavour of romance, had even come to seem preposterous.
Was there a ghost of a chance that he would "find Livingstone," a will-o'-the-wisp in an African marsh? Nobody, he felt, could ever have had a more foolish part to
play in the world than Henry Morton Stanley.

Still, he was at length ready for departure, and on
February 5, 1871, about a month after reaching Zanzibar, his caravan was embarked on four dhows and
reached the mainland in ten hours.

He had set forth into an utterly strange world, as
leader of a troop of strangers. He knew nothing of their
lives or of the motives of their actions; he had to make
himself acquainted with them, and to do this (literally)
step by step. None of his early experiences could be of
much help to him in his present situation, and never before had he been left so entirely to his own resources. If
he did not succeed in breaking with the past, how would

81

he be able to deal successfully with what lay before? He had a premonition of what Africa would demand from him; he sensed the tremendousness of Africa. Already he could hear the beating of that "Great Heart of Africa" which would allure him till the end of his life. Every minute of the day, every hour of the night, brought perplexing novelties. The road he trod (a "road" only in the imagination; not really a road, but only the sketch of a direction) had never before been pressed by a European foot. The reader must continually bear in mind that it was more than sixty years ago, when no European Power had as yet dreamed of colonising these parts, and when, in the maps, most of Central Africa was still represented by blank spaces. It is therefore upon a journey into the unknown that we have to accompany the correspondent of the *New York Herald*, and his feelings may well have resembled those of Captain Cook when he entered the South Seas in 1768, or those of Amundsen when he traversed the North-West Passage in 1905.

Stanley had the most urgent of reasons for getting away with dispatch from the coast town of Bagamoyo, having been warned that if he did not leave before the "masika"—the rainy season—began, it would delay him for six weeks. He knew that rain was a thing to dread. "I had my memory stored with all kinds of rainy unpleasantnesses. For instance, there was the rain of Virginia and its concomitant horrors—wetness, mildew, agues, rheumatics, and the like; then there were the English rains, a miserable drizzle causing the blue devils; then the rainy season of Abyssinia with the floodgates of the firmament opened, and a universal downpour enough to submerge half a continent in a few hours; lastly, there was the pelting monsoon of India, a steady shut-in-house kind of rain." But all these were nothing to the dreadful East African masika, which for forty days in succession transformed the earth into a swamp and the air into a shower-bath.

Stanley divided his caravan into five detachments, which were sent off in serial order, for a young but experienced Mohammedan Hindu trader in Bagamoyo had told him that it was much better and cheaper to send many small caravans than one large one. "Large caravans invite attack, or are delayed by avaricious chiefs upon the most trivial pretexts, whereas small ones pass by without notice." This was a wise precaution, but communications were difficult to maintain between the detachments, which often became widely separated; and the blacks, when left to themselves, were apt to lose their way, so that time would be squandered over the search for them in the trackless wilderness.

During the first days of the march, Stanley made acquaintance with tropical fever. In the course of thirteen months he had twenty-three attacks, some of them so severe as to keep him in his hammock for days at a time, unable to move and barely conscious. Fever was his faithful companion for five-and-twenty years, and never was he to rid his system of its germs. The organs had to adapt themselves to the laws of a morbid change in the composition of the blood, occasioning perhaps a no less abnormal change of the senses and of the character, nay, of the mode of life. It seems probable that there is a definite type of fever-infected human being, a febrile rhythm of existence determined by this African endemic disease.

The difficulties encountered in the crossing of numerous rivers (the Kingani, the Ungerengeri, the Makata, the Rudewa, and the Mukondokwa), enlarged into swamps by the rains, were almost insuperable. Impenetrable thickets and interlacing lianas blocked the path. Lakes of mud were interspersed amid the towering grasses. The lowland jungle exhaled a perpetual miasma; and as soon as the higher and more open ground was reached, the expedition was easily sighted by marauders and was constantly liable to attack. The winding train of porters aroused an uproar among the innumerable birds: green pigeons, daws, ibises, golden pheasants, quails, moorhens, and pelicans.

The gloom of the forest tended to induce a corresponding gloom in the minds of those who were traversing it, paralysing their resolution. The Zanzibar folk were intensely depressed by it, staggering in imminent danger of collapse. Stanley had to exert all his will-power to avoid succumbing to the mental miasma.

Then there were the insect scourges to contend with, among them the tsetse fly, whose bite causes the deadly disease nagana in horses and donkeys. Stanley found the insect harmless to himself—but, as we now know, another species of tsetse is the conveyor of sleeping-sickness to man. He writes of three different flies whose notes formed a chorus—soprano, alto, and tenor. At times their noise was almost as insufferable as their bite.

Thorny growths were destructive, not only to the clothing, but also to face and hands, and to the skin beneath the light covering worn in the tropics. *Acacia horrida* made deep lacerations; the spines of a variety of aloe bored their way into the flesh; and there was another plant (perhaps the *Rhus toxicodendron* or "poison ivy") mere contact with whose leaves would cause burning inflammation and painful ulcers on cheeks and forehead.

One of his horses having died when he was near a village, Stanley had the beast buried. Thereupon the chief arrived upon the scene and made a great to-do because the animal had been interred on his land without permission. The traveller must pay a fine. A long argument ensued "about it and about." At length Stanley lost patience, and said that, since burying the corpse was an offence, he would have it dug up again, and leave the carrion lying in the open to pollute the air. Thereupon the chief wilted, saying: "No, no, Master! Let not the white man get angry. The horse is dead, and now lies buried. Let him remain so, since he is already there, and let us be friends again."

Stanley was forced to meditate upon the peculiarities of the native mind, so hard to understand. He knew, or thought he knew, the Negroes of the Southern States; but these blacks with whom he was now dealing were altogether different. They were savages. What was a "savage"? A cross between child and devil, a being with a mentality wholly unlike his own, one whose thought processes it was not easy to follow. A Welshman by birth, mainly educated in the United States, Stanley had now to undertake the difficult task of acquiring the power of imaginative insight into the mind of a primitive. Otherwise he would never be able to make his way across this sinister continent. He did his utmost to subdue in himself the white man's pride of race, trying various modes of behaviour towards his black underlings, being now too stand-aloof and now too friendly and confiding. Always he was faced with suspicion, fear, impudence, shiftiness. Only one among the whole lot of his followers was really tractable (Selim, the Arab boy from Jerusalem); half a dozen of them were incorrigible; to deal successfully with the mass of them, the nervelessness of a man of steel was requisite. Yet, in the various tribes and peoples, he encountered individuals who were not only well-made physically, having the noble proportions

of a Greek statue from the age of Pericles, but were
likewise noble in thought and feeling; were magnani-
mous, generously proud, and full of kindliness. By degrees he learned to distinguish the good specimens from
the bad, mastered the tones and the gestures which would
best influence them; and, to his astonishment, came to
realise that this was a question of self-discovery and
self-modification, and not (as he had at first believed) a
matter of mere policy and authoritative discipline. He
who wishes to win and to control others, must first enter
into possession of his own self.

In the earlier pages of the description of his march,
we watch him learning by his own blunders, and sometimes using cheap metaphors as he talks of them. Then
comes a delightful scene, which he records with the pen
of a Mark Twain—for, a true Anglo-Saxon, he does not
lack humour and can poke fun at himself sometimes.
He is halting near a village named Kisemo. "Before
night there arrived a small caravan of Wanguana, who
brought with them ... a file of recent *Heralds*. Among
the gratifying intelligence found in them ... was an
account of President Grant's second levee, in which
Jenkins described with laboured verbosity the toilets of
the ladies who attended this notable reception: how a
lavender ostrich-plume waved among the lovely grey
curls of Mrs. A.; how diamonds finished the magnificent
attire of Mrs. B.; ... how Mrs. C. had an overskirt with
ruchings of crimson satin; ... and how the President,

87

with the deep manly voice and the pair of searching grey eyes, was sacrificing himself for the sovereign people on the occasion; ... with much else of the same adulatory tenor. Looking up from this refreshing perusal, I beheld my tent-door crowded with the dark-skinned bodies of the Kisemo girls who had become lost in vain endeavours to penetrate the mystery of those great sheets of paper over which I had been bending so long." Thereupon Stanley diverges into reflections suggested by the contrast between what Jenkins had been describing and the sight actually visible to him; the gaily-bedecked Washington ladies, on the one hand, and, on the other, "one of these plump black girls of twelve or thirteen, ripening into womanhood, with a cock's comb of woolly hair on the top of her head, three pounds of brass-wire ornament on each limb, and streams of beads round her neck; one out of the many who were attending my levee in the natural glory and beauty of nakedness." This is superficial; and when he goes on to make mock of the steatopygian charms, the over-developed rumps, of the black maidens, we feel that it is in very poor taste. He sees only with a stranger's eyes, and therefore does not really see. A stranger's eyes can merely skim the surface of things, and the stranger is moved to idle raillery by the unfamiliar. The black girl's wonderment was a profound thing in comparison with the social philosophy of the newspaper reporter.

He describes a caravan camp in which "the filth of generations of pagazis [porters] had gathered innumerable hosts of creeping things. Armies of black, white, and red ants infest the stricken soil; centipedes, like worms, of every hue, clamber over shrubs and plants; hanging to the undergrowth are the honeycombed nests of yellow-headed wasps with stings as harmful as scorpions; enormous beetles, as large as full-grown mice, roll dunghills over the ground." There were earwigs, fleas, grasshoppers without number; the termites destroyed matting, boxes, clothes, and he wondered sometimes whether they would not devour his very tent.

The Makata valley was a huge one which, being almost unpeopled, abounded with game. At dawn, koodoos and hartebeests, antelopes and zebras, could be seen emerging into the savannas to feed. In the night-time the clamorous hyenas prowled in search of sleeping prey, man or beast.

The porters were tired out, fell sick, and nevertheless must be put upon short rations. When they became exhausted, they dropped in their tracks, were missed when evening came, and had to be fetched. Sometimes a whole detachment of the caravan would be held up by sheer fatigue. "The donkeys stuck in the mire as if they were rooted to it. As fast as one was flogged from his stubborn position, prone to the depths fell another, giving me a Sisyphean labour, which was maddening under pelting rain, assisted by . . . men . . . who could not for

a whole skin's sake stomach the storm and the mud. ...
Surely the sight of the dripping woods enveloped in
opaque mist, of the inundated country with lengthy
swathes of tiger-grass laid low by the turbid flood, of
mounds of decaying trees and canes, of the swollen
river and the weeping sky, was enough to engender
fever" and reduce the leader to despair. Smallpox, the
scourge of East and Central Africa, began to levy its
toll. When the rains were over and the sun shone once
more, the mid-day temperature rose to 100° and even
higher. Farquhar, the leader of the fifth detachment,
was suffering from Bright's disease. Stanley managed to
keep in touch with him by an exchange of letters. It
proved impracticable to hold the expedition together
under a unified leadership.

In Ugogo, Stanley lost his patience and his nerve.
The demands for "honga" had become unendurably
exacting. What is "honga"? Tribute, blackmail, payment for leave to pass through a chief's territory. The
Arab traders had assured him that in this matter nothing
was to be gained by violence; that chaffering and shrewd-
ness were the only resource. The land was under the
sway of a succession of petty despots, each of whom
would expect to fleece the traveller. It would be futile
for him to lay about him with his whip, when the villagers became extortionate in their claims. The best plan
was to talk to them in a friendly way, and to impress
them by some unexpected turn of phrase. Wrath only

aroused their contemptuous laughter, but calmness and self-confidence always had the due effect. What did the anger of a lone white man matter to them since they outnumbered him so vastly? But if he remained tranquil amid multifarious vexations, this would work like a charm.

Stanley seems to have been slow to learn the lesson; but at length he grasped that browbeating and rages availed nothing, were no more than a waste of time and energy.

When the chiefs sent messengers to demand honga, there was an uproar in the camp: vociferations, curses, and threats as from a legion of devils. Stanley got used to it, sat at ease in his tent writing up his diary; but when quiet was suddenly restored, he was aware that the situation had grown serious. The chief must have appeared in person. Then the leader of the expedition knew that it had become incumbent on him to go forth and take a hand in the negotiations.

Palm-groves, beautiful scenery, a general sense of relief. They were within sight of a chain of mountains towering to a height of six thousand feet, and had a view across the salty plain that separates Ugogo from Uyanzi. What size, what distances, what infinity! In the beginning of June, they were uncertain as to their route. They had a choice of three ways: one, more to the north, poorly supplied with water, and leading to Simbo; a second, more to the south, passing through the domains

91

of an exceptionally rapacious chief; and between these a third, leading to a place named Kiti, where there would be both water and food. The Arab traders, whose advice Stanley asked, had not used this Kiti road, and were therefore loth to recommend it. (At all resting-places in the interior, at every place where the habitual routes of travel crossed, there were to be encountered Arab traders with their caravans. They were hospitable and helpful; knew the whole countryside, the best lines of communication, and where danger would threaten. Stanley had to thank them for much useful information.)

The Kiti road, however, was the shortest way to Unyanyembe, the Land of the Moon, a necessary stage on his journey, and Stanley decided in its favour. The porters were afraid of it, since it was an untravelled road. Soon after the caravan had started, the leader became aware that his men, trusting to his ignorance of the locality, were edging off into the southern route. He called a halt, and told the pagazis to obey orders. Instead of doing this, they flung down their loads, and there was every indication of a mutiny. Stanley had a troop of Wangwana warriors in his pay. "I ordered them to load their guns, to flank the caravan, and to shoot any pagazis who should make an attempt to run away. Dismounting, I seized my whip and, advancing towards the first pagazi who had dropped his load, I motioned to him to take it up and march." The man obeyed, and the rest followed his example. Scenes like this were frequent, but in the end Stanley's inflexibility worked wonders, and none of his followers ventured to dispute his commands.

The uninhabited wilderness they were now traversing was kindlier than the peopled land. Sometimes, because of the heat, he marched at night, but the nights were cold. "The thermometer was at 53°, we being about 4500 feet above sea-level. The pagazis, almost naked, walked quickly in order to keep warm, and through so doing many a sore foot was made by stumbling against obtrusive rocks and roots, and treading on thorns." The explorer records death scenes which might have happened during one of the campaigns of Alexander. On a scorching afternoon, "a pagazi, stricken heavily with the smallpox, succumbed, and threw himself down on the roadside to die. We never saw him afterwards, for the progress of a caravan on a forced march is something like that of a ship in a hurricane. The caravan must proceed. Woe betide him who lags behind, for hunger and thirst will overtake him. So must a ship drive before the fierce gale to escape foundering. Woe betide him who falls overboard!"

A picturesque mountain country. Syenite crags thrust skyward like obelisks out of clumps of dwarf trees. Then the expedition re-enters a thickly inhabited region, the Land of the Moon. Are not we reminded of classical designations, such as Ultima Thule? What

need to give here the names of the countless villages
through which he had passed—Mesuka, Kasegera, Ugun-
da, Kwikuru?—they carry no meaning to the European
or American reader. Some of the tribes he encountered
practised sorcery; others lived by slave-raiding. Some
were naked savages, with bodies gruesomely tattooed;
others had come under Arab influence and wore spotless
white robes. Some of the chiefs could be impressed by a
dignified bearing, could be won over by courtesy; others,
however, like Mirambo, the savage ruler of the Land of
the Moon, had war as their only argument and could be
convinced only by the strong hand. Stanley became involved for a time in an ineffective campaign of the Arab
traders against this potentate, who made preposterous
demands for tribute. On September 20th, however, he
shook the dust of Unyanyembe off his feet, and started
on a rapid march towards Ujiji.

Of course Stanley had been everywhere asking for
news of Livingstone, had sent messengers to gather tidings, had pondered all the rumours that came to hand,
had questioned the Arab traders times without number.
So far his inquiries had been unavailing. But hope persisted. Before leaving the Land of the Moon he wrote in
his diary: "Something tells me to-night I shall find him.
Find him! Find him! Even the words are inspiring."
October had come. One of his guides deserted. When he
was crossing the Gombe Nullah, there was a fresh

mutiny, a more serious one this time, for two of his armed men raised their guns against him; and others were in the plot to murder him. He quelled the outbreak by his dauntless contempt for their insubordination; the first ringleader dropped his gun when menaced by the muzzle of Stanley's weapon, the second, more resolute, and still hanging in the wind under the same threat, was disarmed from behind by Mabruki Speke, one of the "faithfuls" of Speke the explorer. Thereafter a "general amnesty" was proclaimed, and the men marched on willingly. Stanley, having been perforce clement, turned his clemency to useful account, insisting on unconditional obedience in future. His followers respected his firmness, and had learned to dread him; he remained the victor.

On, over ravines, up marshy water-courses, in which a man could sink to the neck in the holes where elephants had trod. They traversed a swamp. "Here," said the guides, "an Arab trader with his caravan, consisting of thirty-five slaves, had sunk out of sight and were never more heard of." His men often fell from weakness. At night they sat round the fire shaking with ague, and afraid to sleep because of the roaring of the lions. While the expedition was crossing the River Malagarazi, one of the two remaining donkeys was seized by a crocodile. Stanley no longer had any white companions. Farquhar was dead; and Shaw, who had never been of

95

much use to his employer, having at length completely
lost morale, had been sent back as an invalid.

On the morning of November 3rd, Stanley's expedition met a caravan of eight Waguhha, a tribe which
occupies a tract of country on the south-western side of
Lake Tanganyika. They had come from Ujiji. When
Stanley asked for news, he was amazed and delighted
to learn that very recently a white man had arrived at
Ujiji.

"A white man?"

"Yes, a white man."

"How was he dressed?"

"Like the master" (*i.e.* Stanley himself).

"Young or old?"

"He is old. He has white hair on his face, and is
sick."

"Where has he come from?"

"From a very far country beyond Uguhha, called
Manyuema."

"Indeed! And is he stopping at Ujiji now?"

"Yes, we saw him about eight days ago."

"Do you think he will stop there until we see him?"

"Don't know."

"Was he ever at Ujiji before?"

"Yes, he went away a long time ago."

"Hurrah!" comments Stanley in his diary. "This is
Livingstone. He must be Livingstone. He can be no other.

THE MUTINY ON THE GOMBE RIVER

An illustration from "How I Found Livingstone"

. . . But we must now march quick, lest he hears we are coming, and runs away."

He called his men together and promised them extra pay for forced marches to Ujiji. There must be no needless halts. With redoubled energies, he swept all hindrances (whether imposed by nature or by man) out of his path. He could dream, think, talk of nothing but the old, white-bearded man at Ujiji, perhaps ill, perhaps dying. There was not a minute to spare. Like a hurricane the rescuer, the reporter, the special correspondent, stormed across the territories of Uvinza and Uhha, determined to find a live Livingstone!

Friday, November 10th, 1871, had dawned; the 236th day from Bagamoyo, and the 51st day from Unyanyembe. A happy, glorious morning, the air was fresh and cool, and the caravan was early afoot. "The deep woods are crowned in bright green leafage," writes Stanley; "the water of the Mkuti, rushing under the emerald shade afforded by the bearded banks, seems, with its continuous brawl, to challenge us for the race to Ujiji." The phrasing betrays his impatience! "We ascend a hill overgrown with bamboo, descend into a ravine through which dashes an impetuous little torrent, climb another short hill, then along a smooth footpath running across the slope of a long ridge. We push on as only eager, light-hearted men can do. In two hours I am warned to prepare for a view of the Tanganyika. . . . I almost vent the feelings of my heart in cries. . . . We press forward breathlessly. . . . There it is, a silvery gleam! At last, the Tanganyika, and . . . . the blue-black mountains of Ugoma and Ukaramba. An immense broad sheet, a burnished bed of silver," the great lake which extends north and south over five parallels of latitude. "Lucid canopy of blue above, lofty mountains are its valances, palm forests form its fringes. The green-sworded hill on which I stand descends in a gentle slope towards the town. The path is seen, of an ochreous brown, curving down the face of the hill until it enters under the trees into Ujiji."

Not within the memory of man had so large a caravan reached Ujiji, and the whole population turned out to welcome it. The vociferous crowd surrounded Stanley, overwhelming him with questions. A tall black, wearing a long white shirt, thrust himself forward and hailed the newcomer in English, making himself known as Livingstone's servant. Stanley, in the throes of doubt at the moment when the achievement of his quest was at hand, asked again and again for confirmation of the news that the missionary was in Ujiji and alive; then told the man to run and inform his master. The messenger raced headlong, with his white raiment streaming behind him like a wind-whipped pennant. "The column continued on its way, beset on either flank by a vehemently enthusiastic and noisily rejoicing mob, which bawled a jangling chorus of "yambos" [greetings] to every mother's son of us, and maintained an inharmonious

orchestral music of drums and horns." They reached the
market-place, where Stanley caught sight of the promi-
nent figure of an elderly man. "As I advanced towards
him I noticed that he was pale, with a wearied look."
Then came the world-famous dialogue, laconic, out-
wardly unemotional, such as would only have been possible to members of the English-speaking communities
—who are stiff, reserved, conventional, even in moments
of triumph, release of tension, supreme delight.

"Dr. Livingstone, I presume?"

"Yes," said Livingstone with a kindly smile, lifting
his cap slightly.

Stanley, who had taken off his sun-helmet, replaced
it. Livingstone resumed his cap, and the two men shook
hands. Next an exchange betraying a little more emotion:

"I thank God, Doctor, that I have been permitted
to see you."

"I feel most thankful that I am here to welcome
you."

CHAPTER FOUR

DEFEAT AFTER VICTORY

LIVINGSTONE offered Stanley the use of his house, the services of his cook and all his other retainers, but was speedily informed that the newcomer had no lack of anything. Here was a contrast with Livingstone's own condition, for the missionary was short of the most elementary requirements. At first, therefore, Livingstone was inclined to look upon Stanley as a globe-trotter, as possessed of unlimited means; this outlook made him uneasy and reserved. He had no use for travellers of that sort. But as soon as Stanley had explained his mission, Livingstone was astonished, nay much moved. It had never entered the old explorer's head that the world (that world which had once been his own world) had been in the least concerned about him. Just as he had forgotten that world, so did he believe that the world had forgotten him. By degrees, therefore, he thawed, looked at this remarkable young man with different eyes, found him congenial, listened to Stanley's account of

James Gordon Bennett and of America, was amazed and flattered to discover that America had heard of himself. He took for a personal interest what was only the outcome of sensation-mongering and journalistic appetite. But it is quite affecting to read how, when Stanley gave him the packet of letters from Zanzibar, Livingstone laid it on his knee and made no move to open it. This utter lack of curiosity annoyed Stanley. "But what about your correspondence, Doctor? You will find the news, I daresay, in them. I am sure you must be impatient to read your letters after such a long silence."—"Oh!" replied Livingstone, with a sigh, "I have waited years for letters; and the lesson of patience I have well learned. I can surely wait a few hours longer! I would rather hear the general news, so pray tell me how the old world outside of Africa is getting along."—A tranquil but moving scene, this, between the hermit and the messenger from the outer world.

Stanley spent four months with Livingstone, and found it very hard to break through the missionary's shell. They journeyed together to explore the region, and travelled by boat up and down Lake Tanganyika. What Stanley needed, before all, was something which would serve as definite proof that Livingstone was alive, and that Stanley had found him. Only by the production of such evidence would Stanley be able to justify himself towards the man who had commissioned him.

There must be sufficient proof to satisfy the newspaper-reading public that the expedition had attained its end. Livingstone had no reason for holding back in the matter. Why should he wish to conceal the fact that he was alive? As far as he was concerned, the newspapers might write whatever they pleased. Although at first it had perhaps tickled the remnants of his vanity to know that people's minds and tongues had been busied about him, thus confirming his own conviction that he had done important work as an explorer, ere long, like all else, it became a matter of indifference to him. Still, he would give this "nice fellow" letters to England. No one should have any reason to doubt that the energetic young man had fulfilled his task. But the explorer had no thought of returning to the coast, of accompanying his "rescuer" to Europe in the guise of a living trophy. The time had not yet come for his return to the homeland—perhaps never would come. He knew that death was not far off. It would suit him better to die here in Central Africa than in the old country, in which he was now a stranger. In Africa he had done his work; to Africa he belonged; he would end his days in Africa.

Stanley, therefore, was faced by an unanswerable question. Why, he wondered, did not this weary old man, much older than his fifty-nine years, return home? Livingstone could not but know that his energies were flagging, that his health was shattered, that his financial resources were exhausted. Why, then, did he thus stubbornly resolve to stay in the inaccessible wildernesses of Africa, alone, friendless, uncared for, without any reasonable hope of carrying out his plans? It was beyond Stanley's comprehension that there could be no "going home" for Livingstone in this sense; that the missionary was "at home" in Central Africa, as far as his mind and his mission were concerned. Stanley accepted Livingstone's pretext at its face value, believing the explorer obsessed with the desire to solve a geographical problem. The "rescuer's" only doubts related to the physical capacity of this wonderful man. It was, thought Stanley, the riddle of the Lualaba which had bewitched the indefatigable missionary, who could not rid his mind of the mystery of the great stream running northward, and who burned to know whether it was one of the main sources of the Nile. Such was Stanley's view of the situation, and it became graven into his consciousness more deeply than he realised. In the end, he, at any rate, was obsessed with this idea of discovering by what route the Lualaba found issue into the sea. Stanley had no real insight into Livingstone's mind; he did not grasp the truth. All the same, he became, in so far as he understood Livingstone, Livingstone's disciple, and was inspired with an invincible craving to complete the work of the master. Once more, as has so often happened, a misunderstanding proved the motive force of action. How decisive is this contrast of types, that of the centrifugal and that of the centripetal man! When they come into contact, one of them obliterates the other, and, reinforced by the powers of him whom he has effaced, moves onward more freely and towards higher achievements. Such a collision of types was part of Stanley's destiny. We shall see the same contrast in later years, much cruder and more dramatic, although less spiritually fruitful. When the situation recurred, the counterpart in the second instance was Emin Pasha. Every life is subject to its own peculiar laws of motion.

Of one fact there can be no doubt, that his prolonged association with Livingstone modified and developed Stanley's character. All the rest of Stanley's narrative of these months is unessential; the technical conversations, the accounts of the region and its inhabitants, the discussions of routes and of events, are of little moment. The veiled, the chary, the enigmatic in the nature of the older man could not fail to exert an influence upon the choleric, impulsive, headlong temperament of the younger. The father-son relationship recurred for Stanley in a new form. It was deeper, more intimate, than had been the relationship to his adoptive father. Livingstone was, so to say, confirmed in goodness, one who really lived the Christian life, a visible sacrifice. Stanley frankly admits that every day spent with Livingstone intensified his admiration for the old man.

In the cool of the evening, they would sit on the veranda of their hut exchanging experiences and making

104

plans, just as two gentlemen might talk over their affairs in a peaceful country-house in Kent or Long Island. In the mornings they would stroll up and down the market-place of Ujiji, whence they had a good view of the lake. This was the market to which the neighbouring herdsmen drove their cattle, where the fishermen of Ukaranga sold the fish caught in the lake, and to which the palm-oil dealers from Urundi brought oil which was as hard as butter. There were to be seen the salt-dealers of Uvinza, the ivory-traders of Usova, the boat-builders of Ugoma, and pedlars from far-away Zanzibar; all laughing, chattering, bargaining. This, too, was a picture which Stanley would never forget, for it was part of the spell to which he was subject for the remainder of his life, part of the "Great Heart of Africa."

On March 14, 1872, Stanley set forth on the return journey to the coast. He found it hard to part from Livingstone; nor did the farewell come easy even to the old explorer. Each knew that he would never see the other again. Two months later, Stanley was back in Zanzibar. In the middle of August, Livingstone set out from Ujiji upon his travels once more. Eighteen months afterwards he died on the shore of Lake Bangweolo.

Men of H. M. Stanley's type, all those who lead the sort of life that he led, have to pay for success in the hard coin of disillusionment. Thus was it with Columbus,

whose contemporaries would not believe that he had discovered America. Indeed, I am afraid it began in the
dawn of human history, and will never end as far as
investigators, poets, artists, or the founders of States are
concerned. Always and always the men of the study have
been mortified when men of action achieved the deeds
which the theoreticians had suggested. Still more embit-
tered have ever been those who declared the achievements in question to be impossible.

His cool reception in Zanzibar was already a distress to Stanley, and prepared him for the worse that
was to come. When he reached England, there was, it is
true, a great deal of talk about his disclosures, but
everywhere they were regarded with suspicion. He was
disbelieved, blamed, treated with contempt. His pub-
lisher, Edward Marston, gives a detailed account of this
in a book, *After Work*, two chapters of which are devoted to Stanley. The journalist himself writes only with
reserve about the injustice done him, being restrained by
shame and pride.

Characteristically enough, it was the president of
the Geographical Society who made himself the official
leader of these onslaughts. This authority, Sir Henry
Rawlinson, wrote to *The Times*, saying that it was not
true that Stanley had discovered Livingstone, but that
Livingstone had discovered Stanley. The *Standard*, in
oracular tones, called for the sifting of the discoverer's
story by experts; it "could not resist some suspicions

and misgivings"; it found "something inexplicable and mysterious" in the business. But Stanley, foreseeing these possibilities, had prepared himself for all emergencies. He had brought back Livingstone's letters, and could show Livingstone's confirmation of their meeting. The genuineness of the letters was disputed, above all of the letter which, at Stanley's instigation, Livingstone had written for the *New York Herald*. In a word, Stanley was accused of deliberate forgery. From the various learned societies a chill wind blew upon this American, with his fables from Africa. The impression was conveyed to him that people would rather have settled down to the belief that David Livingstone was irrecoverably lost than that an American journalist should have found him—a journalist, that is to say a man who was not a geographer and an expert.

Comments were rife in which the expedition was made to look ridiculous. Then came a field-day at Brighton at the meeting of the Geographical Section of the British Association. Before an audience of three thousand persons, including a group of great geographers and Eminences of high degree, Stanley had to justify himself as if he had been a man charged with crime. Although his self-possession and composed eloquence made a profound impression upon the audience, he admits in his diary that his stage-fright was so extreme that he could only begin after three trials. He told his story, and read his paper. A special attack was made in the subsequent discussion upon the theory to which Livingstone inclined, that the River Lualaba was the source of the Nile. Stanley himself had grave doubts as to the correctness of that theory, which he was destined ultimately to disprove, but, for Livingstone's sake, he wanted it treated at least with respect. The chairman remarked acrimoniously that they were not there to listen to sensational stories, but to serious facts. Stanley rejoined with a fervent eulogy of Livingstone, and a biting comparison of the armchair geographer, waking from his nap to dogmatise about the Nile, with the gallant old man seeking the reality for years, amid savage and elemental foes. This speech won him all hearts; and when, shortly afterwards, Livingstone's family publicly acknowledged the genuineness of the letters and expressed heartfelt thanks to the heroic traveller who had brought them back, the critics were reduced to silence, for those who had charged Stanley with forgery were now confounded. Lord Granville, Minister for Foreign Affairs, handed him, on Queen Victoria's behalf, a letter of congratulation, and a gold snuff-box set with diamonds. But this public recognition did not put an end to the flow of underground calumny. Reports that in Africa he had treated his men with savage cruelty were continually being revived. These falsehoods hunted him to the end of his life, though he was never able to discover who was responsible for their dissemination. The upshot was that whenever he returned to Europe, and

especially to England, his withers were wrung as if by
the lashings of an invisible whip. Thus early in his career
did fame become a burden. He mistrusted all who extolled him, and had faith in none of those who professed
to love him.

He did not stay long in Europe at this juncture,
feeling uneasy in a dress-coat and when sitting at table
between ladies who pestered him with idiotic questions.
He had no gift for social intercourse and polite conversation. Civilization was to him no more than an idol
regarded with superstitious veneration, and whenever he
came into close contact with it he drew back in alarm.
In the wilds, he could function as one of the pioneers
of civilisation; but when he was in London or in New
York, its institutions oppressed him like a nightmare.
Simple and straightforward in character, he was un-
fitted to play the part of hypocrite; and against the
hypocrisy of others he had no other weapon than a
straightforwardness which was wounding. He was never
able to forget that many notables had wanted to stig-
matise him as a cheat. His sense of honour had been
outraged; so that whenever he was among ordinary mor-
tals the moment would soon arrive when his eyes would
droop and he would fall into a gloomy silence.

Doubtless it was this unhappy mood which led him,
as soon as could be, to shake the dust of England and
America off his feet, and to seize the first opportunity of

returning to Africa. The opportunity came when the Ashantee campaign began, so that a year and a half after he had sailed from the east coast of Africa, he returned to that continent, landing on the Atlantic shore, the so-called Gold Coast, in whose hinterland the most terrible occurrences had taken place.

There is no occasion to say much here about these matters. For half a century or more there had been horrible massacres going on in Ashantee. England had expended much money and sacrificed many lives in the attempt to put a stop to the disorders, the last of these endeavours having been made in the years 1863 and 1864. Now Sir Garnet Wolseley (afterwards Lord Wolseley) was to impose quiet upon the region once for all. The rights and the wrongs of the whole affair, who were attackers and who were defenders, are hard points to settle. This is one of the chapters of colonial history, and perhaps not the most glorious of them. The fighting was extremely savage, and ended in the complete downfall of the Ashantees. Should we approve the conquerors, those who belonged to a race having an enormous preponderance of power at its command, those whose ultimate victory was inevitable despite the numerical excess of the blacks locally, and their desperate resistance? Or are we, on the other hand, to consider that a dark-skinned people, heroically defending its freedom and independence, was unjustly chastised for the endeavour to avoid passing under foreign dominion? These

110

are questions which must still be left open, for the issue has not yet been fought to a finish, nor will be for a long time to come.

In the volume entitled *Coomassie and Magdala, the Story of Two British Campaigns in Africa*, Stanley published a lengthy account of the Ashantee campaign, but his participation in it does not offer the biographer any new elements for a portrait of the man. As in the Abyssinian campaign, so in the raid on Coomassie, he was present merely as a spectator. He was following the profession of a journalist. Though a secret yearning had brought him back to Africa, he did not yet understand the nature of his own passion. An overwhelming urge to activity sometimes led him into foolhardy exploits, but there was little honour to be gained in this expedition. Sir Garnet Wolseley spoke with commendation of his courage and his presence of mind, but that signified little, and availed him nothing. He was something more than, had become something different from, the simple war correspondent, although such was the part he now had to play.

In the case of a man who was still suffering, and was long to suffer, from a sense of moral defeat, aroused by his reception when he returned from "finding" Livingstone, we may well suppose that the horrors of a colonial war wherein both sides were pitiless may have been accordant to his mood. Coomassie, the capital of the Ashantees, was surrounded on either side by a forest

111

hundreds of miles across, full of pestilential swamps so dangerous that ninety per cent. of those who entered them speedily sickened of malarial fever. Even the groves that environed Coomassie were but a continuation of the deadly primeval forest, whose poisonous vapours penetrated into the huts of the natives. The Ashantees had never believed it possible that a British army would be able to reach their lair. The queen dowager had declared that if the invaders did succeed, she would kill herself. But there were signs of ill omen. A meteor fell from the skies; a newborn child began to speak; the great fetish-tree was struck by lightning. During the decisive battle of Amoaful, the war correspondents had been kept behind the rearguard, and had to make their way onward across piles of dead, dying, and wounded. In addition, the Ashantees, following their custom of human sacrifice, had slaughtered hecatombs in order to ensure the favour of the gods. Stanley speaks of the market-place of Coomassie as a Golgotha. He was never able to forget the horrible aspect of the putrefying corpses and the bodiless heads. "The stoutest heart and the most stoical mind might have been appalled."

When he was on his way back from the Gold Coast, at the Isle of St. Vincent, in February, 1874, he received news of Livingstone's death, ten months after "the old man," as Stanley always affectionately called him, had passed away. Thenceforward he knew no rest. His one concern in life had become "the completion of Living-

112

HENRY M. STANLEY

stone's work." It was as if the quest had been the missionary's legacy. We must not forget, however, that there was much else to fortify Stanley in this pious mission: his own bodily gifts; his ambition and his concentrated energy; his contempt for Europe and his infatuation with Africa; his venturesomeness and his lust for discovery. Perhaps these counted, whatever he himself may have thought, for more than the reputation of the man he had known and loved. Besides, he had still to "justify himself"; he had still to force the world to believe in him.

CHAPTER FIVE

THE GREAT HEART OF AFRICA

───────────

1. *The Search*

"I HAVE a spur to goad me on. . . . What I have already endured in that accursed Africa amounts to nothing, in men's estimation. Here, then, is an opportunity for me to prove my veracity, and the genuineness of my narrative. Surely if I can resolve any of the problems which such travellers as Dr. Livingstone, Captains Burton, Speke, and Grant, and Sir Samuel Baker left unsettled, people must needs believe that I discovered Livingstone!"

Such are the words used by Stanley in the *Autobiography*. One may doubt whether he had anywhere encountered a reasonable and respectable person who had taken the absurd accusations seriously; but he was as fixed in his ill-humour as a schoolboy who has been unjustly scolded.

"I strolled over one day to the office of the *Daily Telegraph*, full of the subject. Discussing the matter with the editor, I said: 'The outlet of Lake Tanganyika is undiscovered. We know nothing scarcely—except what Speke has sketched out—of Lake Victoria; we do not even know whether it consists of one or of many lakes, and therefore the sources of the Nile are unknown. Moreover, the western half of the African continent is still a white blank.' "

The editor of the *Daily Telegraph* said he would be ready to finance an expedition if James Gordon Bennett would share the cost. Stanley cabled to New York, and Bennett replied with a laconic "Yes."

On September 21, 1874, Stanley landed at Zanzibar, and in the middle of November he crossed to the continent with a force of two hundred and twenty-four Mohammedan blacks, and with three white men as assistant officers: a certain Frederick Barker and the brothers Pocock, one of whom died on January 17, 1875, in Suna, of typhus.

A different route, a new direction, another goal. He is no longer concerned with finding a man, but with finding a river. Personality has been excluded, and Nature has taken its place. It might be thought that the course of a river, even in a region extending to millions of square miles, would be easier to discover than the dwelling-place of a lost white man who had disappeared into one of the hundreds of thousands of villages in the interior. In both cases alike we have to take into account the difficulties of language and of commissariat, the

115

complete lack of any organised routes, and the immense distances to be covered. But even the stupidest of blacks can understand the search for a man, especially when the man sought for is a person of wide reputation, one who has indeed enjoyed something akin to divine honours; he can understand, and will, if possible, point a finger to help. But what is an ignorant native to reply in answer to questions regarding the sources or the course of a river? If he knows the river at all, he knows it only because he lives on its banks or somewhere near it. In that case he will tell what he knows, which concerns only the reaches of the river in the immediate vicinity of his home. Where it takes its rise and whither it may flow are matters of indifference to him. He may never have heard of the river in question, and in that case he will have no more interest than he has knowledge. He will regard the questioner as an idle chatterer, and will be inclined (it may be from suspicion, it may be from a sense of self-importance, it may be from ill-nature) to misdirect the inquirer. The explorer, who lacks the conveniences obtainable in civilised countries, who has no trustworthy indications to follow, no maps to consult, can be guided only by the compass and by his instinct. If the region he has to explore has been visited or approached by others, there may be at his disposal a few contradictory statements in books written by his predecessors, or handed down to him by word of mouth; and his first task will then most likely

116

be to correct their errors. It will be impossible for him to foresee the difficulties that will be imposed by the nature of the ground; he must be ready to find that a march which, under normal conditions, would occupy three days, will take him thirty, sixty, or one hundred days. The elements will rise in revolt against him; so that, where he had expected easy going on level ground for a space of a few miles, he will find an impassable morass, or perhaps a craggy mountain will have thrust itself into his path. Every foot of his journey has to be conquered, not only in the sense of exploration, but also in the sense of guarding against the menace of the natives, inasmuch as these latter (with good reason) are extremely averse to what Europeans term the "opening-up" of their country.

We have, however, seen—and this must be borne in mind as regards the almost incredible hardships he had to endure—that Stanley was not so much concerned with exploration or with the opening-up of Central Africa, as with justifying himself in the eyes of Europe. Do I mean that his aim was to achieve a dramatic display of valiancy? No, not that. The phrase does not fit him, for he had no vanity. Petty self-admiration, what modern psychologists term narcissism, was completely lacking to him. His breast was animated by a heroic ideal, for whose realisation he was ready to make any sacrifice, just as Livingstone had been ready to hazard his life in pursuit of missionary aims. Like Livingstone,

117

moreover, though in a more ecstatic and stormy fashion, Stanley was one of those lonely beings who never acquire a normal and healthy relationship towards the world in which they have been born, and who must therefore lead loveless, friendless, and unsatisfied lives unless the star of their destiny guides them into a road where they can find adequate self-expression. Unquestionably, Stanley wanted to solve the enigma of the Lualaba; but it is equally clear that he was thinking quite as much of self-discovery, self-revelation, and self-confirmation—a process which, thanks to the passionate tensions of his disposition, led to the most violent discharges of energy. Although he was wholly a man of the nineteenth century, with all the defects and all the merits characteristic of those who belonged to that epoch, he sometimes produces the impression of being a man who does not belong to any particular age, or of being one whose unconscious endeavour it is to transcend the limitations of his era.

The expedition steered its course north-westward, the immediate aim being Lake Victoria Nyanza. It was still uncertain whether, as Speke believed, this was a single lake, or, as Burton, McQueen, and others contended, a group of lakes. The next object of the expedition was to explore Lake Tanganyika. This, being a fresh-water lake, must possess an outlet somewhere. It had not been circumnavigated, and Stanley was determined to settle its problems.

None of Stanley's men had ever traversed the region through which they were marching, and local guides proved untrustworthy. For days they toiled over bush country, interminable plains in which there was no game, no fruit, no grain. Five of the company died of exhaustion. Food could not be obtained either by begging for it, by paying for it, or by threats. At Vinyata, in the land of Ituru, the indigenes began to cut off stragglers. A sick man suffering from asthma lingered behind. The savages pounced on him, dismembered him, and scattered the pieces along the road. He was missed when the roll was called that evening, and men sent back to look for him found his remains. They clamoured for revenge. An example must be given to the savages. "Revenge," said Stanley, "what good will that do? You talk of my giving a lesson to these people. I did not come to Africa to give such lessons. Don't you see that we have so many sick among us that we can hardly stir?"

In truth he earnestly desired to avoid bloodshed, but he was accorded no choice. Next day two brothers went out into the bush to collect fuel. One was speared to death, the other rushed back into camp, a lance quivering in his arm, his body gashed with the flying weapons, his face streaming with blood from the blow of a whirling knobstick. Once more Stanley's men clamoured for reprisals.

119

"Keep silence," he said. "Even for this I will not fight. I cannot afford to lose you. We have a thousand tribes to go through yet, and you talk of war now. Be patient, men, this will blow over."

But while he was arguing for peace, the camp was being gradually surrounded. He had no option but to fight. In this emergency, Stanley showed that he possessed all the gifts of a military commander, and he put the assailants to flight, but with the loss of a fourth of his men. He set about reducing the baggage, and burned every possible superfluous article. He clung to his boat, though sorely tempted to leave it behind, since it required thirty of the strongest men for its porterage. Personal baggage, luxuries, books, cloth, beads, wire, extra tents, were freely sacrificed.

Soon his troubles were relieved when he came to a place where the natives were friendly. "Everywhere we were received with a smiling welcome by the villagers, who saw us depart with regret. 'Come here again,' said they; 'come always assured of a welcome.' "

Throughout the record we have this perpetual alternation between senseless hostility and cheerful hospitality.

After a march of a hundred and four days from the east coast, the expedition reached the shore of Lake Victoria Nyanza. It was to circumnavigate this lake and Lake Tanganyika that Stanley had brought the aforesaid boat from England, in sections, a cedarwood boat,

forty feet long and six feet beam. When he asked for
volunteers to man it, there was a dead silence. His
followers were mortally afraid of the water. "Where
are the brave fellows who are to be my companions?"
The men gazed at one another and stupidly scratched
their hips. "You know I cannot go alone! You see the
beautiful boat, safe as a ship, swift as a seabird. Let
my braves step, out; those men who will dare accompany their master round this sea." Each man at whom
he looked had some fanciful excuse with which to shroud
his fears. At length Stanley gave up the idea of asking
for volunteers, and, choosing eleven of the men, ordered
them to take their places in the boat. With chattering
teeth, they did as they were told, and soon found this
lake-travel pleasant enough—until the inhabitants of the
bordering regions, untutored savages, began hostilities.
A shock-headed native, ugly, loutish, and ungainly in
movement, had agreed, for a consideration, to accompany them as pilot and interpreter of the local dialects.
At one of the first places where they touched, this guide
had many friends, "who told us, for the exceeding comfort of my crew, that it would take years to sail around
their sea, at the end of which time no one would be
alive to tell the tale. On its shore dwelt a people with
long tails; there was a tribe which trained big dogs for
purposes of war; there were people also who preferred
to feed on human beings rather than on cattle or goats."
We seem to be reading a transcript from Herodotus.

Off the northern shore of Lake Victoria Nyanza lies Uganda, a country then well governed by an emperor named Mtesa, who received Stanley with all the honours. The high officials and courtiers came to see him, overwhelming him with questions about his health, his journey, Zanzibar, Europe and its nations, the oceans, the heavens, the sun, the moon and the stars, angels, demons, doctors, priests, and craftsmen in general. After this informal examination, he was conducted to the palace. Mtesa, a tall, clean-shaven man, advanced to greet him, and shook hands. The ruler, like his leading subjects, was especially interested in Europe and in heaven. "The inhabitants of the latter place he was very anxious about, and was especially concerned regarding the nature of angels. Ideas of those celestial spirits, picked up from the Bible, *Paradise Lost*, Michelangelo and Gustave Doré, enabled me to describe them in bright and warm colours. Led away by my enthusiasm, I may have exaggerated somewhat! However, I was rewarded with earnest attention, and, I do believe, implicit faith!"

Mtesa and his people found "Stanley" difficult to pronounce, and re-christened the explorer "Stamlee." One afternoon Mtesa said, "Stamlee, I want you to show my women how white men can shoot." There were about nine hundred of these ladies. By the lake shore they formed up in a crescent line, Mtesa in the midst. "They amused themselves by criticising my personal appearance—not unfavourably, I hope! It was 'Stamlee is this,' and 'Stamlee is that' from nine hundred pairs of lips."

These people were of a fine race. Mtesa himself was slender and tall, over six feet in height. "He has very intelligent and agreeable features, which remind me of some of the faces of the great stone images at Thebes, and of the statues in the museum at Cairo." This Uganda experience was like a beautiful dream, with nothing to parallel it for pleasantness during the rest of the journey. Immediately after leaving Mtesa's hospitable court, Stanley found himself again amid difficulties and dangers.

There were attacks by the natives; extortion of tribute; threats; storms on the lake; fresh onslaughts; short rations; the daily dread of the unknown. The voyage round the giant lake occupied eight weeks. At length, exhausted by hunger and hardship, they returned to the camp at which the main expedition had been left.

"But where is Barker?" asked Stanley of Frank Pocock.

"He died twelve days ago, Sir, and lies there," replied Pocock, pointing to a new mound of earth near the landing-place.

All this glides before our eyes like moving pictures on a screen, but neither the written record nor the illustrations which accompany it can give an adequate idea of the living truth; the story seems to belong to the realm of fantasy.

Having bought sufficient canoes to take the whole caravan back to Uganda, he was again welcomed by Emperor Mtesa, and was provided by this ruler with a couple of thousand men as escort. This enabled him, without danger, to explore a large tract of country towards the west, but he did not, as he had hoped to do, reach the Albert Nyanza, for the Wanyora gathered in such numbers as to make it impossible to resist them. Still, he had succeeded in showing beyond doubt that the Victoria Nyanza was a single tract of water, and it now remained to circumnavigate Lake Tanganyika and to discover its supposed outlet. Having travelled southward to the Tanganyika, he launched his boat thereon, and, voyaging round it, discovered that there was only one outlet, and that a periodical one. At that time its waters were steadily issuing by the Lukuga River, and flowing westward to join the Lualaba; but when a period of drought recurred, the waters of Lake Tanganyika would be lowered, and the Lukuga bed would be filled with encroaching vegetation. So much for the problem of these two great lakes. But what about the Lualaba? He had to trace the course of that river downwards in order to discover whether it became the Congo, the Niger, or the Nile.

When, after circumnavigating the lake, Stanley got back to Ujiji, where he had left Frank Pocock, he found the latter seriously ill. Five of the Wangwana, the armed men brought from Zanzibar, had died from smallpox; many of them had deserted. Then came a desertion which was a great distress to Stanley, that of the boy Kalulu, whom, after his previous visit to this part of the world, he had taken to England and to the United States, and whom he had placed in an English school for eighteen months, during his own absence on the Gold Coast. He had taken a great fancy to the lad, and while on the Ashantee campaign he used to get regular reports from Edward Marston concerning Kalulu's welfare. Here we have one of the few instances in Stanley's life in which we find him showing strong affection, for in general, as I have repeatedly insisted, he was a lonely man. His deep concern about a Negro boy serves but to emphasise his general aloofness. After a few days the runaway was recovered, and Stanley had him whipped. Later, when the boy was drowned in the Congo (in the Kalulu Falls, subsequently called by his name), Stanley mourned his loss bitterly. This is the only episode of the kind mentioned in any of his writings, but it suffices to show us that there were unexplored regions in the great explorer's own soul.

In the district of Uhumbo, which was next visited, no white man had ever been seen before, so we can well understand that Stanley's arrival caused intense excitement. The amazement was reciprocal, for he tells us that never before had he seen such hideous creatures as the inhabitants of this region. Their ornaments, worn about their waists, were likewise repulsive: tags of monkey

125

skin and bits of gorilla bone, goat horn, shells, and the like. Round their necks were heads of mice, skins of vipers, and other fragments from the animal world. They were filthy in their persons, had an offensive smell, and smeared themselves with ochre. The joke was that while the white men were loftily disputing as to whether the beings before them were human, the creatures were actually expressing strong doubts as to whether the whites could be men! It seemed to him that he had been suddenly transferred to another planet, thousands of millions of years younger than our own.

For a time Livingstone had believed that the Lualaba was the upper part of the Congo, but then he had changed his mind. Stanley reports him as having said, "Anything for the Nile, but I will not be made black men's meat for the Congo!" This does not seem to square very well with our knowledge of Livingstone's character. However that may be, Stanley was perfectly willing to risk his life for the Congo. A march of two hundred and twenty miles from the western shore of Lake Tanganyika brought him to the Lualaba, which here, in the very centre of the continent, was fourteen hundred yards wide. "A noble breadth, pale grey in colour, winding slowly from south and by east. In the centre rose two or three small islets, green with the foliage of trees and the verdure of sage. It was my duty to follow it to the ocean whatever might hap during the venture." He pressed on along the river to the Arab colony of Mwana-Mamba, the chief of which was Tippu-Tib, a rich Arab, who owned hundreds of slaves. His was an interesting figure, destined to play a considerable part in Stanley's life, not only at this juncture, but also later, under somewhat sinister conditions, during the Emin Pasha expedition.

So long as Tanganyika and its fertile shores were still close at hand, Stanley had reason to fear lest the Wangwana should desert, so he needed an escort of armed men, and hoped to get the services of Tippu-Tib and his myrmidons at a reasonable price. Tippu-Tib would do anything for a price. Stanley explained his wants. The Arab said he had only two hundred and fifty men.

"They are enough."

"Yes, added to your people, but not enough to bring me back safe after you would leave them, through such a country as lies beyond Myangwe."

"But, my friend, think how it would be with me, with half a continent before me."

"Oh, well, if you white people are fools enough to throw away your lives, that is no reason why Arabs should! We travel little by little, to get ivory and slaves, and are years about it. It is now nine years since I left Zanzibar. What is this river to you? What do you want to know about it?"

Stanley tried to make him understand. Tippu-Tib

shook his head. After a while he called one of his men, Abed by name, who had travelled farther to the west and to the north than anyone else known in those parts.

"Speak, Abed, tell us what you know of this river."

"I know all about the river, praise be to Allah!"

"In what direction does it flow, my friend?"

"It flows north."

"And then?"

"It flows north."

"And then?"

"Still north. I tell you, Sir, it flows north, and north, and north, and there is no end to it. I think it reaches the Salt Sea; at least my friends say that it must."

"Well, point out the direction in which this Salt Sea is."

"God only knows."

The information was too typically oriental to be of much use to Stanley, but Tippu-Tib was open to a deal. He was used to taking risks! For a thousand pounds he would provide the escort Stanley wanted.

Stanley talked the matter over with his companion, Frank Pocock, the only white man left with him. Stanley said:

"These Arabs have told such frightful tales about the lands north of here, that unless Tippu-Tib accepts my offer, the expedition will be broken up, for our men are demoralised through fear of cannibals and pythons,

128

leopards and gorillas, and all sorts of horrible things. Canoes we cannot get. Now, what do you say, Frank? Shall we go south to the Zambesi; shall we explore northeast of here, strike across to Uganda, and thence back to Zanzibar; or shall we follow this great river, which for all these thousands of years has been flowing northward through hundreds, possibly thousands of miles, the great river of which no one has ever heard a word? Fancy, by and by, after building or buying canoes, floating down the river, day by day, to the Nile, or to some vast lake in the far north, or to the Congo and the Atlantic Ocean!"

Pocock's suggestion was:

"Let's toss up; best two out of three to decide it."

"Toss away, Frank; here's a rupee. Heads for the north and the Lualaba; tails for the south and the Zambesi."

Frank tossed again and again, and tails won six times running. But (and this is characteristic of the man), despite the omen of the coin, Stanley decided after all to go northward and down the Lualaba. He could not accept any decision except that which he had spontaneously come to.

Frank Pocock was content, and said:

"Sir, have no fear of me! I shall stand by you"— not knowing that he was pronouncing his own death-sentence.

Ere long matters were settled with Tippu-Tib, who

agreed to accompany the expedition northward with the requisite number of men. A contract was signed, and Stanley gave the Arab a promissory note for one thousand pounds. On November 5, 1876, a force of about seven hundred persons, consisting of Tippu-Tib's slaves and Stanley's expedition, departed from the town of Nyangwe and entered the dismal forestland to the north.

"Outside the woods blazed a blinding sunshine; but underneath that immense and everlasting roof-foliage were a solemn twilight and the humid warmth of a Turkish bath. The trees shed continual showers of tropic dew. Down the boles and branches, massive creepers, and slender vegetable cords, the warm moisture trickled and fell in great globes." Walking in the customary way had become impossible. "Our usual orderly line was soon broken, the column was miles in length. Every man needed room to sprawl and crawl and scramble as he best could, and every fibre and muscle was required for that purpose. Sometimes prostrate forest-giants barred the roads with a mountain of twigs and branches. The pioneers had to carve a passage for the caravan and the boat sections. . . . For ten days we endured it; then the Arabs declared they could go no farther. As they were obstinate in this determination, I had recourse to another arrangement. I promised them five hundred pounds if they would escort us twenty marches only. It was accepted. I proposed to strike for

130

the river. ... Seventeen days from Nyangwe, we saw
again the great river. Remembering the toil of the forest
march, and viewing the stately breadth and calm flow
of the mighty stream, I here resolved to launch my boat
for the last time."

The boat, of course, could carry no more than a
few of the Wangwana besides the leader himself. The
rest of the column, proceeding by land, could not keep
up, so the boat had frequently to wait for it, on one
occasion as long as three days. The men of the marching division were tired out. "Nevertheless, nothing was
to be gained by a halt. We were in search of friendly
savages, if such could be found, where we might rest.
But, as day after day passed, we found the natives increasing rather than abating in wild rancour and unrea-
sonable hate of strangers. At every curve and bend they
'telephoned' along the river their warning signals; the
forests on either bank flung hither and thither the strange
echoes; their huge wooden drums sounded the muster
for fierce resistance. Reed arrows, tipped with poison,
were shot at us from the jungle as we glided by. ...
What a terrible land! Both banks, shrouded in tall
primeval forest, were filled with invisible savage enemies; out of every bush glared eyes flaming with hate;
in the stream lurked the crocodiles to feed upon the
unfortunates; the air seemed impregnated with the seeds
of death!

"On December 18, our miseries culminated in a

131

grand effort of the savages to annihilate us. The cannibals had manned the topmost branches of the trees above
the village of Vinya-Njara; they lay like pards crouching amid the garden plants, or coiled like pythons in
clumps of sugar-cane. . . . For three days, with scarcely
any rest, the desperate fighting lasted. Finally Tippu-Tib
appeared. His men cleared the woods; and by night I
led a party across the river, capturing thirty-six canoes
belonging to those who had annoyed us on the right
bank. Then peace was made. I purchased twenty-three
canoes, and surrendered the others."

Stanley had made his plan. He would keep on un-
hesitatingly down the river. Tippu-Tib would accompany the expedition no further, but Stanley no longer
wanted him. The explorer had got far enough from
Nyangwe. Its seductive life could no longer tempt his
people. Hitherto he had needed Tippu-Tib's slaves to
force his own reluctant followers to obey orders. They
would no longer have any choice. In his own English
boat and in the twenty-three canoes he had just bought,
he would commit himself to the current of the unknown
river. The Arabs might prophesy certain death if they
would. What was the risk of death in the balance against
his burning desire to know, against his love of hazard
for its own sake, against the daimonic lure exerted by
the name of the Congo?

2. *The River*

STANLEY'S seven months' voyage down the Congo across the African continent to the Atlantic ranks with Columbus' voyage and with other great enterprises of the same kind, which are fewer than is commonly supposed, and whose achievement gives the adventurers who carry them out a high place in the history of civilisation. Whatever the primary motive may have been, and no matter whether (measured upon a scale of moral absolutes) it be regarded as a high one or a low one, its effective valuation cannot be made until after the event. Thanks only to such enterprises does it come to pass that there are new things in the world, things which no one had previously seen or imagined, a new law, a new path for mankind, a new idea of the commonwealth, a new image of the Godhead.

I am aware that some of my readers will contend that no such exalted estimate can be taken of that which, they will declare, was at the lowest estimate a mere adventure, and at the highest estimate a journey of geographical exploration. There is something to be said for such a view. Yet what but these were Marco Polo's travels, Magellan's rounding of Cape Horn, John Ross's Arctic voyages, Shackleton's expedition to the South Pole, and many other great excursions of earlier and of recent times? Yet those I have just named brought eternal fame to the men who undertook them. In every case

133

alike there was at work the same craving to enlarge the bounds of geographical knowledge; and when we judge the greatness of the achievement, we have no other standard than the character of the leader, his human capacity, the vigour of his intuitions—and the practical upshot. Stanley's personality places him far above the ordinary level. The man had very remarkable characteristics. I do not see how he can possibly be regarded as a less outstanding explorer than Vasco da Gama, Nordenskjöld, or La Condamine. As to the upshot, as to the practical results, they are obvious to every one. By this one expedition, a flood of light was thrown upon a vast territory, previously unvisited; the darkness was lifted from a huge area of our planet. If mankind does not know how to make the best use of the gifts bestowed on it, that is another story. Great discoverers have never foreseen that the lands they throw open to civilisation are likely to bear Dead Sea fruit.

In this case the mere resolve was amazing. Here was a man with no more than a fleet of nutshells who made up his mind to travel down a river which flowed for thousands and thousands of miles through lands still completely unknown; to face dangers and sufferings as compared with which those previously endured were likely to be no more than child's play; to accept daily and hourly exposure to the risks of illness, famine, and death; to encounter Nature herself in her most savage manifestations as an unceasing and ever-vigilant enemy.

So bold, so amazing, so marvellous was this determination, that even success in carrying it out seems a minor matter. Success, doubtless, crowns a resolve and gives it a firm standing in history; but it has no bearing upon the significance of the resolve as a heroic deed.

Twice in his life did Stanley thus act with unparalleled impetuosity. The second occasion was during the Emin Pasha expedition, when he retraced his footsteps through the deadly forests of Central Africa in search of the Rear Column.

As they make their way downstream, the forests form gloomy walls on either bank, black depths which the eye cannot penetrate. But on the open stream the sunlight is so fiery-hot that one would think it must set the very water aflame. Contemplating the forest and the river, sensing the tremendous tranquillity—these are the hours in which Stanley discovers himself and forgets his troubles. He discovers himself, and he discovers the powers above. His attitude towards Nature is not a vague pantheism, is not the expression of a flight from the divine and from present responsibility, but the humble acceptance of a doom to dwell for ever lonely in the transcendental. At such times, his attitude towards natives who are not actively hostile resembles that of Livingstone in its gentleness. He grieves to recall how narrow is the distance that separates cruelty from the love of our neighbours.

135

Farewell to Tippu-Tib was said on December 28, 1876. A week later, Stanley was in sight of the first cataract, now known as Stanley Falls. The main stream, here more than eight hundred yards wide, and running east-north-east, dashes against a mountainous cliff, so that the air is filled with spray. As it rushes towards the falls, terrible whirlpools are formed. This is no place for boats. The travellers must land, and carry their frail vessels along the bank until quiet water is regained. It is as if an army were turning a hostile position. With incredible labour (which will be repeated again and again, for the river is full of rapids and waterfalls and rocky barriers) they effect the transport through the primeval forest and over pathless heights.

Now there is an interesting change in the scenery. The river glides beneath porphyry caves, on the walls of which the natives have graven mystical signs, squares and cones. Here Stanley cuts his name to commemorate the passing of the first white man who has ever visited the spot, or, as he remarks, the only white man who ever got by without being eaten by the indigenes.

He has compiled a list of two hundred words with the aid of which he can hold parley with the native tribes about matters of primary importance; for, although the dialects vary, they are substantially akin.

In a village named Utikera, where a local war has been going on, all the inhabitants have fled except one ancient, who, with much eloquence, bewails his lot, and

136

who looks like a venerable river-god about to return into the waters. There are, indeed, numerous forsaken islands, numerous deserted villages. Here, as in all parts of the world, men are destroying one another, and then making peace again for a time. In the heart of Africa, migrations, destruction, and reconstruction have probably been going on for hundreds of thousands of years.

After the seventh cataract, the river narrows from a width of a mile to that of half a mile, then a quarter of a mile or less, and divides into channels through which the water races thunderously. It is only by the favour of fortune that the boats escape being smashed. Perpetual fights keep the strange armada busy. From the confluence of the Ruiki with the Congo until reaching the land of Ituka, Stanley's force was engaged in four-and-twenty skirmishes; when the sun went down, the wounded had to be cared for and the dead to be buried; it was dangerous to spend the night in the open stream; so evening after evening a camp had to be fortified on the shore. Continually the boats had to be guarded, and the safety of the wives and children of the Wangwana provided for. Since the mere arrival of the floating expedition aroused the fury of the natives, Stanley had to accept the daily bloodshed, the unceasing combats, as unavoidable; but his self-confidence never waned, and the witchery of the great river held him in thrall. The river had become his faithful companion, his destiny.

137

Here in Ituka, the river threw off the mask behind which, as it were, it had hitherto been hidden, and definitely assumed a westward course, becoming much wider now, ranging up to two miles and more. It was almost as if he were already within sight of the Atlantic, visible at any rate in a mirage; as in a dream he drifted down the mighty stream which it had become his mission to follow to the end. The islands were becoming more numerous, each of them a little paradise. Were it not for the incessant attacks of the natives, for the exhaustion that resulted from the daily struggle for food, he might have been inclined to renounce his aim, and to settle down in search of oblivion in this wonder-world, as Livingstone had done a thousand miles to the east. But with such "filthy, vulturous ghouls," as Stanley calls them in his disgust, there could be no question of making peace. In huge boats, rowed by eighty men, they massed for the onslaught. Their hair was decked with red and grey feathers, every oar was headed with an ivory ball; the drums throbbed, the trumpets blared, the war-songs threatened; there was no time for prayer or for contemplation. "Boys, be firm as iron; wait until you see the first spear, and then take good aim. . . . Don't think of running away, for only your guns can save you."

These blacks were cannibals; among the ashes of their fires lay the scorched ribs and the empty skulls of their foes. But all these troubles were disregarded when, one day, the adventurers reached a huge tributary, the

138

Aruwimi, flowing from the north, and now the westward trend of the main stream became permanent. This could be no other river than the Congo. Doubt was at an end. They were voyaging on one of the world's greatest and most ancient rivers; it was like an aorta flowing out of the heart of Africa.

How luxuriant was the vegetation! "Beautiful was it then to glide among the lazy creeks of the spicy and palm-crowned isles, where the broad, lofty Amomum vied in greenness with the drooping fronds of the Phrynium, where the myrrh and bdellium shrubs exhaled their fragrance side by side with the wild cassia; where the capsicum with its red-hot berries rose in embowering masses, and the Ipomoea's purple buds gemmed with colour the tall stem of some sturdy tree." They had reached the land of Rubunga. Here, at length, the inhabitants were friendly. The call "Sennenneh" (peace) filled them with delight. "I stood up with my ragged old helmet pushed far, far back, that they might scrutinise my face and the lines of suasion be properly seen. With a banana in one hand and a gleaming armlet of copper and beads of various colours in the other, I began the pantomime. . . . I implored the assembled hundreds of Rubunga to yield to the captivating influence of fair and honest barter. I clashed the copper bracelets together, lovingly handled the shining armlet, and allured their attention with beads of the brightest colours, nor were the polished folds of yellow brass omitted; and again the banana was lifted to my open mouth. Then what suspense, what patience, what a saint-like air of resignation! I think I may be pardoned for all that degrading pantomime. I had a number of hungry, half-wild children; and through a cannibal world we had ploughed to reach these unsophisticated children of Nature. We waited, and at length an old chief came down the high bank to the lower landing near some rocks. He nodded!" An agreement had been reached. This is but one pen-picture among thousands, as vivid as those of the Odyssey.

One cannot but ask oneself what charm it was that brought the leader unscathed through all these perils. He gives the answer himself. "Had I been a black man, I should long before have been slain; but even in the midst of a battle, curiosity stronger than hate or blood-thirstiness arrested the sinewy arm which drew the bow, and delayed the flying spear." The blacks were paralysed by astonishment at something they had never seen before—a white man! But the white man must not stir, must not lift a finger, for if he did so the spell would be broken.

His own folk have absolute trust in him. True, they grow impatient at times, asking again and again how it will all end, and whither this interminable journey will lead them. But they do not doubt him. They look up to

140

him as to a god. This, perhaps, is what makes him so strong. A man becomes a hero because of the faith he inspires.

It was the end of February, 1877. The islands, now, were countless; while the numerous bays, lateral channels, and backwaters made it difficult to be sure of the route. But even when they had taken a wrong course, each of these lovely islands offered shelter and protection. "I shall ever and forever remember them," writes Stanley; and we feel that he has fallen in love with the river and the world through which it flows. "These bosky islands: there was no treachery or guile in their honest depths." The words cannot but remind us of Rousseau's enthusiasm for "nature"; or of the Sentimental Journey of an eighteenth-century traveller. When, as in the region of Ikengo, the natives are friendly he forgets all his troubles. "They get angry and sulky again. It was like playing with and coaxing spoiled children. We amused them in various ways, and they finally became composed, and were conquered by good-nature." With a generous scorn of return gifts they presented him with a gourdful of palm wine. "Of all the things which took their fancy, my notebook, which they called 'tara-tara,' or looking-glass, appeared to them the most wonderful. They believed it possessed manifold virtues, and that it came from above. Would I, could I, sell it to them? It would have found a ready sale, but as it contained rec-

141

ords of disaster by flood and fire, charts of rivers and creeks and islands, sketches of men and manners, notes upon a thousand objects, I could not part with it even for a tusk of ivory."

At this stage of the journey, he could hardly ever get any sleep. Clouds of mosquitoes filled his tent; their humming sounded like the distant war-cries of the savages when they were inflaming one another's passions for combat. The noise made him nervous, and his heart beat fast, as if he were in a fever.

In the land of Chumbiri, the king came to greet him in person. There is a picture of this monarch wearing a brimless cylindrical hat which makes him look like a chimney-sweep; and another of his principal wife, with her hair dressed and plastered and puffed until it resembles a ram's horns. The king of Chumbiri had forty wives, and as each of them wore a thick brass collar round her neck, Stanley calculated that the total amount of brass worn by these royal ladies must have been eight hundred pounds. "I asked the king what he did with the brass on the neck of a dead wife. He smiled. Cunning rogue; he regarded me benevolently, as though he loved me for the searching question. Significantly he drew his finger across his throat! He provided me with an escort of forty-five men, in three canoes, under the leadership of his eldest son, who was instructed by his father to accompany us as far as the pool later called Stanley Pool."

142

The river now had a depth ranging from twenty to thirty fathoms. Hitherto the water had been light in colour, a sort of whitish grey, but here it assumed the aspect of strong tea. There had been numerous affluents, so that it had greatly increased in width. But the hope that the expedition would thenceforward be able to float peacefully down to the sea proved deceptive. "It is no longer the stately stream of mystic beauty, noble grandeur, and gentle uninterrupted flow which along the course of nearly nine hundred miles ever fascinated us, despite the savagery of its peopled shores, but a furious river rushing down a steep bed obstructed by reefs of lava, projecting barriers of rock, lines of immense boulders, winding in crooked course through deep chasms, and dropping down over terraces in a long series of falls, cataracts, and rapids. Our frequent contests with the savages culminated in tragic struggles with the mighty river as it rushed and roared through the deep-yawning pass that leads from the broad tableland down towards the Atlantic Ocean." At a distance of only one hundred and fifty-five geographical miles from the summit of the first fall, the broad Congo resumes a peaceful flow at a level lower by nearly eleven hundred feet. "The roar of the rapids was tremendous and deafening. I can only compare it to the thunder of an express train through a rocky tunnel. To speak to my neighbour, I had to bawl in his ear."

Once more the boats had to be carried over a long

portage. Not a portage made familiar by use and wont, for a road had to be built.

At one of these falls they had a terrible loss. Three of the boats, failing to make the bank soon enough, were swept into the centre of the stream and carried over the cataract.

In one of these was the lad Kalulu, with four other followers of Stanley, all good men, while of two of them, as of Kalulu, he was especially fond. None of them was saved. The second of the lost boats had two men on board. These two, strangely enough, escaped destruction, and managed to get ashore below the fall. The third canoe to be swept away, a small and light one, had only one man on board. "We were within hail when he perceived himself to be driving helplessly towards the falls. He shouted to us 'La il Allah il Allah'—there is but one God—'I am lost! Master!' " It was because of the drowning here of the lad of whom he had been so fond that Stanley called this cataract Kalulu Falls.

In the district of Inkisi, the prospects of the voyage seemed almost hopeless. Here there was no clear drop in the waters, "but the river, being forced through a chasm only four hundred yards wide, is flanked by curling waves of destructive fury, which meet in the centre, overlap, and strike each other, while below is an absolute chaos of mad waters, leaping waves, deep troughs, contending watery ridges, tumbling and tossing over a distance of two miles." The gorge was lined by steep cliffs. Stanley climbed to the tableland on the top of one of the cliffs, and took a survey of the situation. To diverge into the wilderness north or south of the river seemed to him impossible, and he could not stay where he was. "Good! I will haul my canoes up the mountain and pass over the tableland, as I must now cling to this river to the end, having followed it so long.

"My resolution was soon communicated to my followers, who looked blank at the proposition. The natives heard me, and, seeing the silence and the reluctance of the people, they asked the cause, and I told them that it was because I intended to drag our vessels up the mountain.

" 'Up the mountain,' they repeated, turning their eyes towards the towering height which was shagged with trees and bristling with crags and hill fragments, with an unspeakable look of horror."

But there was no other way. The only thing was to get to work, surmounting difficulties and dangers. Several of the boats were damaged; so in the forest through which they passed some new boats were built of teak, one of them forty-five feet long, two feet two inches beam, and eighteen inches deep, flat-bottomed. The height of the portage over which the other boats had to be conveyed was more than twelve hundred feet. A smithy had to be erected; a road cut through the forest. Rocks, even, had to be shattered to clear the

145

way. At this time Frank Pocock began to suffer from ulcers on the legs; a number of the native followers sickened from dysentery; others showed symptoms of extreme general weakness. But the work had to be done. The leader, strong of will, would allow of no slacking until the obstacle had been overcome and they could continue their voyage down the open river. The savages were amazed. For them Stanley was already Bula Matari, the Rock-Breaker. This was the name by which he was to become famous throughout all the Congo basin. He was gravely concerned, however, to learn that there were still five waterfalls on the lower reaches of the river.

One incident of this period must not be omitted, for it gives so extraordinarily vivid a picture of Stanley's relationships with those under his command. These were "his own" people—not merely because they were in his pay. He felt very differently towards them as compared with the primitives, the cannibals, against whom he had to defend himself. Mohammedans, with a civilised tradition, they were ages ahead of the Central African natives. The affair we have to describe concerns the behaviour of a man named Uledi, a coxswain, whom Stanley greatly esteemed, and who had saved thirteen members of the caravan from death by drowning. "He was," writes the leader, "the best soldier, sailor, and artisan, and the most faithful servant of the expedition."

146

Now it transpired that "this ennobled, beloved, and honoured servant (a name I do not like to apply to him) had robbed me!" A sack of beads had been ripped open, and a considerable quantity had been abstracted. "Beads abstracted! At such a period, when every bead is of more value to me than its bulk in gold or gems, when the lives of so many people depend upon the strictest economy, when I have punished myself by the most rigid abstinence from meat in order to feed the people!"

He asked various members of the company, and their suspicions were all concentrated upon Uledi. Stanley had the latter's mat opened, and found in it over five pounds of the fine Sami-Sami beads, sufficient for nearly two days' provisions for the whole expedition. The thief was placed under guard. The leader assembled the whole of his company to judge the case. Having explained what had happened, he turned to the boat's crew and said: "Now, you boys, you who know Uledi so well and have followed him like children through a hundred rough seas, speak, what shall be done to him?"

Mpwapwa, one of the steadiest of these men, replied: "Uledi is like our elder brother, and to give our voice for punishing him would be like asking you to punish ourselves. But the fathers of the people have demanded that he shall be beaten. Yet, Master, for our sakes, beat him only just a little."

"And you, Marzouk, Uledi's companion on the rock

147

of the fourth cataract of the Stanley Falls, what do you say?"

"Verily, Master, Mpwapwa has spoken what my tongue would have uttered. Yet I would say, remember it is Uledi."

"And you, Shumari, who are Uledi's brother, what punishment shall I mete to this thief who would starve everybody, you and me?"

"Oh, dear Master, your words are as lead. Spare him! Or at least, since the chiefs say he must be flogged, give me half the flogging, and knowing it is for Uledi's sake, I shall not feel it."

"Now, Siawa, you who are his cousin, what do you say?"

"Will the master give his slave liberty to speak?"

"Yes, say all that is in your heart, Siawa."

"The master is wise. All things that happen he writes in a book. Each day there is something written. We, black men, know nothing, neither have we any memory. What we saw yesterday is to-day forgotten. Yet the master forgets nothing. Perhaps if the master will look into his books he may see something about Uledi. How Uledi behaved on Lake Tanganyika; how he rescued Zaidi from the cataract; how he has saved many men whose names I cannot remember from the river; how he worked harder on the canoes than any three men; how he has been the first to listen to your voice always; how he has been the father of the boat-boys; and

148

many other things. If, as the chiefs say, Uledi should be punished, Shumari says he will take a half of the punishment. Then give Siawa the other half and set Uledi free. Siawa has spoken."

"Very well," said Stanley. "Uledi, by the voice of the people, is condemned, but as Shumari and Siawa have promised to take the punishment on themselves, Uledi is set free and Shumari and Siawa are pardoned."

Uledi, upon being released, stepped forward and said: "Master, it was not Uledi who stole, it was the devil who entered into his heart. Uledi will be good in future, and if he pleased his master before he will please his master much more in time to come."

Stanley's action here was wise as well as clement, and could serve only to heighten his authority. In the simplicity and naturalness of the description, the scene gives us an even finer and truer picture of the leader than of the led.

The inhabitants of Mowa, who had hitherto been friendly, came to the camp one day in great numbers, bearing arms, and with a threatening mien. When Stanley asked them what was the matter, they told him that they were afraid of the tara-tara. The day before some of their people had watched him making marks in it. "This is very bad. Our country will waste, our goats will die, our bananas will rot and our women will dry up. . . . We have gathered together to fight you if you do not burn that tara-tara now before our eyes. If you burn it, we go away, and shall be friends as heretofore."

Stanley was in a quandary. He could not possibly sacrifice his invaluable diary to the superstition of the natives. Going to his tent, he rummaged his book-box, and came across a volume of Shakespeare, which, worn and well-thumbed, was of the same size as the diary, and with a similar cover. That would do. He took it out to them. "Is this the tara-tara, friends, that you wish burned?"

"Yes, yes, that is it!"

"Well, take it, and burn it, or keep it if you like."

"No, no, no, we will not touch it. It is fetish. You must burn it."

"I! Well, let it be so. I will do anything to please my good friends of Mowa."

"We walked to the nearest fire," writes Stanley, "I breathed regretful farewell to my genial companion, which during many weary hours of night had assisted to relieve my mind when oppressed by almost intolerable woes, and then carefully consigned the innocent Shakespeare to the flames, heaping the brush fuel over it with ceremonious care."

"Oh, oh," breathed the poor deluded natives, sighing their relief.

When, on its westward journey, the exploring party first came into contact with blacks provided with European firearms, their feelings of satisfaction may have

150

been not unmingled with regret. Plainly the lowlands must be near, the mouth of the river, where white men had established colonies, from which trade routes led into the interior. I cannot but wonder whether Stanley had any anxious reflections upon this matter; whether, thenceforward, he may have been inclined to take a milder view of the resistance the aborigines in the interior had offered to his passing, that of the first white man they had ever seen. Their instincts may have been savage and cruel, but the instincts were sound enough, seeing what they had to expect from the white invasion. The white invaders, in their turn, were but simpletons if they expected to be received with open arms by these unsophisticated folk among whom they established themselves by force and by guile, bringing with them all the blessings of civilisation—such as distilled spirits, syphilis, forced labour, speedy degeneration, a fall in the value of all produce, and the dispossession of the natives from their lands. We gather, however, that Stanley had no such forebodings. In these matters he was as innocent as a child. He had no doubt as to the superiority of the white race, or as to the benefits which their mental and material goods would confer upon the blacks. When, half a century later, a man of wide knowledge, André Gide, visited the Congo region, he was to be reduced to shame and despair by the study of what had happened to the natives under the rule of civilised nations.

On June 3, 1877, Frank Pocock fell a victim to the mighty river. His boat was swamped in one of the rapids, he was drowned, and his body was not recovered until more than a week later. Stanley's sorrow was keen, for Pocock had become a friend. On the Wangwana, the effect of the tragedy was amazing. "It stupefied them, benumbing their faculties of feeling, of habit, and of action. From this date began that exhibition of apathetic sullenness and lack of feeling for themselves and for their comrades which distinguished their after-lives in the cataracts. The slightest illness would cause them to lean against a rock, or crouch by the fire in a posture of despair. They never opened their lips to request help or medicine, and as they were inaccessible to solicitude for themselves, they had none to bestow on others. After this fatal day, I could scarcely get a reply to my questions when anxious to know what their ailments were. Familiarity with many forms of disease, violent and painful deaths, and severe accidents had finally deadened, almost obliterated, that lively fear of death which they had formerly shown."

This apathy lasted for many days. Then, one evening, Stanley called them together and asked them what was amiss. "They could say nothing, except that they were tired and were not going to work more. Death was in the river; a wearisome repetition of frightful labour waiting for them each day on the rocks. Their stomachs were hungry; they had no strength."

152

Stanley replied: "And I have none, my friends, I assure you. I am as hungry as any of you. I could get meat to make me strong, but it would be robbing you. I am so tired and sorry that I could lie down smiling and die. My white brother, who was lost the other day, is far happier than I. If you all leave me, I am safe, and there is no responsibility on me. I have my boat, and it is in the river. The current is swift, the fall is only a few yards off. My knife can cut the rope, and I can then go to sleep forever. There are the beads, take them, do what you will. While you stay with me, I follow this river until I come to the point where it is known. If you do not stay with me, I still will cling to the river, and will die in it."

This speech had its due effect. The men came to their senses, and recovered their self-control.

Throughout history such situations have always been met in the same way. It was thus that Alexander quelled a mutiny by an eloquent address to his soldiers; it was thus that Ulysses instilled new courage into the faint-hearts among his companions; it was thus that Columbus put an end to disaffection among his ship-mates. Such recurrences show how our minds always react in like wise to like situations.

In thirty days they made only three miles' progress, and there were more drownings. Waterfall followed rapid and rapid followed waterfall; and the most difficult were still in front of them. In the rapids, the boats were tied together with rattan cables; and when they wanted to land they had to climb the cliffs by means of ladders made of the same material. Stanley, his spirit attuned to the spirits of his Mohammedan companions, found himself in a fatalist mood, hearkening to an inner voice that said, "What will be, will be." Below Mbelo Falls the stream, brown-black and menacing, entered the main river from behind the rocky islets; they were whirled round twice by the eddying pool, precipitated into a dancing, seething, hissing cauldron, just as if the river were boiling over. Stanley's men believed, for a while, that their master had been drowned.

"When they saw me advancing towards them, I was like one risen from the dead to them. 'Yes, we shall reach the sea, please God!' said they. 'We see the hand of God, now. But you must not tempt the wicked river any more, Master. We shall do it ourselves. Better far that we die than you. You shall not go to the river again until we are beyond the falls.' " This spontaneous avowal of loyalty and trust, renewed Stanley's confidence.

At Isangila, on July 30, he learned that the sea was only five days distant, and, since there was now no shadow of doubt that he was on the Congo, and there were several more waterfalls to pass, he decided to follow the advice of the natives and make an overland

154

march. The boats were drawn up on the strand and were left to their fate. "A wayworn, feeble, and suffering column were we, when, on August 1, we filed across the rocky terrace of Isangila, a sloping plain, and strode up the ascent to the tableland. Nearly forty men filled the sick-list with dysentery, ulcers, and scurvy, and the victims of the latter disease were steadily increasing." Only one of the company marched forward indomitably, the leader Bula Matari. Their way led across a hot and arid plain, whose inhabitants were dirty, and neglected-looking (thanks to the nearness of civilisation!), and would only sell food in exchange for gin. " 'Gin! And from me! Why, men, two and a half years ago I left the Indian Sea, and how can I have gin? Give us food that we may live, or beware of hungry men.' They gave us refuse of their huts, some peanuts, and sodden bananas."

On August 4, in the village of Nganda, Stanley wrote an appeal for help, addressed "To any Gentleman who speaks English at Boma"; adding as a postscript, "You may not know me by name; I therefore add that I am the person who discovered Livingstone in 1871."

The white traders on the coast, for whom the arrival of this letter was a first-class sensation, hastened to send a caravan with the required aid. On August 12, 1877, nearly three years after he had set out from the Indian Ocean, he reached Boma, where he was given a warm welcome by the representatives of the various firms which had branches in the settlement. The news of his arrival had been cabled all over the world before he went to sleep that night.

His first care, now, was for his companions, the payment of their wages, the healing of their sicknesses, and the chartering of a ship to take them home to Zanzibar. Instead of sailing direct from Boma to England, he accompanied them round the Cape, and would not bid them farewell until they had been restored to their own country. I have been told that this faithfulness of a white master to his men has become legendary in Zanzibar.

CHAPTER SIX

ILLUSION

THE most remarkable characteristic of such a nature as Stanley's is its inexhaustible supply of bodily and nervous energy, and therewith the capacity for physical renewal, which proceeds without rest, without recreation, without any periods of recuperation. It was as if his father and his forefathers, his mother and his foremothers, had stored up all their internal energy, all their will to live, for him alone, so that he had become the sole user of their accumulated capital of vitality. The user and the consumer—for such persons are not content with the interest, but spend the capital as well, making an end of it rapidly. They have no taste for economy. By spending heedlessly, thriftlessly, they give their ancestors to understand that, as far as they of the new generation are concerned, the reproduction of the race has become superfluous.

From the time of his arrival in Boma, he never lost the conviction that he had discovered a continent, or at

157

least the largest and most important part of a continent; had discovered it and won it for Europe. But discovery and a nominal taking possession of this part of the world in the name of the white race were only the first steps. The next, more responsible if not more difficult, was the introduction of civilisation. He had laid open a tract comparable in extent and resources to the basin of the Amazon or the Mississippi. What his vision saw, what his supreme effort was given to, was the transformation of its millions of people from barbarism: the transformation of those who were oppressed by all the ills of ignorance, superstition and cruelty, into happy and virtuous men and women.

His aim (declares his widow, the loving editor of the journals and memoirs that were still unpublished when he died) was as pure and high as Livingstone's. No one has any right to doubt this, although his efforts were based upon a fundamental misunderstanding. His recipe for the moralisation of the African natives was typically simple. Africa and Europe were to enter into trade relations, and, thereupon, as a result of conjoined philanthropic zeal and scientific labour, within a brief space of time the Golden Age would come into being for Africa. "When I hear the unceasing complaints about bad trade," he exclaims, "about looms that are standing still and blast furnaces that are cold, I always wonder what has become of the spirit of enterprise which once made England famous in the commercial world."

158

As a Briton by birth, he thought first of England, and England's advantage. This was natural in view of the existing relationships of political power. Disappointment quickly followed, however. The curse of Central Africa, he said, had been its isolation. Though a commonplace, the statement was true, inasmuch as it was the expression of geographical conditions which, at that date, were unalterable. Switzerland cannot be removed from the central highlands of Europe to the sea coast! Shrewder was his remark that the only contact of Central Africa with the outer world had been through the ferocious slave-trade, carried on by Europeans on the western shore of the continent through four centuries, until suppressed under English leadership, but still maintained by the Arabs, working wholesale ruin from the east.

The Congo seemed to him a natural channel, and an invitation to legitimate and wholesome commerce. To open it for traffic was indispensable. In his impatience, he would have liked to telegraph instantly to all the rulers of Europe and to institute a competition among them. The obstacle which had prevented the use of the river was a strip of two hundred miles next the sea, where a succession of cataracts and rapids, through rough and sterile hills, made navigation impossible. This strip must be pierced, first by a wagon road, later by a railway. Its human obstacles, chiefly the rapacious African traders or middlemen, shrewd, greedy, and jealous of the white

159

man's intrusion, must be propitiated, or if necessary swept out of the way by the strong hand. Then, from mouth to source of the river, stations must be established as centres of trade and of friendly intercourse.

With this plan, thought out by him in all its details, he went to London, having, as a preliminary, written to the papers disclosing the immense political possibilities open for realisation by Great Britain with the aid of the newly discovered territory. He counted upon widespread popular support, and he counted upon the Government. With scarcely a breathing space, he threw himself into the work of persuading, preaching, imploring the ruling powers in British commerce and in public affairs to seize this grand opportunity. He spoke in all the commercial centres, especially in Manchester and Liverpool, setting forth the immense advantages of such an enterprise. He negotiated with shipowners, with joint-stock companies, with the leading bankers; he had audience of ministers of State. Every one listened to his eloquence; many seemed interested in his schemes; but in the end no one lifted a finger. The common people proved indifferent; the middle classes were otherwise engaged; the Government was disinclined to embark upon a new colonial enterprise. Times were unfavourable, for the troubles in Egypt were engrossing the attention of the Foreign Office and of the City. Once again he was laughed at as a Don Quixote. Others styled him an "adventurer" or a "buccaneer." Others professed to be

HENRY M. STANLEY AND HIS BOY

shocked, and said he put commerce before religion. He received no help or encouragement from Britain.

The one ruler who was quick to interest himself in Stanley's plans was King Leopold of Belgium, a keen man of business as well as an able monarch. When Stanley first got back to Europe in the end of 1877, he was met at Marseilles by messengers from Leopold, who urged him to come to Brussels for a conference, and for the initiation of further African enterprises. He excused himself upon the plea of physical exhaustion, but his real reason for refusing was his hope that England would take up his schemes. Having failed in the land of his birth, in August, 1878, he met King Leopold's commissioners in Paris. The vague purpose, to do something scientific or commercial in the basin of the Congo, crystallised into Stanley's plan as given above. There was close study, with a careful analysis of details; the papers were sent to Leopold, and Stanley kept in touch with the project. But again he urged upon England to take the lead, and again fruitlessly. Although England had the widest colonial experience, the most abundant financial resources, the outstanding prestige, she would do nothing in the matter. Thereupon, at length, Stanley put himself wholly at King Leopold's disposal. An organisation was formed under the name Comité d'Etudes du Haut Congo; plans were adopted on a modest scale; the sum of £20,000 was subscribed for immediate use, and Stanley was put in charge of the work. Colonel Strauch,

161

of the Belgian army, was chosen president of the society; and he and his associates selected Stanley's European assistants, acting as his base of supplies during the five and a half years (from January 1879 to June 1884) which he spent in the work.

On August 15, 1879, he returned to the mouth of the Congo, almost exactly two years after he had left it. "Having been the first to explore the great river, I am to be the first who shall prove its utility to the world." He was going to civilise the Congo basin; to establish peaceful settlements on the banks of the river; to transform them, in accordance with modern ideas, into national States, in which justice, law, and order would prevail, and the cruel slave-trade would be abolished for ever. Illusion! Yet they were the views of a man who already knew life to its depths, who had travelled hither and thither on so many of its roads, who in general could judge the affairs of the world without prejudice, who had never in other respects shown himself inclined to regard the characters and the doings of friends and foes through rose-tinted spectacles. Illusion! People are always talking to us about the sober judgment and the keen understanding of practical men, of the clear-sightedness of men of action. When blinded by an idea, they grow more fanciful and are more hopelessly out of touch with reality than the dreamiest of poets!

He had brought with him seventy Zanzibaris and Somalis. With the aid of local recruits, this force was now increased to two hundred and ten blacks, with whom, under the officership of fourteen Europeans besides himself, and with four tiny steamers, he set out "for the mastery of the river." In his previous journey he had traced it from the source. Now he was attacking it by proceeding inland from the mouth. A few hours' steaming away from the trading establishments at Boma, at the head of the navigable lower reaches, he founded the first station, Vivi. Wooden huts brought from England were set up, and wagon roads were made. Now, a labour of Hercules, transport must be found for steamers and goods through a long strip of rugged hills. After exploration, the route must be chosen; then the stubborn, dogged labour of road-building over mountains and along precipices. The chief, hammer and drill in hand, showing his men how to use their tools; endless marching and hauling; and at last, a whole year's work had been done. Forward and backward they had travelled 2,532 miles, and as a result they had won a practicable way of fifty-two miles. Not a holiday affair this! Strenuous toil, a diet of beans, goat's flesh, and sodden bananas; the muggy atmosphere of the Congo cañon, with fierce heat from the rocks and bleak winds through the gorges! Six European and twenty-two native lives, and thirteen whites invalided and retired, were part of the price.

It would be monotonous to follow these indefatigable activities through all their phases. Stanley has himself described them most minutely. In his books, we cannot see the wood for the trees; we lose sight of the man amid the multitude of incidents. The incessant movement distracts us from the central figure of him who, intoxicated by his mission, utterly honest and perfectly straightforward, is the real centre of the whole affair. Names and figures; names and figures. What does it mean to us when we read that the second station was called Isangika; the third, Manyanga; the fourth, Leopoldville? A more enlightening detail is that at Manyanga he had so violent an attack of fever that death seemed near. He prescribed for himself the huge dose of sixty grains of quinine, was insensible for twenty-four hours, and then recovered. With incredible labour, he fought his way to Stanley Falls, and tells us triumphantly that the navigable waterways now opened up amount to about six thousand miles, the district they water being estimated as a square of seven hundred and fifty-seven miles either way, a superficies of fifty-six thousand four hundred square miles, nearly the dimensions of the future Free State. It is as if a landowner were measuring his estate, as if a prince were surveying the princedom he had inherited; it is the pride of possession, the delight of the ruler; and also, though this must be less obvious at first sight, it is the age-long passion of the peasant for the soil. But inasmuch as this "farm" of

164

his is a great realm, his passion for it has superhuman elements.

What a Jack of all trades he has to be!—though he is not, as in the old saw, master of none. Nay, he is master of them all. He is road engineer, house builder, land surveyor, machinist, overseer, mason, the writer of diplomatic reports, negotiator, geographer, soldier, schoolmaster, and doctor. He writes home that it is necessary to build a railway along the river. The committee approves. But before anything can be done he must get the consent of hundreds of chiefs, and he holds parley with hundreds of chiefs. Since the white assistants sent him from Europe are young fools of no account, shady adventurers, men who can be of no use to him as collaborators, he demands that they shall be chosen with greater care. His remonstrances prove unavailing, and (his health, too, demanding a change) he goes back to Europe for a time. He must have men he can trust. During his absence at home, however, he is terribly worried at the thought of what incapables, sluggards, and traitors he has left in charge, and how they will make a muddle of everything. His fears are only too well grounded. When he gets back to the Congo, he finds that the stations have been terribly neglected. Leopoldville, from which he had hoped so much, is nothing but a ruin. Wherever he goes, he learns that his subordinates have failed in their duty.

By his tact, firmness, and kindliness, he gradually

165

induces four hundred of the chiefs to renounce their political supremacy. For suitable rewards, they assign him jurisdiction over their territories, so long as their private rights shall be respected. Thus is the foundation stone of the Congo Free State laid. But think what this means, in time, in patience, in personal endeavour, in nervous energy—to go through the same ceremonies four hundred times, to repeat the same arguments, to use the same seductive arts. He has to have an inexhaustible supply of trade goods, bales of cloth, copper wire, beads. Soon these natives will be wearing the red caps of soldiers and the discarded liveries of Brussels footmen; their fields will have been occupied by factories and trading companies; they will have sold their birthright for whisky and gin; and in the eyes of megalomaniac officials from Europe, equipped with unrestricted powers, the privileges they have been granted will be mere scraps of paper. Stanley does not know this, and had a prophet foretold it, he would not have believed. The vision which has obsessed him makes it impossible for him to draw logical inferences from actual experience. But as far as he himself is concerned, he remains free from megalomania. He remains free from the presumption that is so common in the apostles of European civilisation, whose inflated sense of power is often in an inverse ratio to their real worth in the human scale, and who incline to seek compensation for their natural inferiority in the wilderness where no writ runs. Nothing

166

of the sort ever happens in Stanley's case. He has a very modest, almost too modest, conceit of himself, being genuine and sterling in this matter as in all others. Note, for instance, with how little pride he refers to the fine nickname bestowed on him by the natives: "It is for the work of pulverisation of rock that the Vivi chiefs, won-deringly looking on while I taught my men how to wield a sledge-hammer effectively, bestowed on me the title of Bula Matari—Breaker of Rocks—with which, from the sea to Stanley Falls, all natives of the Congo are now so familiar. It is merely a distinctive title, having no privi-leges to boast of, but the friend or 'son' or 'brother' of Bula Matari will not be unkindly treated by the Bakongo, Bateki, or By-yanzi, and that is something surely."

There is a delightful tale of a young chief in the Stanley Pool district, who needed a lesson because of a breach of contract. Stanley staged a little scene to im-press him, a sort of conjuring of spirits with the aid of a gong, upon the striking of which a troop of armed men, previously hidden in the surrounding bush, sud-denly appeared upon the scene. This chief was a braggart, a liar, greedy, capricious, abjectly supersti-tious, and mischief-making. Stanley handled him as an experienced schoolmaster handles a recalcitrant pupil, with inexhaustible patience and without any parade of moral prejudices. He and Stanley had been "blood

167

brothers" before, and when the chief had mended his ways, he was admitted to "blood brotherhood" once more, with crossing of arms, incisions, and solemn pronouncements by the great fetish-man of the tribe, in token of renewed fraternity and fidelity. We may suppose that Stanley took so much trouble about this rapscallion on the principle that one convert makes many. Anyhow, he made a success of the affair. He succeeded in other instances, times without number. He was never preachy-preachy; he left doctrinal religion and the catechism alone; he gave object lessons, set an example; it was always by some clever practical instance that he secured his effects. In this connexion, he quotes a passage from Livingstone's last journals, under date October 28, 1870: "Muini Mukata, who has travelled farther than most Arabs, said to me, 'If a man goes with a good-natured, civil tongue, he may pass through the worst people in Africa unharmed.'" Elsewhere Livingstone declared, and more than once, that he had only encountered resistance and enmity in places where other white men had been before him, or where reports of what white men were like had found their way. In the uncorrupted wilds, he had always met with the most cordial hospitality.

Except in times of depression, Stanley showed the utmost friendliness towards the natives, and sometimes a boyish exuberance of spirits. He tells us with gusto of the welcome given to frolics, to races, and to the gambols

168

indulged in by one of his white followers, a Dane named Albert. "The dark faces light up with friendly gleams, and a budding good will may perhaps date from this trivial scene. To such an impressionable being as an African native, the self-involved European, with his frigid, imperious manner, pallid white face, and dead lustreless eyes, is a sealed book."

Like all Europeans, he started, and with good reason, from the fundamental assumption that the white man has higher intelligence than the black. In those days, intelligence was still of comprehensive value, and was highly prized. He spoke of the "intelligence which brings blessings in its train." But in his case, at any rate, this higher intelligence was never a means for cheating the innocent natives; he never entered into treaties which aimed at dispossessing them of their lands, as became the rule in later years when he had left the Congo. He did not despise the blacks because their primitive ways of thought rendered them incapable of even understanding the business acumen of the whites, and still less of coping with it. His honest endeavour was to protect them, for the very reason that he was endowed with a "higher intelligence." What disastrous results that higher intelligence was destined to bring in its train remained hidden in the future. Yet all too soon his beloved "Free State" was to become the arena for conscienceless exploitation and oppression.

People are apt to speak of the Negroes, especially

169

in their native haunts, as stupid. If stupid they be, this stupidity has nothing to do with what Europeans mean by that term, depending, rather, upon certain fallacies in their logical process, upon gaps in their thought. Stanley, of course, understood this well enough, and relates some amusing instances of it. "Another man was so ludicrously stupid that he generally was safe from punishment because his mistakes were so absurd. We were one day floating down the Congo, and, it being near camping time, I bade him, as he happened to be bowman on the occasion, to stand by and seize the grass on the bank to assist the boat when I should call out. In a little while we came to a fit place, and I cried, 'Hold hard, Kirango!'— 'Please God, Master,' he replied, and forthwith sprang on shore and seized the grass with both hands, while we, of course, were rapidly swept down river, leaving him alone and solitary on the bank. The boat's crew roared with laughter at the ridiculous sight; but, nevertheless, his stupidity caused the tired men a hard pull to ascend again, for not every place was available for a camp. He it was, also, who, on an occasion when we required a branch which overhung the river to be cut away, to allow the canoes to be brought nearer to the bank for safety, actually went astride of the branch and chopped away until he fell into the water with the branch and lost our axe. He had seated himself on the outer end of the branch!"

I do not think that Stanley ever attained any insight into the mysterious side of native life, that he ever studied the African modes of religious worship, or the secret traditions of the indigenes. At any rate, he never writes of such matters. Bred as he was in the spirit of the nineteenth-century "enlightenment," permeated with the liberal spirit of the epoch, these things did not interest him. They lay outside his range, altogether apart from the fact that he was not a man of culture. He would probably have been amazed at such researches as those of Lévy-Bruhl, had they been made in his day. Yet we can hardly suppose that he failed to notice the behaviour of the savages in their daily life, and especially how different from those of white men were their sexual actions and ideas. Had an anthropologist had opportunities for private conversation with him upon the matter, he could doubtless have disclosed many remarkable facts, but he never referred to such topics in his books. His lips were sealed by personal shamefacedness and national prudery.

He was, however, made of the stuff proper to a coloniser in the grand style. His relations with the blacks led to a decisive change in the general view of the African races held by Europeans—but, all the same, he himself was never freed from the European delusion of the need for the "occupation" of Africa. Hence, in part, the tragedy of the Congo Free State. In his inner self, the "white" was probably victorious over the "black." Besides, though personally he set a good example in his

171

treatment of the natives, his white subordinates did not follow in his footsteps. Perhaps, too, his best impulses were overridden by the inborn contempt of the European or the American for the "nigger." As a leader, moreover, he was alone, terribly alone. Never had he felt more lonely than during these years. The officers in his service, men combed out of all the nations of Europe, did not belong to the fine flower of their respective countries; and they were extremely young—not a mature man among them. "How can he who has witnessed many wars," he exclaims, in his *Autobiography*, "hope to be interested by one whose most shocking sight has been a nose-bleed?"

Yet these youthful adventurers hastened to disregard Stanley's instructions directly his back was turned, saying that they had not come to Africa in order to work, and being much more concerned with their boat-clubs and other amusements than with the daily round of toil. They rough-handled the chiefs, the Arab traders, their own black underlings, whenever they had a chance; each of them, within his own little circle, playing the military dictator. They were narrow-minded, lazy, ignorant; knew nothing of the manners and customs of the natives; lacked the remotest conception of the real standing of their leader. They looked upon him as an upstart, a mere journalist; were annoyed at his insistence upon strict discipline, sent complaints home to the Committee to the effect that Stanley was "hard"; and, when they were

172

alone among themselves, made mock of his ideals and of his Negrophilism. There were exceptions, no doubt, but very few. Their attitude should assuredly have convinced him how little support he could expect from Europe, how little enthusiasm he could hope to arouse there, and how scant were the prospects of his being able to make his Congo Free State into the Eldorado that he hoped. His illusion persisted!

He was under an illusion, likewise, as to the possibility of abolishing the slave-trade. In the Africa of those days, there was as little chance of anything of the kind as there was, in the Russia of half a century ago, a likelihood of a republic being proclaimed. The slave-trade had grown out of extant African social conditions, was almost sanctified by use and wont, and protests that were not backed up by force were empty flourishes. One of the most tragic pages in the story of his return to the Congo describes his coming upon a series of villages just ravaged by a ferocious slave-raid of the Arabs, and of his afterwards encountering a herd of the wretched captives chained and guarded. It is a terrible picture. Over a hundred villages had been devastated; and the five thousand carried away as slaves stood for six times as many slain, or dying by the roadside. The hot impulse rose to strike a blow for liberation, but it would have been hopeless and useless. An army would have been needed. He describes his thoughts and feelings as he looks upon the slave convoy.

173

"Every second during which I regard them the clank of fetters and chains strikes upon my ears. My eyes catch sight of that continual lifting of the hand to ease the neck in the collar, or as it displays a manacle exposed through a muscle being irritated by its weight or want of fitness. My nerves are offended with the rancid effluvium of the unwashed herds within this human kennel. The smell of other abominations annoys me in that vitiated atmosphere. . . . Many of those poor things have already been months fettered in this manner, and their bones stand out in bold relief beneath the attenuated skin, which hangs down in thin wrinkles and puckers. Who can withstand the feeling of pity so powerfully pleaded for by these large eyes and sunken cheeks? What was the cause of all this vast sacrifice of human life, of all this unspeakable misery? Nothing but the indulgence of an old Arab's wolfish, bloody, starved, and ravenous instincts. He wished to obtain slaves, to barter profitably away to other Arabs. . . . If we calculate three quarts of blood to each person who fell during the campaign of murder, we find that this one Arab caused to be shed two thousand eight hundred and fifty gallons of human blood, sufficient to fill a tank measuring four hundred and sixty cubic feet, quite large enough to have drowned him and all his kin!"

It is difficult to say whether the vividness or the bitterness of the description is more striking. But what will be the result if such Dantesque pictures are sent

174

home to the civilised world? A few missionary societies will be stirred to send out their emissaries. This will do nothing to cut at the roots of the system. It will merely salve the conscience of the man of illusions!

He feels that the task is beyond his strength, that it is certainly too·much for any one to tackle unaided. His thoughts turn to General Gordon. "There was a man at that time in retreat, near Mount Carmel. If he but emerged from his seclusion, he had all the elements in him of the man that was needed: indefatigable industry, that magnetism which commands affection, patience, and perfect trust; that power of reconciling men, no matter of what colour, to their duties; that cheerful promise that in him lay security and peace; that loving solicitude which betokens the kindly chief. For six months I waited his coming; finally letters arrived announcing his departure for the Sudan; and, soon after, there appeared Lieutenant-Colonel Sir Francis de Winton, of the Royal Artillery, in his place."

England was, in fact, making a move to secure her share of the spoils. General Gordon had arranged to take the governorship of the Lower Congo, under Stanley, who was to govern the Upper; and together they were to destroy the slave-trade at its roots. This idea was congenial to Gordon's piety. As soon as Sir Francis de Winton came, Stanley transferred to him the government of the Congo, and returned to England.

175

A few weeks later, the new State was recognised by the Powers. England's contribution was mainly indirect. For centuries Portugal had had settlements on the coast at the mouth of the Congo. England had previously made a treaty with Portugal, allowing her a strip of African coast, as the result of which all other nations could have been excluded from the Congo. In view of the menace to the world's trade by the Anglo-Portuguese treaty, Bismarck now took a hand in the game. He summoned a conference at Berlin, to which the leading European Powers sent delegates. All at once, every one wanted to have a finger in the pie. There were also delegates from the United States, and with these Stanley was present as "technical adviser." The political and legal arrangements resulting from this conference must, presumably, have brought much gratification to Stanley, although he probably disapproved of the dominant role which the crafty king of the Belgians had assigned to Germany. There is no evidence in his writings to show whether the illusion which had mastered him for years had at length been dispelled, but his cry for help from Gordon suggests that this was so.

TIPPU-TIB

An illustration from "In Darkest Africa"

CHAPTER SEVEN

A NEW MISSION

THE last, most remarkable, and most famous of Stanley's
exploits, in which another extremely interesting and
enigmatical personality was concerned, was the Emin
Pasha Relief Expedition. In every one over fifty years of
age the mention of this name will arouse youthful impressions, remembrances of adventurous doings, such
as, in general, are recorded only in the mouldering folios
of old days, or are hatched in the brains of the writers
of romance. But few people of the younger generation,
with the exception of specialists and persons with an itch
for universal information, have ever heard of Emin.
Yet the whole affair in which he was concerned was great
after its fashion. It was one of those real dramas recorded, as it were, only upon the margin of history, and
finding no place in the main text; but of a kind to give
a profounder insight into human nature—this by-play—
than the movement in the middle of the stage of those
principal figures which, because they are in the lime-

177

light, imagine themselves to be in the centre of the world.

On January 26, 1885, General Gordon, who had gone to the Sudan in the hope of making headway against the fanatical movement led by the Mahdi, was killed at Khartoum, the Egyptian garrison being massacred, the population reduced to slavery, and all the vast Sudan submerged by barbarism. The Mahdi was one of the most dangerous fanatics who have ever troubled the peace of mankind—at all times hanging by a thread. The only Egyptian force in the Sudan which escaped from the disaster was the one led by Emin Pasha.

Emin had sought refuge among the savage tribes in the neighbourhood of Wadelai, on the left bank of the Nile, about thirty-five miles north of the Albert Nyanza. Fearing that he would be unable to hold out, he wrote letters to the Egyptian Government, Mr. Mackay (a missionary in Uganda), the Anti-Slavery Society, and Sir John Kirk, imploring assistance before he should be overwhelmed. The messengers had to make immense detours, so that Emin's missives did not reach their respective destinations until a good many months had elapsed. His situation was made worse by the fact that Uganda was in an uproar, so that he could not hope to escape by this route towards the east coast. The way to the north was blocked by the Mahdi. To the south and to the west, the unknown, dreaded, and reputedly impassable forest of Central Africa extended for hundreds of miles.

178

Nations have their caprices, just like individuals. The British had been profoundly moved by the heroic death of General Gordon, who was regarded as a national martyr. Now, Emin's danger and appeals for help, following upon the catastrophe in Khartoum, aroused more excitement than any previous happenings in these parts of the world. The Press fanned the flames of sensation. Day after day there appeared articles describing how one of Gordon's officers, at the head of a small army, was in imminent danger of suffering the same fate as Gordon and the garrison and inhabitants of Khartoum. Moving descriptions of Emin's personal character inflamed public anxiety yet further. The demand for a relief expedition became irresistible. As a first step there was formed a Relief Committee, under the presidency of Sir William Mackinnon, and this latter, an old friend of Stanley's, offered him the leadership of the expedition. "I replied that I would lead it gratuitously; or, if the Relief Committee preferred another leader, as was very probable, I would put my name down for five hundred pounds as a subscription to the fund. Without awaiting the issue of his appeal to his friends, I sailed for America to commence a lecturing tour. Thirteen days after my arrival in America I was recalled by cable, and on Christmas Eve, 1886, I was back in England." By this time, £11,000 had been collected in that country, and the Egyptian government had provided a further sum of

179

£10,000. On December 31, 1886, Stanley was formally commissioned to begin preparations.

To avert, as far as might be, the chance of failure, the undertaking was conceived on a grand scale. By way of trade goods, orders were given for about thirty thousand yards of cloth, three thousand six hundred pounds of beads, and one ton of wire—brass, copper, and iron. Another order was for the purchase of forty pack-donkeys and ten riding-asses; and another was for the construction of a steel boat. From Egypt there were sent to Zanzibar five hundred and ten Remington rifles, two tons of gunpowder, three hundred and fifty thousand percussion caps, and one hundred thousand rounds of Remington ammunition. A dozen British firms were at work for weeks in fitting out the expedition. Pages of figures relating to this matter are given in the first volume of Stanley's *In Darkest Africa*. Who had more knowledge than he of what was needed for equipment? Everything—tents, provisions, medicaments—was thought out down to the minutest detail.

Forthwith Stanley was overwhelmed with appeals from the brave and adventurous young. Persons of all classes and professions wanted to take part in the enterprise. Had the financial resources been on the same scale, he might have set forth as commander of a great army; the barracks, the military colleges, the public schools, even the nurseries would have been emptied! Finally, from among a host of applicants, he selected the following: Lieutenant W. Grant Stairs, of the Royal Engineers, who had applied by letter; William Bonny, an army surgeon, who had just left service in one of the Army Medical Department's hospitals; Major Edmund Musgrave Barttelot, of the Seventh Fusiliers, who had been highly recommended; Captain Nelson, who had served in the Zulu campaigns; A. J. Mounteney Jephson, a young man regarded by some members of the selection committee as of too "high class," but accepted because he was so keen on going, and because the Countess de Noailles had made in his favour a subscription of £1,000 to the Relief Fund, "an argument that the Committee could not resist"; James S. Jameson, who had travelled in Mashonaland and Matabeleland, to collect trophies of the chase, to study birds, and to make sketches (he did not appear remarkably strong, but his previous African experience spoke in his favour); T. H. Parke, of the Army Medical Department, who was appointed surgeon to the expedition, since William Bonny was not considered entirely fit for this job.

Almost every one of these men had his own tragedy to go through in the heart of Africa.

The outstanding question was, by which route, from which side, it would be best to approach the region in which Emin Pasha, concerning whom the news that came to hand was more and more disquieting, was, to all intents and purposes, held prisoner. There was the more reason for urgency because Emin was short of ammunition, and one of the most important parts of Stanley's commission was to take him powder and cartridges. As to the choice of a route, numerous persons, both experts and the uninstructed, were devoting themselves to what had become a fashionable puzzle. It seemed as if every one were ready to regard himself as a connoisseur in African matters, and felt himself responsible for the rescue of Emin Pasha. One advised that the Mobangi-Welle would prove an excellent way to Emin. Another was convinced that a way by Abyssinia would be found feasible. Yet another, interested in the African Lakes Company, proposed that the expedition should adopt the Zambesi–Shire–Nyassa road, and thence by way of Tanganyika north to Muta-Nzige and Lake Albert, and a missionary from the Tanganyika region warmly endorsed this recommendation. Dr. Felkin, in the *Scottish Geographical Magazine*, came to the conclusion that a road west of Lake Victoria and Karagwe, through Usongora to Lake Albert, possessed certain advantages over any other.

Stanley himself considered that there were four almost equally feasible routes. The first of these, via Masai Land, was decidedly objectionable while carrying a vast store of ammunition which absolutely must reach Emin. There was great scarcity of water and grain on this route; and its nearness to the east coast would encourage the tendency of the Zanzibaris to desert. The route by way of the Victoria Nyanza and Uganda, which was the best as far as natural conditions were concerned, was rendered impossible for a small expedition by the hostility of Uganda. The third possibility was to travel by Msalala, Karagwe, and Ankori, and thence by Unyoro and Lake Albert. Immense loss of men and goods would, however, assuredly follow any attempt from the east coast. Fifty per cent. loss was inevitable, and no precautions would avail to prevent desertion. Besides, Karagwe was garrisoned by the Waganda, who would be persistently hostile. The fourth possibility, and probably the best in Stanley's opinion, was to go up the Congo, for this would shorten the land journey by five hundred miles, and the choice of the Congo route would quiet the fears of the French and the Germans that, behind a professedly humanitarian quest, the expedition might be really designed to effect annexations. The drawbacks of the Congo route were: first, that there were not enough transport vessels available in the upper portion of the river to convey the expedition easily to Yambuya; and, secondly, the possibility that the forest between Yambuya and the destination might prove an insuperable hindrance.

We may well suppose that, from the first, Stanley inclined strongly towards the Congo route, inasmuch as the whole of the great river as far as Stanley Pool was, so to say, his own realm, with which he was intimately familiar. Nor was he seriously afraid of the forest, being

183

accustomed to its dangers and difficulties, which were perhaps even a lure. When, at this juncture, King Leopold promised the support of the Belgian Government and offered the use of the ships plying on the Congo, there was no longer any reason for hesitation; and Stanley found no difficulty in convincing the Committee and Sir William Mackinnon of the advantages of "his own" route. He declared, however, that King Leopold's impulsive offer was rather vaguely worded. It would be necessary to find out how many ships Leopold would place at the disposal of the expedition.

A glance at Stanley's diary relating to this period gives us a picture of febrile activity.

"January 8, 1887.—Received letters from the King. He lays claim to my services. Offers to lend whole of his naval stock for transport except such as may be necessary for uses of administration. Wired to Mackinnon that I felt uneasy at the clause; that it was scarcely compatible with the urgency required. Colonel de Winton wrote in the same tenor. Effects of expedition are arriving by many cwts. De Winton worked with me until late in the night.

"January 9, 1887.—Colonel Grant, Colonel de Winton, and myself sat down to consider His Majesty's letter, and finally wrote reply requesting he would graciously respond with greater definiteness respecting quantity of transport and time for which transport vessels will be granted, as so many matters depend upon quick reply.

"January 10, 1887.—De Winton visited Foreign Office and was promised as soon as possible to attend to the detention of mail steamer and government transport round the Cape of Good Hope. Messrs. Gray, Dawes, & Co. write Postmaster-General willing to detain Zanzibar mail steamer at Aden, to await *Navarino*, which sails from London on the 20th with the ammunition and officers.

"January 12.—Was notified at 2 p.m. by the Earl of Iddesleigh that he would see me at 6 p.m., but at 3.13 p.m. the Earl died suddenly from disease of the heart.

"January 13.—Goods arriving fast. Will presently fill my house. Went down with Baroness Burdett Coutts to Guildhall, arriving there 12.45 p.m. I received Freedom of City of London, and am called youngest citizen. Afterwards lunched at Mansion House, a distinguished party present and affair most satisfactory. Telegraphed to Brussels to know if Friday convenient to King. Replied. 'Yes, at 9.30 a.m.' "

On January 20, Lieutenant Stairs, Captain Nelson, and Mr. Mounteney Jephson sailed upon the *Navarino* to Suez, as per programme. Next evening, Stanley himself left London for Egypt. He had to attend various conferences in Cairo, and to engage in a series of negotiations there. At the railway station in Cairo he was met by Sir Evelyn Baring, of whom he had read in Gordon's diaries. "We drove to Sir Evelyn's house, and I was told in his straightforward and clear manner that there was a hitch somewhere. The Khedive, and Nubar Pasha, the Prime Minister, were doubtful as to the wisdom of the Congo route." It was tiresome that he should have to prove once more what he had already proved a hundred times. If only he could have done with these infernal speeches, explanations, festivities, greetings, and farewell dinner-parties! Sir Evelyn Baring also told him that Professor Schweinfurth and Dr. Junker had both been struck with consternation at the idea of the Congo route and by their manner had expressed that the idea was absurd. Well, this was nothing new to Stanley, for he had always been at loggerheads with the experts.

From Dr. Junker he learned a number of important details concerning Emin Pasha. Emin was German by nationality and Jewish by blood; his real name was Eduard Schnitzer. He was tall, thin, and exceedingly shortsighted; a great linguist, Turkish, Arabic, German, French, Italian, and English being familiar to him; to these languages could be added a few of the African dialects. He had made zoological researches of considerable importance, was a qualified medical man, and had done good service to Gordon as a doctor. Gordon, however, prized Emin still more for his diplomatic talents and his capacity as an official, and had therefore appointed him governor of Equatoria. A strange man, and a remarkable career. Few who knew him seem to have admired him much. Certainly the impatient tone of his letters for help showed that prolonged isolation (he had at this time been in Equatoria for about seven years) had undermined his morale. He wrote: "Egypt does not care for us, and has forgotten us; Europe takes no interest in what we do."

Stanley felt it incumbent upon him to convey to Emin news that a relief expedition was on the way. Egyptian ministers of State assured him that this should be seen to. Writing himself to Emin Pasha, Stanley explained that he hoped to find Emin at the southern end of Lake Albert Nyanza; and warned him against needlessly hazarding his life by a premature attempt to escape through Uganda.

The Khedive gave Stanley a Firman addressed to Emin Pasha and couched in the following terms: "As a mission for the relief has been formed under the command of Mr. Stanley, the famous and experienced African explorer, whose reputation is well known throughout the world; and as he intends to set out on his expedition with all the necessary provisions for you so that he may bring you here with officers and men to Cairo, by the route that Mr. Stanley may think proper to take—we have issued this Firman to you, and it is sent to you by the hand of Mr. Stanley to let you know what has been done, and, as soon as it reaches you, I charge

187

you to convey my best wishes to the officers and men—
and you are at full liberty with regard to your leaving
for Cairo or your stay there with officers and men. . . .
Those who wish to stay there, among the officers and
men, may do so on their own responsibility, and they
must not in that case expect any assistance from the
Government. Try to understand this document well, and
make it known to all the officers and men, that they may
be aware of what they are going to do."

Inasmuch as one of Emin Pasha's most salient characteristics was a morbid irresolution, it can hardly be
said that the foregoing dispatch was so worded as to
help him to make up his mind. On the contrary, it could
only serve to provide him with arguments for continuing
to play his tragical role of cunctator.

In Zanzibar our old friend Tippu-Tib came to the
front of the stage once more. During the ten years since
Stanley had last seen the Arab adventurer, the latter
had acquired considerable wealth and had become a
person of great importance in Central Africa. Lesser
Arabs of his own kidney had enrolled under his banner,
so that he had become the uncrowned king of the territories lying between Lake Tanganyika and Stanley
Falls. Stanley knew the man to be double-faced, hopelessly untrustworthy, extremely avaricious, and he knew
that Tippu-Tib had a secret understanding with the king
of Uganda; but the Arab princeling was necessary to his
purposes. "With due caution, therefore, I sounded

Tippu-Tib on the first day, and found him fully prepared for any eventuality—to fight me or to be employed
by me. He chose the latter, and we proceeded to business.
His aid was not required to enable me to reach Emin
Pasha, or to show the route. There are four good routes
to Wadelai from the Congo; one of them was in Tippu-
Tib's power, the remaining three were clear of him and
his myriads. But Dr. Junker informed me that Emin
Pasha possessed about seventy-five tons of ivory. At
eight shillings per pound this ivory would be worth
£60,000. The subscription of Egypt to the Emin Pasha
Fund had been large for her depressed finances. In this
quantity of ivory we had possibility of recuperating her
treasure (with a considerable sum left towards defray-
ing expenses, and perhaps leaving a handsome present
for the Zanzibari survivors). Why not attempt the carriage of this ivory to the Congo? Accordingly, I wished
to engage Tippu-Tib and his people to assist me in
conveying the ammunition to Emin Pasha, and on return
to carry the ivory. After a good deal of bargaining, I
entered into a contract with him by which he agreed to
supply six hundred carriers, at £6 per loaded head—
each round trip from Stanley Falls to Lake Albert and
back."

The contract was formally signed in the presence
of the British consul-general, but thereupon Stanley, who
did not trust the old Arab in the least, remarked that,
quite apart from this matter, there was a bone to pick

189

with him. Tippu-Tib had waged war upon the settlement founded by Stanley at Stanley Falls in the year 1883— a war fought from behind a mask, so to say, so that Tippu-Tib could at any time repudiate personal responsibility. So persistently, however, had he harassed the settlement that, in the end, it had been abandoned, and the commander, when withdrawing his garrison, had set fire to the station. Since then the middle regions of the Congo had been kept in a state of unceasing disquiet by Tippu-Tib's mercenaries, but the wily old slave-trader had always managed to cover up his tracks. Tippu-Tib, on his side, found it a grievance that white men should have intruded into "his" part of Central Africa at all!

When these dissensions had been cleared out of the way, Stanley went on to make a remarkable offer to Tippu-Tib. The Arab was what he was, and was the man of power in the region to be traversed; it was necessary to come to terms with him. King Leopold had authorised the plan Stanley now proceeded to unfold.

"Look here," he said, "King Leopold proposes that you try your hand at governing that station. He will pay you every month what he would pay a European officer. But there are certain little conditions that you must comply with before you become governor."

Tippu-Tib opened his eyes and snapped them rapidly, as his custom was. Then he asked, "Me?"— "Yes, you. You like money; I offer you money. You have a grudge against white men being there. Well, if

190

you do your work rightly there will be no need for any white men except him we will have to place under you to see the conditions are not broken."

"Well, what are they?"

"You must hoist the flag of the State. You must allow a Resident to be with you, who will read your reports to the King. You must neither trade in slaves, nor allow anybody else to trade in them below Stanley Falls. Nor must there be any slave-catching; you understand? Such trade as you make in ivory, gums, rubber, cattle, and anything else, you may do as much as you please. But there is to be no pillaging of native property of any description whatever below your station. A monthly allowance will be paid into the hands of your agent at Zanzibar. Don't answer right away. Go and discuss it with your friends, and think of what I offer you. My ship sails on the third day. Give me your answer to-morrow."

Stanley's plan, as will have been seen, was to make the goat gardener, in the hope of robbing the beast of its horns. 'Tis an old political expedient! Tippu-Tib, whose vanity was tickled by the thought of this dignified position, soon made up his mind to agree to the terms. As we shall learn by and by, he had his own schemes to serve in the matter. Really, it was a bad bargain for Stanley, although these negotiations with Tippu-Tib seemed likely to ensure a peaceful march from the Congo through his territory. At any rate, no Arab would now persuade the Zanzibaris to desert, as their custom was whenever a white man's expedition passed near their settlements. Tippu-Tib would not dare countenance such proceedings in this case.

On February 25, 1887, Tippu-Tib and his people, together with every one connected with the expedition, were on board the *Madura,* which steamed away round the Cape of Good Hope to the mouth of the Congo.

I shall not devote much space to an account of the difficulties and disappointments Stanley had to encounter on arrival. There were the usual troubles: passive resistance on the part of the administration, incapacity of subalterns, waste of material, lack of trained assistance. Stanley was informed that there was a famine in the country; that the villages along the road to the Pool were abandoned; that the "Stanley" was seriously damaged; that the mission steamers "Peace" and "Henry Reed" were in some unknown parts of the Upper Congo; that the "En Avant" was ashore without machinery or boiler; that the "A. I. A." was five hundred miles above Stanley Pool; and that the "Royal" was completely rotten and had not been employed for a year—in fact, that the whole of the naval stock promised did not exist at all except in the imagination of the gentlemen in the bureau at Brussels. Besides, "the boats were only to assist you if they could be given without prejudice to the service of the State."

192

In face of these hindrances, to transport his caravans and equipment, with several hundred men's burdens, was a very difficult task. He had to take the land route to Stanley Pool, and thence, having laboriously repaired the small steamers on the upper reaches, to make several trips to and fro on the Upper Congo and beyond to the village of Yambuya, in Basoko Land, far in the interior, on the bank of the river Aruwimi. A tremendous piece of work, taxing his energies to the utmost. Characteristic of the man was that, throughout these delays, his conscience was pricking him. "In my ears rang the cry in England, 'Hurry up, or you may be too late'; and singing through my memory were the words of Junker, 'Emin will be lost unless immediate aid be given him'; and Emin's appeal for help, 'For, if denied, we shall perish.' "

By the middle of June, 1887, he was at Yambuya, thirteen hundred miles from the Sea, almost in the centre of the continent. He estimated that the unexplored territory lying between Yambuya and the Albert Nyanza was about five hundred miles long and three hundred miles wide. According to such reports as he had received of it, which were confirmed by his subsequent experience, this region was mainly covered by forest —the vast and terrible primeval forest of Central Africa. That was what he had to cross. How was the crossing to be effected? We must linger a while upon

193

the matter, for, connected with Stanley's experiences during this part of the Emin Pasha Relief Expedition, there are problems still unsolved. In his *Autobiography* Stanley writes: "Now was the time, if ever, to prove that our zeal had not cooled. Six weeks, probably two months, would pass before the entire force could be collected at Yambuya. If Emin were in such desperate straits as he had described, his total ruin might be effected in that time, and the disaster would be attributed to that delay—just as Gordon's death had been attributed to Sir Charles Wilson's delay at Metemmeh. To avoid such a charge, I had no option but to form an Advance Column, whose duty it would be to represent the steady progress of the expedition towards its goal, while a second column under five experienced officers, would convey to us, a few weeks later, the reserve stores and baggage. If Tippu-Tib was faithful to his promise to supply the second column with six hundred carriers, the work of this Rear Column would be comparatively easy. If the Arab chief was faithless, then the officers were to do the best they could with their own men; to follow after me, in that case, was obviously their best course."

Major Barttelot was appointed to command the Rear Column, with Jameson and Bonny as his subordinates. Stanley wrote detailed instructions in the form of a letter addressed to Major Barttelot. On the same

194

day he had a long conversation with the Major, who said he desired to speak about Tippu-Tib.

"I should like to know, sir, something more regarding this Arab. When I was delayed a few days ago at the Falls, you were pleased to deliver some rather energetic orders to Lieutenant Stairs. It strikes me that you are exceedingly suspicious of Tippu-Tib, and if so, I really do not see why you should have anything to do with such a man."

"I have nothing to do with Tippu-Tib," replied Stanley, "but from necessity, for your sake as well as mine. He claims this as his territory. We are on it as his friends."

Had he not made an agreement with Tippu-Tib, went on Stanley, the expedition would have been at the Arab's mercy. Knowing what Tippu-Tib was capable of, he could not, in default of such an agreement, possibly have left Barttelot alone in Yambuya with eighty rifles against several thousand. For Tippu-Tib the Congo Free State was a thorn in the flesh. In Zanzibar the old man had breathed threatenings and slaughter against all the whites in the Congo. Stanley had had no choice but to make him and his formidable nephews less dangerous by coming to terms with them.

"Well, now, do you think Tippu-Tib will keep his contract, and bring the six hundred people he promised?" asked the Major.

"You ought to know that as well as I myself. What did he say to you before you left him?"

"He said he would be here in nine days, as he told you at Bangala. Inshallah!" replied the Major, mimicking the Arab.

"If Tippu-Tib is here in nine days, it will be the biggest wonder I have met."

"Why?" asked the Major, in surprise.

"Because to provide six hundred carriers is a large order. He will not be here in fifteen days or even twenty days. We must be reasonable with the man. He is not a European—taught to be rigidly faithful to his promise. 'Inshallah!' That means to-morrow, or the day after, or five days hence, or ten days. But what does it matter to you if he does not come within twenty days? The 'Stanley' will not be here until the 10th, or perhaps the middle of August; that will be about seven weeks hence. He has abundance of time. Wait for him patiently until the 'Stanley' comes, and if he doesn't appear by that time he will not appear at all."

"But it will be a severe job for us, if he does not appear at all, to carry five or six hundred loads with two hundred carriers, to and fro, backwards and forwards, day after day!"

"Look at your written instructions. Which would you prefer: to say here and wait until I come back with Emin from Lake Albert, or to advance in pursuit of us

196

day by day, even if it means covering the same piece of ground twice or thrice over?"

"Oh, my God! I think staying here for months would be a deuced sight the worse."

"Exactly what I think, and that is why I made these calculations for you. I assure you, Major, if I were certain that you could find your way to Lake Albert, I would not mind doing this work of yours myself and appoint you commander to the Advance Column, rather than have any anxiety about you."

"But tell me, Mr. Stanley, how long do you suppose it will be before we meet?"

"God knows. None can inform me what lies ahead here, or how far the forest extends inland. Whether there are any roads, or what kind of natives, cannibals, incorrigible savages, dwarfs, gorillas. . . . Is it all forest? If so, it will be an awful work. How far does the forest reach inland? One hundred—two hundred—three hundred miles? There is no answer. . . . But it is immaterial. The thing has to be done. We will go ahead, we will blaze the trees, and mark our track through the forest for you. We will avail ourselves of every advantage— any path easterly will suit me until I bore through and through it, and come out on the plains and pasture-land. And where we go you can go. If you cannot go on, you will hear from us somehow. . . . In seven weeks from now you will leave Yambuya, and I shall expect you at the

south-west corner of Lake Albert, at or near Kavalli. . . .
Are you satisfied?"

"Perfectly," he replied. "I have it all here"—
touching his forehead—"and this paper and letter will
be my reminders."

"Good. In conclusion, my dear Major, I should like
to say another word to you about Tippu-Tib. Never trust
him for a moment, and yet don't let him see that you
suspect him. One thing more. Your friend introduced
you to me as a distinguished officer full of dash and
courage; upon which I said that those qualities were
common characteristics of British officers, but I would
prefer to hear of another quality which would be of
equal value for peculiar service in Africa—and that was
forbearance. You will excuse me, I hope, for saying that
I read on your face immense determination and something like pugnacity. Now a pugnacious fellow, though
very useful at times, is not quite so useful for an expedition like this (which has to work in an atmosphere
of irritability), as a man who knows not only how and
when to fight, but also how to forbear. . . . As a last proof
of how I regard Tippu-Tib, don't forget that written
order to Lieutenant Stairs a few days ago to rake his
settlement with the machine-gun upon the least sign of
treachery. You have read that letter. You ought to know
that the gage of battle is not thrown in the face of a
trusted friend. . . . Shake hands upon this, Major. For

198

us the word is 'Right onward'; for you, 'Patience and forbearance.'"

The camp was surrounded with a stockade and a dry ditch. Written orders were given to the officers of the Advance Column, to Stairs, Nelson, Jephson, and Parke, who were to accompany Stanley, but in separate detachments. On June 28, they all said good-bye to Barttelot, and the Advance Column, in four sections, set forth into the unknown forest.

CHAPTER EIGHT

THE FOREST PRIMEVAL

"WE marched out of the gate, company after company, in single file. Each with its flag, its trumpeter or drummer, each with its detail of supernumeraries, with fifty picked men as advance guard to handle the bill-hook and axe, to cut saplings, 'blaze,' or peel a portion of the bark of a tree a hand's breadth, to sever the leaves and slash at the rattan, to remove all buttressing branches which might interfere with the free traverse of the hundreds of loaded porters, to cut trees to lay across streams for their passage, to form zarebas or bomas of bush and branch around the hutted camp at the end of the day's travel. The advance guard are to find a path, or, if none can be found, to choose the thinnest portions of the jungle and tunnel through without delay, for it is most fatiguing to stand in a heated atmosphere with a weighty load on the head. If no thinner jungle can be found, then through anything, however impenetrable it may appear; they must be brisk, or an ominous murmur will

200

rise from the impatient carriers behind. They must be clever and intelligent in woodcraft; a greenhorn must drop his bill-hook, and take the bale or box. Three hundred weary fellows are not to be trifled with."

The eyes of these hearty men, resolute, going forth to meet their fate, are already shadowed by the sufferings and the terrors that await them.

"Until December 5, over one hundred and sixty days, we marched through the forest, bush, and jungle, without ever having seen a bit of greensward of the size of a cottage chamber floor. Nothing but miles and miles, endless miles of forest, in various stages of growth and various degrees of altitude, according to the ages of the trees, with varying thickness of undergrowth according to the character of the trees which afford thicker or lighter shade. . . . It is an absolutely unknown region opened to the gaze and knowledge of civilised man for the first time since the waters disappeared and were gathered into the seas, and the earth became dry land. Beseeching the reader's patience, I promise to be as little tedious as possible, though there is no other manuscript or missal, printed book or pamphlet, this spring of the year of Our Lord 1890, that contains any account of that region of horrors, other than this book of mine." (*In Darkest Africa, or the Quest, Rescue, and Retreat of Emin, Governor of*

Equatoria, was not penned until three years after the opening of the events it describes.)

Although Stanley was not an imaginative man, the forest would seem to have stirred his imagination profoundly, and even to have aroused his fears, for many years afterwards he admitted that it was with a quickly beating heart that he had set out to cross it. "The longer I hesitated, the blacker grew its towering walls, and its aspect more sinister. My imagination began to eat into my will. But when all the virtue in me rose in hot indignation against such pusillanimity, I left the pleasant day and we entered as into a tomb. I found it difficult to accustom myself to its gloom and its pallid solitude. I could find no comfort for the inner man, or solace for the spirit. A man can look into the face of the Sun and call him Father; the Moon can be compared to a mistress, the stars to the souls of the dear departed, and the Sky to our Heavenly Home: but when man is sunk in the depths of a cold tomb, how can he sing or feel glad?

"The daily routine began about six o'clock. After roll calls, the pioneers filed out, followed, when a little headway had been gained, by each company in succession. At this hour the forest would be buried in a cheerless twilight, the morning mist making every tree shadowy and indistinct. . . . Soon after sunset, the thick darkness would cover the limitless world of trees around; but within our circle of green huts and sheds a cheery light would shine from a hundred camp-fires. By nine o'clock, the men, overcome by fatigue, would be asleep; silence ensued, broken only by sputtering fire-logs, flights of nightjars, hoarse notes from great bats, croakings of frogs, cricket-cheeps, falling of trees or branches, a shriek from some prowling chimpanzee, a howl from a peevish monkey, and the continual gasping cry of the lemur. But during many nights we would sit shivering under ceaseless torrents of rain, watching the forked flames of the lightning and listening to the stunning and repeated roars of the thunder-cannonade as it rolled through the woody vaults.

"Ever before us rose the same solemn and foodless forest, the same jungle to impede and thwart our progress with ooze, frequently a cubit deep, the soil often as dangerous as ice to the barefooted carrier, creek beds strewed with sharp-edged oyster shells, streams choked with snags, chilling mist and icy rain"—which, almost without transition, would be followed by suffocating heat.

Lieutenant Stairs was a born soldier, a man who never forgot his duty, "an inestimable merit in a tropical country where duty has to be done." He was a little rough in his manner to his underlings, but "a leader in a climate like that of Africa cannot sugar-coat his orders, and a certain directness of speech must be expected." Surgeon Parke was unsophisticated and simple, with a cheerful temperament. He soon, with his inex-

203

haustible wit and humour, won Stanley's affection, and, being extremely competent in his profession, earned the trust of the men under his medical charge. There was plenty for him to do! Stanley writes: "Few people at home know what an African ulcer is like. It grows as large as the biggest mushroom; it destroys the flesh, discloses the arteries and sinews and, having penetrated to the bone, consumes it, and then eats its way round the limb. The sight is awful, the stench is horrible; yet Parke dressed from twenty to fifty of such hideous sores daily, and never winced. . . . When Stairs was wounded with a poisoned arrow, the Doctor deliberately sucked it, though, had the poison been fresh, it might have been a highly dangerous proceeding." Again, speaking of what a comfort Parke was to him in his own illnesses, Stanley says: "When consciousness returned to me, out of many delirious fits, his presence seemed to lighten that sense of approaching calamity that often pressed on me."

Nelson and Mounteney Jephson were likewise satisfactory subordinates. Subsequently, the leader spoke of them with high praise, although he was chary in this respect at the time. There can be no question that the young men suffered from an invincible timidity in his presence. They could not feel that they were in close touch with him; there was no intimacy about him; by repute he was hard and unfeeling; he was taciturn and averse from company. When the day's work was done he used to withdraw into his own tent, "keeping himself to himself," as the folk say; he was never hail-fellow-well-met, but always strict and formal, with an inclination to melancholy and bitterness. This was hardly calculated to be a stimulating atmosphere for his underlings. They always felt as if a mighty but incomprehensible being was driving them forward towards a goal to reach which they would have to make the utmost sacrifices.

One of the chief articles of diet was manioc—tapioca—prepared from cassava roots, which were not easy to come by, and had to be obtained from thickly barricaded plantations. The roots had to be boiled in three successive waters, for without this they are poisonous. Every day, scouts were sent forth in all directions, to gather information about the unknown country, which was full of unanticipated dangers. The march was a very slow one, and if the expedition could advance, on the average, as much as three hundred yards an hour, it had often good reason to be satisfied with its progress. There were continual skirmishes with the natives, who, using poisoned arrows, were by no means to be despised as adversaries. Sometimes the rain was so heavy that campfires could not be lighted at night. Occasionally, since they were marching near the Aruwimi, it was possible to use their boat in order to make progress up-stream; but the disadvantage was that they were then exposed to attack by swarms of native canoes. During the first days of

July, the perpetual rainfall made them so chilly that they decided to break camp, brave the mire, and wade through the brooks waist-deep. On July 10th they reached the rapids of Gwengwere. Here there were seven large villages bordering the rapids and extending from below to above the broken waters. All the population had fled, probably to the opposite main, or to the islands in mid-river, and every portable article had been carried away except the usual wreckage of coarse pottery, stools, benches, and back-rests. Writing of the forest not far beyond this place, Stanley waxes almost enthusiastic, as he thinks of his remoteness from civilisation: "The forest world remains restful, and Nature bides her day, and the river shows no life; unlike Rip Van Winkle, Nature, despite her immeasurable long ages of sleep, indicates no agedness; so old, incredibly old, she is still a virgin locked in innocent repose."

He describes chaffering with the savages: "The sign of peace with these riverine natives appears to be the pouring of water on their heads with their hands. As newcomers approached our camp, they cried out: 'We suffer from famine, we have no food, but up-river you will find plenty, O Monomopote! (Son of the Sea) but we suffer from want of food, and have not the strength to proceed unless you give us some.' " Thereon the savages produced fat ears of Indian corn, plantains, sugar-cane, and tobacco, which they were ready to trade for trifles,

206

such as empty sardine tins, jam and milk cans, and cartridge cases.

One difficulty of travelling on the river by boat was that the passengers were so liable to be attacked by angry wasps, whose stings made the men half crazy with pain. As far as Panga Falls by the island of Nepanga, the caravan had suffered no serious loss, only one of the porters having died. But these were early days; it was but five weeks since they had set out.

Not until it had become necessary to divide forces did serious troubles begin. For instance: "At noon on August 15, the land column filed out of the palisaded villages of Avisibba, led by Mr. Jephson, the officer of the day. As a captive had informed us that there were three cataracts ahead, not far off, I instructed Mr. Jephson that he was to follow the river and halt at the most convenient spot about 2.30 p.m.; that I would halt the river column, now consisting of the boat and fourteen canoes, until the rearguard under Captain Nelson had left the settlement; but as the canoes would proceed faster than the land caravan, I should probably overtake him, and camp at the first fit place I could find after an hour's row, in which event he would proceed until he found us. The instructions were also repeated to the leading men of the pioneers. I ought to have said that our start at noon was occasioned by the delay caused by the discovery at the morning muster that five men were absent. They ultimately turned up at ten o'clock; but this perpetual straying away without leave was most exasperating." It was a desperate task to discover such strays. The paths were beset with poisoned wooden skewers; there might be a lurking cannibal behind every plantain stock, a cunning foe lying under a log or behind a buttress, and there were sunken pits covered with undergrowth but having pointed pales at the bottom. When, on this occasion, the lost men returned, a late start was made. "We pulled upstream at the rate of a knot and a half an hour, and at 2.45, having discovered a convenient camp, halted for the night. We waited in vain for Mr. Jephson, and the column fired signal guns, rowed out into the stream, and with a glass searched the shore up and down, but there was no sign of a camp-fire or smoke above the woods, which generally cover the forest as with a fog in still weather, no sound of a rifle-shot, blare of trumpet, or human voice."

All through that night, Stanley was terribly anxious. The whole of the next day there was no news of the missing men, and at length, on the following day, a boat was sent downstream to follow the trail of Jephson's column. When these scouts came back, they informed the leader that they had struck the trail, and that Mr. Jephson had evidently taken a wrong direction. Stanley had to leave it at that for the moment, and stay where he was in the riverside camp. "We had thirty-nine canoe-men and boatmen, twenty-eight sick people, three Europeans, and

208

three boys, and one of the Europeans (Lieutenant Stairs) was suffering from a dangerous wound, and required the constant care of the surgeon. One man had died of dysentery at Avisibba. We had a dying idiot in camp, who had become idiotic some days before. We had twenty-nine suffering from pleurisy, dysentery, incurable debility, and eight suffering from wounds. One man was half strangled with a wound in his windpipe; another, wounded in the arm, appeared dangerously ill, his arm was swollen, and gave him great pain. . . . Across the river the people of Itiri, perceiving that we were so quiet on our side of the river, seemed to be meditating an attack."

In spite of this danger from the savages, Stanley now sent three more parties to scout for news of the missing column, but on the night of August 18th, he wrote despondently: "If three hundred and eighty-nine picked men, such as we were when we left Yambuya, are unable to reach Lake Albert, how can Major Barttelot with two hundred and fifty men make his way through this endless forest? We have travelled, on an average, eight hours per day for forty-four days since leaving Yambuya. At two miles per hour we ought, by this date, to have arrived on the lake shore. But, instead of being there, we have accomplished just a third of the distance. The poet says we must not 'nourish despair,' for to do that is to lie down and die, to make no effort, and abandon hope."

Further rain and wind storms come to afflict them. The river had become unnavigable. "The moaning and the groaning of the forest is far from comforting and the crashing and fall of mighty trees is far from assuring, but it is a positive terror when the thunder rumbles above. . . . It would be a vast relief for our sick and wounded to be free of such sounds. . . . They seem to fancy that daylight will never appear again; at least so I judge from the faces steeped in misery. They appear stupefied by terror, worry, sickness, loss of friends, hunger, rain and thunder, and general wretchedness. They may be seen crouching under plantain-leaf shades, native shelters, cotton shelters, straw mats, earthen and copper pots above their heads, even saddles, tent canvas covers, blankets, each body wreathed in blue vapour, self-absorbed with speechless anguish. The poor asses, with ears drawn back, inverted eyes, and curving backs, represent abject discomfort."

On the 19th and the 20th, they were still without news of Jephson. Young Saadi, who had been wounded by a poisoned arrow on the morning of the 14th, was suffering from tetanus. Another wounded man had a painful rigidity of neck and spine. Morphia injections gave no relief. Hour after hour Stanley was wondering what had become of Jephson and his men. "It is strange that out of three hundred people and three officers, not one has sense enough to know that he has lost the road, and

210

that the best way of recovering it would be to retrace their steps to Avisibba."

At length, at 5 p.m. on August 21, the missing detachment turned up, although the tale was not complete, for three men had died—two from wounds and one from dysentery. All the members of this land column were utterly exhausted. Though Jephson had obviously blundered, we gather that Stanley made no recriminations, his only comment being in his diary that evening to the following effect: "The dearest passion of my life has been to succeed in my undertakings; but the last few days have begun to fill me with a doubt of success in the present one." This is no longer the confident tone of Bula Matari. We have to remember that he is now six-and-forty years of age, and that for thirty years he has been imposing unwarrantable demands upon his bodily strength.

On August 30th, having taken observations of latitude and longitude, he writes: "We have one hundred and sixty-three geographical miles in an air line to make yet, which we could never accomplish within sixty-four days, as we have performed the western half of the route. The people are in an impoverished state of body, and mentally depressed, ulcers are raging like an epidemic, anæmia has sapped their vitality. I told them the half-way camp was reached, but they replied with murmurs of unbelief.

211

"How can the Master tell? Will that instrument show him the road? Will it tell him which is the path? Why does it not tell us, that we may see and believe? Don't the natives know their own country better? Which of them has seen grass? Do they not say that the whole world is covered with trees and thick bush? The master talks to us as if we were children and had no proper perception."

He understands their state of mind, and can only reassure them with kindly words. If he were harsh to them, he would drive them crazy.

The afternoon of the next day, August 31st, was signalised by a great disappointment. Stanley's European servant came running up at a mad pace, crying out as he ran:

"Sir, oh, sir, Emin Pasha has arrived."

"Emin Pasha?"

"Yes, sir, I have seen him in a canoe. His red flag, like our Egyptian flag, is hoisted up at the stern. It is quite true, sir!"

A race began, master and man striving for the lead. In camp, the excitement was also general. But the servant had been mistaken. It was not Emin. The men in the boat with the red flag were nine Manyuema, serving one called Uledi Balyuz, known to the natives by the name of Ugarrowwa, who was reported to be settled about eight marches up-river, and commanding several hundred armed men.

There were Arabs, then, so far inland, on the Upper Aruwimi. Stanley was extremely annoyed to learn this. There was a camp of fifty, six miles above the point he had now reached. As soon as Stanley's men learned of this, desertions began. The first to run away was a porter named Juma, who left with half a hundredweight of biscuit that night. Next morning, September 1, 1887, Stanley rowed up to the village where the Manyuema were said to be camped, to find the place abandoned. The deserters, it seemed, had told them that Stanley might make trouble because they had recently captured slaves with them, and for that reason they had decamped. At the gate of the camp there was a dead male child, literally hacked to pieces; within the palisades was a dead woman, who had been speared. The same day, five more of the Zanzibaris deserted, taking five loads with them, four of ammunition and one of salt. "A search-party was despatched to hunt news of the missing men, and returned with one man, a box of ammunition, and three rifles. The search-party had discovered the deserters in the forest, with a case of ammunition open, which they were distributing. When the attempt was made to surround them, the deserters scudded away, leaving three of their rifles and a case behind them. On September 3rd, five more deserted, carrying away one case of Remington cartridges, one case of Winchester cartridges, one box of European provisions, and one load of fine Arab clothing, worth £50. Another was detected with a box of

213

provisions open before him, having already abstracted a tin of sago, a tin of Liebig, a tin of butter, and one of milk. Ten men had thus disappeared in a couple of days. At this rate, in sixty days the expedition would be ended."

On September 16th, at 4 p.m., Stanley had camped just below Ugarrowwa's station. "A roll of drums, the booming of many muskets, and a flotilla of canoes announced the approach of the Arab leader. About fifty strong, robust fellows accompanied him, besides women, every one of whom was in prime condition of body." The Arab chief, having heard in what poor case the European caravan was, showed no longer any fear of it, but had hopes of doing trade with Stanley. "When I asked him if there was any prospect of food being obtained for my people in the vicinity of his station, he admitted that his followers in their heedless way had destroyed everything, that it was impossible to check them because they were furious against the 'pagans' for the stupid retaliation and excesses the aborigines had committed against many and many of his countrymen during their search for ivory." In one day he had lost forty men. He had an Arab guest at his station who had lost every soul out of his caravan.

It is in small matters as in great. Evildoers always complain when the measure they have meted is meted unto them again. According to his own story, this slave-raider was a most gentle creature who could not under-

214

stand how any one could think him capable of violence. Stanley had to conceal his indignation, for he needed help from the Arab, and wanted information as to the route. The information was by no means encouraging. As to the supply of healthy and vigorous men, to do the work which his own men were now too sick to do, this could be managed at a price. Well, the price was forthcoming.

"At Ugarrowwa's settlement, I saw the first specimen of the tribe of dwarfs who were said to be thickly scattered north of the Ituri. She measured thirty-three inches in height and was a perfectly formed young woman of about seventeen, of a glistening smooth silkiness of body. Her figure was that of a miniature coloured lady, not wanting in a certain grace, and her face was very prepossessing. Her complexion was that of a quadroon, or of the colour of yellow ivory. Her eyes were magnificent but absurdly large for such a small creature, almost as large as that of a young gazelle, full, protruding, and extremely lustrous. Absolutely nude, the little demoiselle was quite self-possessed, as though she were accustomed to be admired and really enjoyed inspection." Stanley writes as if her nudity were a reason for not admiring her! We cannot but feel, though he does not say so, that this strange little creature seemed to him emblematic of the wilderness by which, in his inmost soul, he was allured.

215

There was an unceasing struggle to obtain food. On October 10th Stanley writes: "In the morning I had eaten my last grain of Indian corn, and my last portion of everything solid that was obtainable. At noon the horrid pains of the stomach had to be satisfied with something. Some potato leaves brought me by one of the headmen were pressed fine and cooked. They were not bad, but the stomach still ached from utter depletion."

The same day he records further desertions. "Kajeli stole a box of Winchester ammunition and absconded. Salim stole a case containing Emin Pasha's new boots and two pairs of mine, and deserted. Wadi Adam vanished with Surgeon Parke's entire kit. Swadi left his box on the road, and departed for parts unknown. Bull-necked Uchungu followed suit with a box of Remington cartridges." Stanley had to take drastic measures to put a stop to these desertions. Ugarrowwa sent him back three of the deserters, and he decided to make an example. He mustered his men, and put the case before them. They agreed that the desertions were imperilling all their lives, and that there was no choice but to punish these offenders with death.

"Very well, then, you have condemned them to death," said Stanley. "One shall die to-day, another to-morrow, and another the next day; and from this day forward, every thief and deserter who leaves his duty and imperils his comrades' lives shall die." The three men had to draw lots as to which of them was to die that

216

day, and the one upon whom the lot fell was instantly hanged. It was the report of these unavoidable severities which subsequently raised up many enemies against Stanley among the pious and the philanthropic in England. Actually they were repugnant to him, as is shown by what followed in the case of the two other men under death sentence. Next day, Stanley had a talk with Rashid, the chief of his Zanzibaris, and asked whether he thought that there was any possibility of checking the desertions without proceeding to the last extremity as concerned the two remaining offenders.

"I would say, Sir," replied Rashid, "that all ways are good, but without doubt the best is that which will leave them living to repent."

Once more the men were mustered, and the noose was placed round the neck of him who had been condemned to die that day.

"Now, my man, have you anything to say to us before you join your brother who perished yesterday?"

The man remained silent and scarcely seemed conscious that Stanley spoke. The leader turned to Rashid and asked: "Have you anything to say before I give the word?"

Rashid nudged his brother chiefs, at which they all rushed up, and threw themselves at Stanley's feet, pleading forgiveness, blaming in harsh terms the thieves and murderers, but vowing that their behaviour in future would be better if mercy were extended for this one

217

time. During this scene the Zanzibaris' faces were worth observing. "The eyes dilated, and the lips closed, and their cheeks became pallid, as with the speed of an electric flash the same emotion moved them!"

"Enough, children!" said Stanley. "Take your man, his life is yours. But see to it. There is only one law in future for him who robs us of a rifle, and that is death by the cord."

"Then," writes Stanley, "such a manifestation of feeling occurred that I was amazed. Big tears rolled down many a face, while every eye was suffused and enlarged with passionate emotion. Caps and turbans were tossed into the air. Rifles were lifted, and every right arm was up as they exclaimed: 'Until the white captain is buried, none shall leave him! Death to him who leaves Bula Matari! Show the way to the Nyanza! Lead on, we will follow!' "

The prisoner likewise wept, and after the noose was flung aside, knelt down and vowed to die at Stanley's feet. Stanley shook hands with him and said: "It is God's work; thank Him."

Such happenings seem to take us back to the days when the human race began. Nature, the primeval forest, has called them into being. Will the caravan never reach the other side of this gloomy wilderness? The strongest and the best of the men are falling sick. It is a train of shadows which, day after day, totters onward through the endless obscurity.

218

For the last two weeks Captain Nelson had been suffering from a dozen small ulcers, which had gradually increased in virulence. Now, when the condition of the river was such that further boat travel had become impossible, he and fifty-two of the Zanzibaris were utterly unfit and incapable of land travel. After Stanley and Nelson had talked matters over, it was agreed that Stanley, taking with him the men who were still fit to march, should make his way to the station of an Arab named Kilonga-Longa, which was only three days' march distant, leaving Nelson and the rest of the sick in camp beside the Ituri, to follow him as soon as their condition had improved. When they parted, Stanley and Nelson believed that the separation would be for a few days only, but it was five months before they met again. How strong was the leader's sense of responsibility towards his sick comrades was shown by the fact that he left Dr. Parke with them, much though he must have needed the surgeon with his own column.

The expedition had started from Yambuya with three hundred and eighty-nine men and two hundred and thirty-seven loads. Now, after three and a half months, there were only two hundred men left. Death and desertion accounted for the loss of seventy-one; fifty-six had been left invalided at Ugarrowwa's station; fifty-two stayed in camp with Nelson. Obviously, then, Stanley had more loads than bearers, and therefore, though it went much against the grain, he had to leave

219

some of the ammunition intended for Emin Pasha in Nelson's camp, eighty-one loads in all, besides ten boats.

"No more gloomy spot could have been selected for a camp than that sandy terrace encompassed by rocks, and hemmed in narrowly by dark woods, which rose from the river's edge to the height of six hundred feet, and penned in the never-ceasing barrier created by the writhing and tortured stream and the twin cataracts, that ever rivalled each other's thunder. . . . Think of the night, with its palpable blackness, the dead black shadows of the wooded hills, that eternal sound of fury, that misery engendered by loneliness and a creeping sense of abandonment; then will be understood something of the true position of these poor men."

Yet, as he quotes:

> Return we could not, nor
> Continue where we were; to shift our place
> Was to exchange one misery with another,
> And every day that came, came to decay
> A day's work in us.

"On October 7th we set out at a funereal pace through the trackless region on the crest of the forest uplands, starting at 6.30 a.m. We picked up fungi and wild fruit as we travelled, and after seven hours' march we rested for the day. . . . Each officer had economised his ration of bananas. Two were the utmost I could spare for myself."

It was a question of life and death for them

220

whether the Arab station said to exist at Ipoto was really there. Even the officers were sceptical. The most experienced foragers were sent to look for food, stimulated by the promise of liberal rewards if they were successful.

They passed through a sinister valley, then had to clamber over thickly wooded hills, while their exhausted hearts palpitated at the exertion. The remaining donkey was famished and near death, so, to end the beast's misery, Stanley shot him. "The meat was as carefully shared as though it were the finest venison, for a wild and famished mob threatened to defy discipline. Then a free fight took place over the skin, the bones were taken up and crushed, the hoofs were boiled for hours, there was nothing left of my faithful animal but the spilled blood and hair; a pack of hyenas could not have made a more thorough disposal of it." For three hundred and thirty-six hours the pangs of hunger had to be endured, but at length the pioneers suddenly found themselves in a blazed trail. Soon there were plantations of maize and rice; then Arab houses; universal rejoicing.

Yet there were gloomy surroundings to this settlement of ivory-hunters and slave-traders in the midst of the forest. "Towards the Lenda and Ihuru rivers, they had levelled into black ashes every native settlement. Their rage for destruction had even been vented on the plantain groves; every canoe on the rivers had been split into pieces, every island had been searched;

221

and into the darkest recesses where a slight track could be traced they had penetrated with only one dominating passion, which was to kill as many of the men and capture as many of the women and children as craft and cruelty would enable them. . . . They had reduced the forest land into a howling wilderness, and throughout all the immense area had left scarcely a hut standing."

The leaders of these raids took their percentage of the family slaves and all the ivory; while the great entrepreneurs such as Tippu-Tib lived peacefully on the Congo or the Lualaba, delighting in the pleasures of the table, and professing that the joys of the harem were troubled if any stories reached them of the horrors perpetrated in the distant forest. "Every tusk," writes Stanley, "every scrap of ivory in the possession of an Arab trader has been steeped and dyed in blood. Every pound weight has cost the life of a man, woman, or child; for every five pounds a hut has been burned; for every two tusks a whole village has been destroyed; every twenty tusks have been obtained at the price of a district with all its people, villages, and plantations. . . . Because ivory is required for ornaments or billiard balls, the rich heart of Africa is laid waste." These notes were made in Stanley's diary towards the end of the year 1878. To-day, forty-five years later, things have come to such a pass that, great game-preserves notwithstanding, it seems not unlikely that the last of the African elephants will soon be shot. Meanwhile, the slave-

222

trade continues to flourish; or if, in semblance, it has
been abolished, its place has been taken by what is
euphemistically termed "forced labour," and by refined but still brutal methods of exploitation. The modern system may be less obviously and palpably cruel,
but it goes on sucking the blood of the natives like a
gigantic vampire.

In view of the devastation that had been wrought
throughout the surrounding country, the welcome extended to him by the Manyuema seemed to Stanley
hypocritical, nay, an outrage. Not only did all his sym-
pathies flow towards the oppressed natives, but he was
far too straightforward a man to mask his feelings for
the sake of a temporary advantage. Furthermore, the
Arabs were disappointed to find that the caravan was
not sufficiently well equipped to provide them with rich
gifts, so that their cordiality did not last long, and,
although they avoided an open breach, they began to
tempt the Zanzibaris to sell shirts, caps, knives, belts, and
the like. These were the men's own property, so the leader
could not interfere. But the next stage was that "the
unthrifty and reckless fellows sold their ammunition,
accoutrements, bill-hooks, ramrods, and finally their
Remington rifles—all to secure food." Another execution was necessary to stop these thefts, and Stanley had
to threaten the Manyuema with desperate measures in
the way of vengeance upon the receivers of stolen goods.

Still, he needed the Arabs' support, and therefore, a day or two later, he came to an agreement with their chiefs, who undertook:

"To send thirty men to the relief of Captain Nelson, with four hundred ears of corn for his party.

"To provide Captain Nelson and Surgeon Parke, and all sick men unable to work in the fields, with provisions, until the return of the expedition from Lake Albert.

"The service of a guide from Ipoto to Ibwiri, for which they were to be paid one bale and a half of cloth on the arrival of the Rear Column."

Mounteney Jephson was commissioned to lead the relief expedition back to Captain Nelson and Dr. Parke. This marching hither and thither through the woods was a source of perpetual suffering; the primeval forest was a torture chamber, and the tortures it inflicted left the victims with no resource but to acknowledge their impotence.

The climax of horror was reached at the so-called "clearings" in the Balesse country. Stanley writes of them as follows: "Some of these are very extensive, quite a mile and a half in diameter, and the whole strewn with the relics, debris, and timber of the primeval forest. Indeed, I cannot compare the Balesse clearing to anything better than a mighty abattis surrounding the principal village, and over this abattis the traveller has to find his way. As one steps out of the shadow of the forest, the path is at first, maybe, along the trunk of a great tree for a hundred feet, it then turns at right angles along a great branch a few feet; he takes a pace or two on the sail, then finds himself in front of a massive prostrate tree stem, three feet in diameter or so; he climbs over that, and presently finds himself facing the outspreading limbs of another giant, among which he must creep and twist and crawl to get footing on a branch, then from the branch to the trunk he takes a half turn to the right, walks along the tree from which, increasing in thickness, he must soon climb on top of another that has fallen across and atop of it, when, after taking a half turn to the left, he must follow, ascending it until he is twenty feet above the ground. When he has got among the branches at this dizzy height, he needs judgment, and to be proof against nervousness. After tender, delicate balancing, he places his foot on a branch —at last descends cautiously along the steep slope until he is six feet from the ground, from which he must jump on to another tapering branch, and follow that to another height of twenty feet, then along the monster tree, then down to the ground; and so on for hours, the hot, burning sun, and the close steamy atmosphere of the clearing, forcing the perspiration in streams from his body. I have narrowly escaped death three times during these frightful gymnastic exercises. One man died where he fell. Several men were frightfully bruised. Yet it is not so dangerous with the naked feet, but with boots in the

225

early morning, before the dew is dried, or after a rain, or when the advance-guard has smeared the timber with a greasy clay, I have had six falls in an hour. The village stands in the centre. We have often congratulated ourselves on coming to a clearing at the near approach to camping time, but it has frequently occupied us one hour and a half to reach the village. It is a most curious sight to see a caravan laden with heavy burdens, walking over this wreck of a forest and timbered clearing. Streams, swamps, water-courses, ditches, are often twenty to twenty-five feet below a tapering slippery tree, which crosses them bridge-like. Some men are falling, some are tottering, one or two have already fallen, some are twenty feet above the ground, others are on the ground creeping under logs. Many are wandering among a mass of branches, thirty or more may be standing on one delicate and straight shaft, a few may be posted like sentries on a branch, perplexed which way to move. All this, however, is made much harder and more dangerous when, from a hundred points, the deadly arrows are flying from concealed natives, which, thank Heaven, was not common. We have been too cautious for that kind of work to happen often, though we have seldom been able to leave one of these awful clearings without having some man's foot skewered and some one lamed.

"Never was such a series of clearings as those around Mambungu, and the neighboring settlement of Njalis. The trees were of the largest size, and timber

226

enough had been cut to build a navy; and this lay, in all imaginable confusion, tree upon tree, log upon log, branches rising in hills above hills; and among this wild ruin of woods grew, in profusion upon profusion, bananas, plantain, vines, parasites; ivy-like plants, palms, convolvuluses, etc.; through which the poor column had to burrow, struggle, and sweat, while creeping, crawling, and climbing in, through, and over obstacles and entanglements that baffle description."

The men prisoned in such a forest grow irritable towards one another, just as, we have all read, those who have to pass the long Polar night in a block-house become snappish. Each man finds that the others get on his nerves, and each shows his worst side. They know one another, as far as this worst side is concerned, through and through; and in the case of most human beings, to know one another too well means to hate one another. There is perpetual wrangling. So was it here among Stanley's men. The Manyuema rough-handled the Zanzibaris, and the Zanzibaris swore to be revenged on the Manyuema. The blacks blamed the whites for having led them to destruction, the whites regarded the blacks as cowardly and treacherous slaves, on whom a kindly word would be wasted. Stanley alone rose superior to these base feelings, to the lusts of anger and hatred; he was the leader, the guide, the master, the judge. His only thought was for his men. But one night, as he sat

227

alone in his tent, gloom overpowered him when he thought of the sufferings the Arabs at Ipoto had brought upon his poor fellows, and he made a fiercely worded memorandum, as if it were an account that he would be able some day to render.

To Messrs. Kilonga-Longa & Co., Ipoto

Drs. to Messrs. Stanley, Officers, and Men of the E.P.R. Expedition.
November 17, 1887.

To having caused the sentence to death between Lenda River and Ibwiri of 67 men; because we had crossed that river with 271 men—and in camp with those due here shortly there were only 175, and 28 inclusive of Captain Nelson and Dr. Parke, therefore loss of men ... 67

To 27 men at Ipoto too feeble to travel, many of whom will not recover

To spearing to death Mufta Mazinga   1

To flogging one man to death   1

To flogging Ami, a Zanzibari, 200 lashes

To condemning to starvation Captain Nelson and Dr. Parke

To instigating robbery of 2 boxes of ammunition

To receiving 30 stolen Remington rifles

To various oppressions of Zanzibaris

To compelling Sarboko to work as their slave

To various insults to Captain Nelson and Dr. Parke

To devastating 44,000 square miles of territory

To butchery of several thousands of natives

To enslaving several hundreds of women and children

To theft of 200 tusks of ivory between May, 1887 and October, 1887

To many murders, raids, crimes, devastations, past, present, and prospective
         To deaths of Zanzibaris   69
           To mischiefs incalculable!

One of these "mischiefs incalculable" had happened that very afternoon. The brutality of the Manyuema, and the association of Stanley's expedition with them in the minds of the natives, had aroused the countryside. A man named Simba who had left the camp to draw water from the stream came back with an arrow piercing his belly, shot by a lurking savage in the woods. "Realising from our anxious faces the vital nature of the wound, soon after he had been taken into his hut, he loaded a Remington rifle near him and made a ghastly wreck of features which were once jovial and not uncomely. The reflections of the other Zanzibaris on this suicide were curious, and were best expressed by Sali, the tentboy: 'Think of it; Simba! A poor devil owning nothing in the world, without anything or anybody dear to him, neither name, place, property, nor honour, to commit suicide! Were he a rich Arab, a merchant Hindu, a captain of soldiers, a governor of a district, or a white man who had suffered misfortune, I could understand, but this man, who was little better than a slave, to go and kill himself like a man of wealth! Pitch him into the wilderness and let him rot. What right has he to the honour of a shroud and a burial?' "

Soon came slight indications, growing stronger day by day, that the end of the forest was approaching. The sky was open towards the east. They could hardly believe it at first, and then the word was passed with delight from mouth to mouth.

229

"From south-east to south extended a range of mountains between 6,000 and 7,000 feet above the sea. One woman captive indicated south-east as our future direction to the great water that 'rolled incessantly on the shore with a booming noise, lifting and driving the sand before it.' But I preferred aiming east. Old Boryo, chief of Ibwiri, had drawn with his hand a semicircle from south-east to north-west as the course of the Ituri River, and said that the river rose from the plain at the foot of a great hill or a range of hills. To the south-east of Pisgah we could see no plain, but a deep wooded valley, and unless our eyes deceived us the forest seemed to ascend up the slopes of the range as far as its summits. This was still the primeval forest, drowsy, like a great beast, with monstrous fur thinly veiled by vaporous exhalations, resting in its infinite sullenness, remorseless and implacable as ever."

Then they found a man who promised to lead them into the open plain, but he proved a blind guide, and they thought they had lost their way once more. At length they came to a village, or rather a district, consisting of several small settlements or conical huts thatched with grass. Thatched with grass! They must indeed be near the open. On the morning of December 4, 1887, leaving the Ituri, they crossed a narrow belt of tall timber on its left bank, marched on along a broad elephant track for about six hundred yards, "and then, to our undisguised joy, emerged upon a rolling plain, green as an English lawn, into broadest, sweetest daylight and warm and glorious sunshine to inhale the pure air with an uncontrollable rapture. To judge of the feelings of others by mine, we felt as if we had thrown all age and a score of years away, as we sped with invigorated limbs on the soft sward of young grass. We strode forward at a pace most unusual, and, feeling unable to suppress our emotion, the whole caravan broke into a run. Every man's heart seemed enlarged and lifted up with boyish gladness. . . . We gazed at the sun itself, undaunted by its glowing brightness. . . . Until breathlessness forced a halt, the caravan had sped on the double-quick, for this was also a pleasure that had been long deferred." Then, when they saw a fine black cow and her calf issue out of a defile in the rocks, there were clamours of "Beef, Beef, ay, Beef, how are you? We have not seen you since we were young!"

231

CHAPTER NINE

WHERE IS THE REAR COLUMN?

BUT their way to the east was encumbered with difficulties and dangers. It led across a fertile plateau, thickly beset with fields of grain, for the natives were agriculturists. But they were also warriors, and for a time the expedition had to fight even for a pitcher of water. These blacks of the open country were much bolder and stronger than the inhabitants of the forest. At times Stanley almost despaired of reaching the lake, but, pious man that he was, he read his Bible every night before he turned in, to find there words of consolation.

On December 13th they reached the edge of the plateau. The waters of the Albert Nyanza could now be seen, 1,500 feet below them. Stanley's men shouted and danced, thronging around him with congratulations for "having hit the exact spot so well," and convinced that he must have divine powers. He himself was less exuberant, and writes: "A chill came over me, as I thought of the very slight chance there was, in such a country

232

as this, of obtaining a canoe fit to navigate the rough waters of the Albert." The region they were looking down upon was known as Unyoro. Beyond the lake it was bounded by a range of hills. The plain was clothed with sere grass, gently rising as it receded south, and finally producing scrubby wood, acacia, and thorn.

The descent to the level of the lake occupied three hours, frequent halts being necessary to repel the pursuing savages. Then, when a village in the plain was reached, it was to find people who were at enmity with Kabba Rega, king of the Unyoro, although they themselves spoke the same harsh, rasping speech; and they believed that the newcomers, having traversed Kabba Rega's territory, must be friends of his. They did not, however, actually show fight.

"They would not accept our friendship, nor make blood-brotherhood, nor take even a gift. They would give us water to drink, and they would show the path along the lake."

When Stanley explained the object of his expedition, they replied:

"You seek a white man, you say? We hear there is one at Kabba Rega's." (This had been Casati.) "Many, many years ago a white man came from the north in a smoke-boat." (Mason Bey.) "There has been no strange boat on our waters since. We hear of strange people being at Buswa, but that is a long way from here. There, northward along the lake, lies your way. All the wicked people come from there. We never heard any good of men who came in from the Ituri either."

This was not encouraging! Thinking matters over, Stanley decided that it would be futile, for the moment, to push on in search of Emin. They had no boat, and it would be necessary to return in order to get one. His officers were both shocked and grieved. Stanley encouraged them as follows:

"Oh, gentlemen, don't look so. You will make my own regrets greater. Let us face the facts. If the island of Kasenya has no canoe to give us, we must retrace our tracks; there is no help for it. There is no cultivation on this arid lake terrace, nothing nearer than the plateau. Our principal hope was in Emin Pasha. I thought that he would make a short visit in his steamers to this end of the lake and tell the natives that he expected friends to come from the west. What has become of him, or why he could not reach here, we cannot say. But Katonza's villagers tell us that they have never seen a steamer or a white man since Mason Bey was here. They have heard that Casati is in Unyoro. Without a boat it means a month's journey for us to find him. In our present condition we cannot risk that."

Stanley decided, then, to return to Ibwiri, eighteen days' march; to build a fortified camp there; thence to send a detachment to Ipoto to fetch the steel boat, trade goods, all the officers and men that had recovered; to await the arrival of the Rear Column under Major

Barttelot; then, when their forces had been reassembled, to return with the boat to Lake Albert and carry out his mission. Many unforeseen difficulties and dangers might arise, but no other course was possible.

They climbed back, therefore, on to the plateau, crossed it, and re-entered the forest. On January 7, 1888, the caravan reached Ibwiri, where Stanley built a fort, to which he gave the name of Fort Bodo. It was surrounded by a high stockade, which included some cultivable land. Corn, beans, and tobacco were planted. Everything was done with wonderful speed, but there were various troubles, as from rats, flies, fleas, and ants, each plague requiring special methods to avert it.

On January 19, 1888, Lieutenant Stairs set out for Ipoto with a force of one hundred men, and on February 18th he returned with Nelson, Dr. Parke, and all of the Zanzibaris who had sufficiently recovered to undertake the journey. They had the boat with them, in sections. Parke was in fine fettle. Nelson, on the other hand, looked aged, his face being wrinkled, and he tottered like an octogenarian. "They suffered from the want of the necessaries of life day after day, while we revelled in abundance," writes Stanley in self-condemnation— as if he had been really revelling, instead of enduring great hardships. "The worst of all to bear," he said, "was that the Manyuema chiefs had not kept their word,

235

and had shamefully ill-treated the men left in their care."

Well, what was to be done now? The headmen and their white leaders had a talk that evening. "I discovered that all the headmen were unanimous for proceeding to Nyanza to launch the boat and search for news of Emin. My desire was equally great to obtain news of the Pasha; nevertheless, I think very little would have been required to induce me to abandon the search for the Pasha, in order that I might obtain news of Major Barttelot, but officers and men were alike unanimous in their demand that we should solve the fate of Emin." (Once more Stanley is engaged in the search for a man who has disappeared. The Livingstone situation has been renewed. How are we to explain it, that in the case of certain individuals, not merely do their peculiar relationships to other persons recur, but the very same tasks are allotted to them again and again, that identical or closely similar experiences befall them?) At this juncture Stanley himself was more concerned about Barttelot and the Rear Column than about Emin. It was seven months since he had left the Major, and throughout that time he had heard no word of his subordinate. Surely Barttelot ought to have reached him long ere this! In the end a compromise was effected. It was determined that couriers should be sent with letters to Major Barttelot, with a map of the road, and such remarks as would be of practical use to him. It was also decided that Lieu-

236

tenant Stairs, after two days' rest, should escort these couriers as far as Ugarrowwa's and see them safely across the river, and that on returning he should bring along convalescents, who, too feeble to march, had been housed in that settlement on September 18th; that in order that Lieutenant Stairs should "participate in the honour of being present at the relief of Emin Pasha," Stanley would wait for him until March 25th.

The men were mustered on the morning of February 16th, twenty volunteers, who must be in prime physical condition, were asked to convey the letters for Major Barttelot, and Stairs vanished with them into the depths of the forest once more. It seemed almost like a child's game! This sending out and return, and once more the sending forth of those who had returned, to look for missing members of the party. Tedious weeks had now to be got through. Stanley was laid up with severe gastritis, needing large doses of morphia, so that when he began to get better on March 13th he had little memory of the illness he had passed through. On his recovery he found that his men had captured a queen of the pigmies, a pretty little woman about four feet four inches in height, and perhaps nineteen or twenty years of age.

When March 25th arrived, forty-six days since Stairs had set out, as there was no news of him or the twenty volunteers who had accompanied him, Stanley decided to wait no longer. Not a word had come about

237

Barttelot. "Tippu-Tib has evidently been faithless," writes Stanley, "and the Major is therefore working the double stages, some hundreds of miles behind. . . . Stairs has found so many men yet crippled with ulcers that he is unable to travel faster." To idle any longer in the fort was intolerable. It was not "idling," really, for there were road-making, field work, war against the pigmies. These things filled the time out, but did not enable him to ignore his anxieties. Still, Stairs was given a few more days' grace. March was over. No Barttelot, no Bonny, no Stairs, no signal, no messengers. Time was up, and on April 2, 1888, "we filed out at noon with a view to attempt a second time to find the Pasha, or at any rate to penetrate the silence around him. We took with us our steel boat in twelve sections." The weaklings and the sick were left in the fort, which had been made impregnable.

I skip the encounters with the natives, the palavers with the chiefs, the attempts of the savages to extort tribute, their excitement over the gift of a red or a green rag. It is always the same story. In these respects Stanley's descriptions are excessively prolix—a mistake common to almost all travellers, especially to African explorers. Africa seems to encourage diffuseness; it upsets Europeans spiritually and morally; being itself amorphous, it makes them the same. Moreover, Stanley was a pedant, a strange mixture of the pedant and the

238

man of illusions; he had a taste for dilating upon details and at the same time a passion for the boundless. In him it was ever but a step from the schoolmaster to the adventurer. As a writer he was eminently a man of his time, although as a hero he had timeless characteristics; he was a brilliant journalist with the soul of a neglected child; he was an observer who could never classify his experiences, but only pile them one on another. For instance, his account of the appearance and of the manners and customs of the natives of Undussuma is cursory and superficial. He speaks of their refined features, their aquiline noses, their slender necks, their small heads, their excellent manners; he tells of their venerable traditions, their inviolable customs, their satiny skins. Yes, he describes these things, but so unconvincingly that I see nothing as I read him; the indigenes do not become real to me; I know nothing about their inner qualities, their lives, their mentality. I am holding a picture-book in my hand and the pictures convey nothing to me.

Moreover, he quite forgets to explain why this same tribe, which had been so fiercely hostile to the caravan on the first occasion when it emerged from the forest, should now greet Stanley and his men most hospitably, and show every determination to be helpful.

At Uzansa, the expedition was met by two messengers from Kavalli, who told him that their chief had a little packet for him, received from another chief, who

239

in turn had had it from a white man. Stanley went hot-foot to Kavalli, and was there given the packet, wrapped in American oilcloth. It contained a letter from Emin Pasha, dated Tunguru on Lake Albert, March 25, 1888. The letter informed Stanley that the wife of the chief of Nyamsassi [I cannot help it if the reader finds these African names difficult!] had arrived that day, had told him (Emin) that she had seen Stanley and his men, and was willing to convey a message from Emin to Stanley. Emin went on: "Be pleased, if this reaches you, to rest where you are, and to inform me by letter, or one of your people, of your wishes. I could easily come, and my steamer and boats would bring you here. On the arrival of your letter or man, I shall at once start for Nyamsassi, and from there we could concert our further designs."

How cold, how reserved, how official! "Be pleased to rest where you are." Is not this almost equivalent to "Go to the devil"? Stanley himself was so little inclined to display enthusiasm that he may not have taken the phrasing amiss, may not even have noticed that it was chilly. Perhaps it harmonised with his own stiffness in intercourse with fellow-Europeans. He answered civilly, but with the same lack of emotion—this being in marked contrast to what he says about the effect of Emin's missive upon the rest of the expedition. "The letter was translated to our men, upon hearing which they became mad with enthusiasm; nor were the natives of Kavalli

240

COURTESY OF SCHREITERSCHE VERLAGSBUCHHANDLUNG

EMIN PASHA

less affected (though not with such boisterous joy), for they perceived that the package they had carried with such jealous care was the cause of such happiness." In his letter to Emin, Stanley mentioned the Egyptian Firman, and summarised its contents, in case the document should not yet have reached the Pasha. He explained why he had chosen the Congo route, and pithily described the hardships the expedition had undergone in crossing the forest. He begged Emin to bring him three or four milch cows, if it was true (as he had been informed) that the Pasha had plenty of cattle. In conclusion he said that he would await Emin's coming at Nyamsassi. The steel boat was put together, was floated on the waters of the lake, and was provided with sails. Stanley's reply was entrusted to Mounteney Jephson, whose voyage to Emin Pasha's headquarters would take a couple of days.

On April 18th, Jephson set out, and on the 29th he returned with Emin, who was accompanied by Captain Casati and another officer. Stanley asked which of the three was Emin Pasha. Thereupon one of them, with a rather small, slight figure, wearing glasses, and having a greyish beard, addressed him in excellent English. Stanley was amazed, inasmuch as Dr. Junker's description had led him to expect an exceptionally tall man.

"I owe you a thousand thanks, Mr. Stanley; I really do not know how to express my thanks to you."

"Ah, you are Emin Pasha. Don't mention thanks,

241

but come in and sit down. It is so dark out here we cannot see one another."

Once more the exceptional situation of a meeting in the wilds, a meeting which it has been so hard to bring about. Once more a profound contrast between the temperaments and the whole mentality of the two men. This time, moreover, misunderstanding and estrangement. Emin and Stanley are "worlds apart": on the one hand, the Anglo-American, a man of electrical tensions, always concentrated upon some immediate aim; on the other, the unpractical, visionary, purposeless and homeless German Jew. But on this occasion, we have not the apprentice standing before the master craftsman, the disciple before the teacher. The man who has come from afar represents force, authority, is endowed with a much more vigorous personality; whilst the man he has come to seek, and has at length found, is weak-willed, and has to struggle against an adversary equipped with titanic resolution.

Having had two long conversations with Emin, that evening and the next, Stanley writes in his diary: "After all, I am unable to gather in the least what the Pasha's intentions may be." Whenever Stanley had spoken of their returning together, of the march towards the sea, Emin, with a mannerism he had, would tap his knee, and would smile "in a kind of 'we shall see' manner." It was evident, thought Stanley, that Emin found it

242

difficult to renounce his position in a country where he had held viceregal powers.

Ambiguously, Emin remarked: "The Khedive has written to me that the pay of myself, officers, and men will be settled by the paymaster-general if we return to Egypt, but if we stay here we do so at our own risk and on our own responsibility, and that we cannot expect further aid from Egypt. Nubar Pasha has written to me a longer letter, to the same effect. Now, I do not call these instructions. They do not tell me that I must quit, but they leave me a free agent."

Stanley's rejoinder was: "Our instructions were to carry a certain quantity of ammunition to you, and to say to you, when we delivered it, 'Now we are ready to guide and assist you out of Africa, if you are willing to accompany us; but if you decline going, our mission is ended.'"

Emin continued to raise difficulties, and to put forward alternative proposals. When Stanley gave cogent reasons for his leaving, the Pasha replied:

"What you say is quite true, but we have such a number of women and children, probably ten thousand people altogether! How can they all be brought out of here? We shall want a great many carriers."

"Carriers for what?"

"For the women and children. You surely would not leave them, and they cannot travel."

"The women must walk; for such children as can-

243

not walk, they will be carried on donkeys, of which you say you have many. . . . Our women walked on my second expedition across Africa; your women, after a little while, will do quite as well. . . . You have plenty of cattle, some hundreds, I believe. Those will furnish beef."

But Emin would not come to a decision, and said they had better postpone further talk of the matter until next day. When the next day came, he had additional difficulties to put before his would-be rescuer, who seemed to him altogether too dictatorial.

"What you told me last night," he began, "has led me to think that it is best we should retire from Africa. The Egyptians are very willing to go, I know. There are about fifty men of them, besides women and children. . . . But of the Regulars, the Nubians, who compose two battalions, I am extremely doubtful. They have led such a free and happy life here that they would demur at leaving a country where they enjoy luxuries such as they cannot hope for in Egypt. . . . Now, supposing the Regulars refused to leave, you can imagine my position would be a difficult one. Should I be right in leaving them to their fate? Would it not be consigning them to ruin? I should have to leave them their arms and ammunition, and on my retiring all recognised authority and discipline would be at an end. There would presently arise disputes, and factions would be formed. The more ambitious would aspire to be chiefs, and from rivalries

244

would spring hate and mutual slaughter, involving all in one common doom."

Stanley answered that Emin need merely read the Khedive's letter to the troops, and that there was no occasion to trouble about those who decided to remain, since they would take the risk of their own free will.

"That is very true," replied the Pasha; "but suppose the men surround me and detain me by force?"

"Unlikely, I should think, from the state of discipline I see among your men. But of course you know them better than I do."

Stanley then said he would like Emin to ask Captain Casati (who was ignorant of English, as Stanley was of Italian) whether he wanted to stay in Equatoria, or to return to the coast with the relief expedition.

Casati answered through Emin Pasha: "If Governor Emin goes, I go; if he stays, I stay."

"Well, Pasha," said Stanley, "in the event of your staying, your responsibilities will be great, for you will involve Captain Casati in your own fate."

Casati said that he absolved Emin Pasha from all responsibility, being governed by his own choice entirely—from which Stanley inferred that Casati entertained secret designs of his own!

Emin went on to explain some of the considerations that made him disinclined to leave: "As to the pay, there can only be about two thousand and odd pounds due. What is such a sum to a man about to be shelved?

I am now forty-eight, and one of my eyes is utterly gone. When I get to Egypt they will give me some fine words and bow me out. A fine prospect, truly!"

Stanley took considerable pleasure in Emin's society, for the Pasha was an amiable and well-educated man, whose vacillations and irresolution were, however, extremely irritating. There was nothing plain or straightforward about him. His words, his deeds, his motives were obscure. Danger menaced from two sides. From the disturbed state of Uganda; and from Kabba Rega of Unyoro, whom the arrival of Stanley's expedition had made uneasy, and who, when the first tidings of its approach came, in the beginning of February, had seized Casati and treated him roughly. Casati, indeed, had barely escaped with his life. Here were additional reasons for a speedy decision, but Emin continued to procrastinate. He asked Stanley to write out a proclamation which could be read to the soldiers, stating the instructions Stanley had brought, and that Stanley now awaited the men's decision. Stanley agreed to do this. In a subsequent conversation he told the Pasha that there were three possibilities open. The first was that Emin should continue to be an obedient soldier, and should return with Stanley to Egypt. The second possibility (and here Stanley was playing a political card which hitherto he had kept up his sleeve) was that Emin, with such soldiers as remained loyal to him, should accompany Stanley to the north-east corner of the Victoria

246

Nyanza, where Stanley would establish the Pasha as resident in the name of the East African Association. This scheme was hatched, one may presume, to give a tit for tat to Germany, which had recently gained a footing in those parts; and it is evident that the suspicions with which the Germans had regarded Stanley's expedition were not wholly devoid of justification. The third possibility, the most surprising of all, and involving even graver political considerations, was that Emin should remain where he was as governor of Equatoria and that that province should be affiliated to the Congo Free State. Stanley had been authorised, he said, by Leopold, King of the Belgians, to make this proposal.

Here we see Stanley in a new role—that of political agent—a role forced upon him as the founder of the Congo Free State, "his" State. The Pasha listened most attentively to these remarkable schemes, and Stanley went on to explain at considerable length what an advantage it would be for Equatoria to be affiliated to the Congo Free State. The affair would not be difficult to carry through. On the one side was Egypt, lacking power and lacking funds, so weak that she had not even been able to check the revolt of the Mahdi; and, on the other, the great realm recently founded in the Congo basin, founded without violence and subsisting without violence; a realm with inexhaustible natural resources, the very heart and soul of the African continent.

Tempting as his scheme might appear, and though

247

Emin was a born adventurer, he had now lost all desire for so bold a hazard. He had burned his fingers too often; so it suited his turn to play the honest man whom no temptation could corrupt.

"My duty to Egypt comes before anything else. While I am here, the provinces belong to Egypt, and remain her property until I retire. When I depart, they become no-man's-land. I cannot strike my flag in such a fashion, and change the red for the blue. I have served the first for twenty years; the latter I never saw. Besides, may I ask you if, with your recent experience, you think it likely that communication could be kept open at reasonable cost?"

"Undoubtedly not at first. Our experiences have been too terrible to forget them soon. But we shall return to Yambuya for the Rear Column. I anticipate, with much less suffering. The pioneer suffers most. Those who follow us will profit by what we have learned. Turn the matter over in your mind pending the arrival of the Rear Column, which I am going to fetch. You have certainly some weeks before you to consider the question thoroughly."

As to Emin's protestations of loyalty to Egypt, Stanley went on to show him the Foreign Office despatches supplied to the leader of the relief expedition by order of Lord Iddesleigh. Among these was a copy of Emin's letter to Sir John Kirk, wherein, in 1886, he offered Equatoria to England, and stated that he would

248

be most happy to surrender the province to the British Government, or, indeed, to any other power that would undertake to maintain it.

"Oh," said the Pasha, "they should never have published that letter. It was private. What will the Egyptian Government think of my conduct?"

The fact was that Stanley inspired him with awe. Subsequently he referred on many occasions to the spell Stanley had exercised upon him, so that he had been unable, in the Englishman's presence, to think his own independent thoughts.

Another month had gone by without any word from the Rear Column. Stanley's patience was exhausted. In order to bring his communications to Emin to a close for the time being, he drafted the proclamation which Emin had asked for. Mounteney Jephson read it to the troops. It was penned in a curt military style, its tone being very similar to some of Napoleon's manifestos of the sort—a proof that like situations find expression in like words. It gave a summary account of the misfortunes from which Egypt had suffered through the rising of the Mahdi and the loss of Khartoum, explained the object of the relief expedition, and that Stanley had come in order to show them the way to Zanzibar, where they would be put on board a steamer for Suez, and thence taken to Cairo. (Stanley had realised that it would be impossible for him to lead this miscellaneous body of men, women, and children through the forest to the

Congo. He had had daily evidence of the insubordination of the forces under Emin's "command," having
assisted the Pasha in a punitive campaign against King
Kabba Rega.) The manifesto went on to tickle the vanity of the Egyptians, saying that the writer was assured
of their loyalty to the Khedive, and promising them
reward and promotion in the event of their continued
obedience. "The Khedive and his vizier, Nubar Pasha,
have all along kept you in mind. They have heard by
way of Uganda how you have held to your post, and
how staunch you have been to your duties as soldiers.
Therefore, they send me to tell you this; to tell you that
you are well remembered, and that your reward is waiting for you, but that you must follow me to Egypt to get
your pay and your reward. At the same time, the Khedive says to you, through me, that if you think the road
too long, and are afraid of the journey, you may stay
here, but in that case you are no longer his soldiers;
that your pay stops at once, and that in any trouble
which may hereafter befall you, you are not to blame
him but yourselves." Of course this was designed much
more to influence Emin than his disorderly cohorts! The
concluding paragraph runs: "I go to collect my people
and goods, and bring them to the Nyanza, and after a
few months I shall come back here to learn what you
have to say. If you say 'Let us go to Egypt,' I will then
show you a safe road. If you say 'We shall not leave
this country,' then I will bid you farewell and return

to Egypt with my own people. May God have you in His keeping. Your good friend, Stanley."

This proclamation was read on May 22. On the 24th, Stanley said good-bye to Emin, and set out on his return to Fort Bodo. When the two men had parted, Emin sent a courier after Stanley with a letter in which there were a number of courteous but non-committal assurances. The most noteworthy words are the concluding ones: "I have lived too long in Africa not to have became somewhat 'negrofied.' " We cannot doubt that, in his secret heart, he was delighted to be quit of this blunt deliverer. Now he would have plenty of time in which to think things over, and to change his intentions again and again. It was, in fact, more than nine months before Stanley returned.

For my own part, I consider that this renewed march through the forest, two months from Fort Bodo to Yambuya, and nearly four months back again—a total distance of over a thousand miles—was the most remarkable of all Stanley's achievements. There was no longer the lure of the unknown, there was nothing new to discover; it was a pure act of self-sacrifice to which nothing impelled him but his sense of responsibility towards his subordinates or his comrades (call them which you will); nothing but his anxiety about their unknown fate in conjunction with his eagerness to succeed in the undertaking to which he had put his hand.

251

He would not, must not, fail. Should he fail, he would make himself ludicrous in the eyes of Europe. If he had been criticised and slandered in the days when he had effected what he had set out to do, and had returned victorious, what a storm would now arise should he go back under the shadow of defeat! No doubt such thoughts must often have passed through his mind as he sat alone in his tent when the day's march was over, and must have been pondered through many a sleepless night. Now, as always, he was a lonely man. Those who accompanied him were simply drawn along in his train; they could not really see his face and knew nothing of his true mind. What a torment it must have been to him, the conviction that he had put his trust in men who had perhaps proved unworthy of it; in men who had been unable to profit by the example he had set them; to think of them as quailing before difficulties which he had taught them could be overcome.

He was sick and depressed. Malarial fever had got a permanent grip upon his system; Emin's shilly-shallying had profoundly upset him; and one might think he had excellent reasons for resting at Fort Bodo. Stairs, Nelson, and Parke were there. They had recovered health and strength while he had been away. He could have sent one of them, two of them, or all three of them, with a hundred men, to march to Yambuya and see what had become of Barttelot and the Rear Column. No one would have blamed him for such a course, which

252

would have been regarded as eminently reasonable. Stanley, however, would not delegate this responsibility to anyone. He was fond of saying: "If you want a thing done, do it yourself!" He determined to traverse the dreadful forest again, to endure many months of darkness, exhaustion, daily peril, melancholy, and despair. He must go to Yambuya himself. He must find out for himself what could have made Barttelot, who had shaken hands with him upon their agreement, unfaithful. Assuredly it was heroic, this resolve of his to solve the enigma in person.

On June 16th he marched out of the fort with more than two hundred men. Wishing to be burdened with as little baggage as possible, he did not take any of his white officers with him, except Dr. Parke, who was to accompany him as far as Ipoto in order to convey back to Fort Bodo the boxes of ammunition which had been left at the former place. He did not even take with him his fox-terrier Randy, although the dog had borne the fatigues of the march to the Albert Nyanza so well, had been such a good friend in an hour of great need, and had become the pet of everyone. "I committed him to the care of Lieutenant Stairs, in order to save him the thousand-mile journey before us. But the poor dog misjudged my purpose and resolutely refused his food from the moment I left him, dying of a broken heart the third day after my departure."

The last evening at Fort Bodo, talking matters over with Lieutenant Stairs, Stanley said: "Evil hangs over this forest as a pall over the dead; it is like a region accursed for crimes; whoever enters within its circle becomes subject to the divine wrath. . . . Our atonement shall be a sweet offering, the performance of our duties. Let us bear all that may be put upon us, like men bound to the sacrifice, without one thought of the results. Let me depart from you with the conviction that in my absence you will not swerve from your duty here, and I need not be anxious for you. . . . Give me a reasonable time, over and above the date I have named, December 22nd. Then, if I return not, consult with your friends, and afterwards with your men, and do what is best and wisest. As for us, we shall march back to the place where Barttelot may be found, even as far as Yambuya, but to no place beyond, though he may have taken everything with him down the Congo. If he has left Yambuya and wandered far away south-east instead of east, I will follow him up and overtake him, and then strike through the forest in the most direct way to Fort Bodo." The tone of gloomy determination is that of a man who is no longer so sure of himself and his star as he was wont to be in earlier days; one who no longer believes that fortune smiles on him.

Back through the forest; back to the former camps, beside the rivers, through the clearings, past the waterfalls. Many of the paths they had cut have already been overgrown. The old enemies, the pigmies and the other savages, are still on the watch, and their attacks have to be warded off. Sickness, hunger, and exhaustion, as before! Men who had deserted on the first journey are picked up again. The Manyuema are raiding as of old. The hothouse atmosphere of the jungle is as enervating as ever. Stanley is thinned to a shadow, his physical strength having been undermined. In camp, one night, he overhears a conversation between his tent-boy Sali and another Zanzibari. The boy says he believes the Master will not last long. "Please God," rejoins the other, "we shall find goats or fowls in a few days. It is meat he needs."

Canoe voyages, marches, day after day, for two months. In his consuming unrest, Stanley overcomes every obstacle, having even ceased to record the number and the names of those who lie down to die. Some of the messengers whom, six months before, he had sent out for tidings of Barttelot, return. God knows whither they have wandered, but now they bring no news, and still he presses on.

"It was this nervous anxiety about the missing people that drove me through the Great Forest at such a rate. That which had taken us one hundred and twenty-nine days was now performed in sixty-two. On August 17, 1888, the eighty-third day since quitting the Pasha on Lake Albert, I came in view of the village of Banalya, ninety miles east of Yambuya." At this point the River Ituri makes a curve. It was a sombre morning; the village had been destroyed, but amid the ruins there was a stockade.

"Presently white dresses were seen, and, quickly taking up my field-glass, I discovered a red flag hoisted. Suspicion of the truth crept into my mind. A light puff of wind unrolled the flag for an instant, and the white crescent and star were revealed. I sprang to my feet and cried out, 'The Major, boys! Pull away bravely!' A vociferous shouting and hurrahing followed, and every canoe shot forward at a racing speed.

"About two hundred yards from the village we stopped paddling, and, as I saw a great number of strangers on the shore, I asked, 'Whose men are you?'— 'We are Stanley's men.' "

Then Stanley recognised a European near the gate; it was William Bonny. Pressing his hand, Stanley said:

"Well, Bonny, how are you? Where is the Major? Sick, I suppose?"

"The Major is dead, sir."

"Dead? Good God! how dead? Fever?"

"No, sir, he was shot."

"By whom?"

"By the Manyuema—Tippu-Tib's people."

"Good heavens! Well, where is Jameson?"

HENRY M. STANLEY

"At Stanley Falls."

"What on earth is he doing there?"

"He went to get more carriers."

"Well, where are the others? Where is Ward, where is Troup?" (These two men had been Barttelot's technical assistants, to see to the steamboats and the transport service.)

"Mr. Ward is at Bangala."

"Bangala! Bangala! What can he be doing there?"

"Yes, sir, he is at Bangala, and Mr. Troup was invalided home some months ago."

Stanley can hardly understand, and is as if petrified. Days pass before he grasps the full extent of the disaster, and even then its causes have not been fully explained. It is as if we were looking at a film, with the sensational title: "The Mystery of Yambuya."

The following facts are clear. Within a few weeks after Stanley's departure from Yambuya, reports of his death were current, although the origin of these rumours never became clear. The Major, to whom information on the subject was brought, said he did not believe it, but all the same he sent down to Bangala all Stanley's clothing, maps, and charts, reserve medicines for the expedition, and so on. The result was that when Stanley got back, and expected to be able to get a fresh rig-out from his private boxes, he found that nothing of the kind was forthcoming. He had to beg an old pair of

257

trousers from Mr. Bonny, to cut another pair from a white blanket left by a deserter, and another from a curtain in his tent. Barttelot's precipitation in sending down-river boxes of jams, sardines, herrings, wheaten flour, sago, tapioca, arrowroot, etc., was all the more puzzling, seeing that there were thirty-three men in the camp who were dangerously ill, and for whom these delicacies might have been most useful.

Even the more puzzling was the fact that on August 14, 1887, six weeks after Stanley's departure, Troup delivered over to the Major one hundred and twenty-nine cases of Remington rifle cartridges, in addition to the twenty-nine cases left by Stanley at Yambuya. Now these one hundred and fifty-eight cases contained 80,000 rounds. But by June 9th of the year 1888, according to Barttelot's report, this supply had dwindled to 35,580 rounds. Yet there had been no fighting, no marching. What had become of the 40,000 rounds that had disappeared? Two-thirds of the bales of cloth had vanished, and half of the gunpowder. The Rear Column had originally consisted of two hundred and seventy-one men, rank and file. A year later, while the Rear Column was still in the same camp, its strength had fallen to one hundred and thirty-five men, rank and file. The others were dead or had bolted.

If Barttelot had followed instructions, he would have set out in Stanley's tracks about the middle of

258

August, 1887; he was to do so in any circumstances, no matter whether he believed the leader dead or not. Since the transport service by river had worked efficiently, and all the requisite supplies had come, there was nothing to hinder his start. Yet he stayed at Yambuya. Why? Why did Bonny, Jameson, and Barttelot, instead of doing everything they could to get away promptly from Yambuya, spend their time in futile journeys to and fro between the camp and Stanley Falls?

Stanley asked Bonny what he thought the reason could have been. Bonny admitted that the whole thing seemed absurd, but could give no reason. Had all these men, presumably able and shrewd, disciplined soldiers and officials, suddenly gone mad?

Stanley learned that Barttelot, in apparently hopeless perplexity, had had a cable sent from St. Paul de Loanda, asking the Committee to wire advice and information. The Committee had replied by referring him to Stanley's orders of June 24th. Thus a company of five officers in Yambuya were in doubt as to the meaning of perfectly plain orders, when a Committee six thousand miles away had no doubt whatever as to the spirit of the instructions.

Nay, more, Bonny showed Stanley a letter written by the Major at Yambuya, under date April 22, 1888, to the following effect: 'In event of my death, detention by Arabs, absence from any cause from Yambuya camp,

259

you [Bonny] will assume charge of the Sudanese company, etc., etc. Relief to Mr. Stanley, care of the loads and men, good understanding between yourself and the Arabs must be your earnest care." What cause of absence was he thinking of? What was left for the faithful Jameson, "whose alacrity, capacity, and willingness to work are unbounded," to do? Where was the "promising, intelligent, and capable" Ward? What position was reserved for the "methodical, businesslike, and zealous" Mr. Troup? Why on earth was Bonny, whose competence was, to say the least of it, questionable, to be suddenly elevated to the command of the Rear Column in the event of any unhappy accident to Major Barttelot?

Commenting on these matters, and on the impression they produced upon him, Stanley writes: "My first fear was that I had become insane. But at length a conviction flashed upon my mind that there had been a supernatural, malignant agency at work to thwart every honest intention." Stanley was amazed when Bonny told him that, at a meeting of the officers, one of them had proposed that Stanley's instructions should be disregarded, and that the ideas of Major Barttelot should be carried out in future. What ideas? Had Barttelot ever spoken of any plans apart from those he had been instructed to carry out? Apparently not!

We seem to be reading some ancient saga of doom when we scan the following comment by Stanley: "Also, on a fatal date, fatal because that resolution to wait

260

sealed their fate, an officer of the Advance Column was straying through an impenetrable bush with three hundred despairing men behind him, and on this fatal date the next year, Mr. Bonny, the sole survivor of the English band, pours into my ears a terrible tale of death and disaster, while at the same hour poor Jameson breathes his last, tired and worn out with his futile struggles to 'move on' at Bangala, five hundred miles west of him; and six hundred miles east of him, the next day, Emin Pasha and Mr. Jephson walk into the arms of the rebel soldiery of Equatoria—this is all very uncanny, if you think of it. There is a supernatural diablerie operating which surpasses the conception and attainment of a mortal man."

To try to follow up at least one thread of this inextricable tangle of lying, misrepresentation, blundering, and neglect of duty, Stanley went on to inquire what could have been the origin of the rumours that he was dead. The report ran, it appeared, that he had not died of illness, but had been murdered. "Quantities of human bones are said to be discovered by some reconnoitring party, human limbs are said to be found in cooking-pots; sketches by an amateur artist are said to have been made of whole parties indulging in cannibal repasts; it is more than hinted that Englishmen are implicated in raids, murder, and cannibalism, that they have been making targets of native fugitives—all

261

for the mere sake of infusing terror, alarm, and grief among quiet English people, and to plague our friends at home. The instruments this dark power selects for the dissemination of these calumnious fables are as various in their professions as in their nationalities. It is a deserter one day, and the next it is an engineer of a steamer; it is now a slave-trader, or a slave; it is a guileless missionary in search of work, or a dismissed Syrian; it is a young artist with morbid tastes, or it is an officer of the Congo Free State." The feeling strengthens that all these poisonous legends must have emanated from one and the same focus. Some details as to the course of events are worth giving. On August 17, 1887, the steamer "Stanley" had delivered all the goods and ammunitions that the Rear Column had been waiting for. There seems to have been no reason why a start should not have been made. The officers met to deliberate, and unanimously decided that the wisest plan would be to await Tippu-Tib. Tippu-Tib was late in coming, so Ward was sent down to Stanley Falls to inquire, returning on the 29th with a reply from Tippu-Tib wherein that worthy promised to collect the carriers needed and send them within ten days. A few days later there appeared a small troop of Manyuema, reported to be the vanguard of the carrier contingent, which Tippu-Tib would shortly bring in person. Now, however, trouble broke out on the Lumami, and Tippu-Tib was obliged to hurry to the scene to settle it. The Yambuya garrison, therefore, went on waiting for him. At length, on October 1st, another visit to Stanley Falls was made, this time by Major Barttelot in person. Four weeks afterward the Major reappeared, stating that Tippu-Tib, unable to muster six hundred carriers in the Stanley Falls region, had been obliged to proceed to Kasongo, about three hundred and fifty miles above Stanley Falls, and that this journey of seven hundred miles to Kasongo and back would occupy forty-two days.

Barttelot was informed that during his absence, Majato, a headman of the Manyuema, had been behaving badly, "intimidating the natives who marketed with the garrison, with a view to starving the soldiers and Zanzibaris, or by reaping some gain through acting as middlemen or factors in the exchange of goods for produce." Thereupon Major Barttelot sent Mr. Ward to Stanley Falls (the third visit) to complain of Majato, who was recalled. In the beginning of 1888, Salim bin Mohammed, one of Tippu-Tib's nephews, arrived at Yambuya for the second time, and presently became so active in enforcing harsh measures against the natives that the food supply of the camp was wholly cut off and never renewed. He also began the construction of a permanent camp of substantial mud-built huts at half a bow-shot's distance from the palisades of Yambuya, thus completely investing the fort on the land side, as though he were preparing for a siege of the place.

263

After a futile effort to bribe Salim with the offer of £1,000 to lead a Manyuema contingent to follow the Advance Column, Major Barttelot and Mr. Jameson, about the middle of February, undertook a fourth visit to Stanley Falls. Salim, fearing unfavourable accounts of his behaviour, accompanied them. The party met two hundred and fifty Manyuema, who were permitted to scatter over the country in search of ivory. Barttelot returned to Yambuya on March 25th, with the information that Jameson, the indefatigable Jameson, had gone up the Congo to Kasongo, believing that, if he could only find the old fox, he would be able to make Tippu-Tib fulfil the bargain to supply carriers.

By the end of March, Barttelot was on bad terms with Salim bin Mohammed, and made a fifth visit to Stanley Falls to secure the latter's removal. In the middle of April, Barttelot was back at Yambuya, bringing orders that Salim was to leave. Salim, however, instead of proceeding to Stanley Falls, started to raid a large village below Yambuya. He came back a few days later, stating that he had heard a rumour to the effect that the Advance Column was descending the upper waters of the Aruwimi. Salim's raiding activities made it increasingly difficult for Major Barttelot to secure food for his men. In May, therefore, Barttelot made a sixth visit to Stanley Falls, and on the 22nd of the same month returned with Jameson and a large party of Manyuema. Three days later Tippu-Tib actually arrived, eleven

264

months behind time. But if the Major and his subordinates believed that the old Arab had come to give them serious aid, they were speedily disillusioned. Tippu-Tib said that loads sixty pounds in weight were too heavy for his people; the officers were asked to reduce them to forty, thirty, and twenty pounds weight, to suit his views. This was no easy task, but it had to be performed. The delay suited the purposes of Tippu-Tib, who seized the opportunity for making extortionate demands. The Major, however, had lost patience, or perhaps his conscience had begun to prick. At any rate, on June 11, 1888, Barttelot, Jameson, and Bonny left the camp they should have left not later than August 25, 1887, with a following of Zanzibaris, Sudanese, Somalis, and Manyuema, aggregating nearly nine hundred men, women, and children, intending to make a "strenuous quest" for the lost commander, and to relieve Emin Pasha. Barttelot, however, did not accompany the expedition all the way to Banyala. On the thirteenth day he quitted it for a seventh visit to Stanley Falls, leaving the column to struggle on without him. It reached Banyala on the forty-third day of a march of ninety miles [!]; and "on the same day the restless and enterprising Major entered Banyala on his return from Stanley Falls." Next day, on July 19, 1888, he was shot by an Arab.

Banyala was one of Tippu-Tib's many stations, and had been established since Stanley had left. Bonny's

265

report describes what happened on the morning of July 19th: "Early this morning a Manyuema woman commenced beating a drum and singing. It is their daily custom. The Major sent his boy Soudi, who is only about thirteen years old, to stop them, but at once loud and angry voices were heard, followed by two shots by way of defiance. The Major ordered some Sudanese to go and find the men who were firing; at the same time, getting up from bed, and taking his revolvers from his case, he said: 'I will shoot the first man who starts firing.' I told him not to interfere with the people's daily custom, to remain inside, and not to go out, inasmuch as they would soon be quiet. He went out, revolver in hand, to where the Sudanese were. They told him that they could not find the men who were firing. The Major then pushed aside some Manyuema, passed through them towards the woman who was beating the drum and singing, and ordered her to desist. Just then a shot was fired through a loophole, in an opposite hut from within, by Sauga, the woman's husband. The charge penetrated just below the region of the heart and passed out behind, lodging finally in a part of the veranda under which the Major fell dead."

Barttelot seems to have met his fate as the natural outcome of a nervous irritability shown by a commander towards an expedition which he had allowed to get out of hand. He can hardly be regarded as accountable for his actions. Who was now to lead the Rear Column?

266

Three days after the tragedy, Jameson appeared at Banyala, and assumed command, but on the 25th he undertook a fresh journey to Stanley Falls (the eighth!). For what purpose? Stanley says that it was "in the hope that by making liberal offers of gold to satisfy the avaricious Tippu-Tib, he might induce the Arab either to head the Rear Column himself, or else send one of his fiery nephews." It may have been so, and Stanley may have believed that it was so. In any case, twenty-eight days after the tragic death of Major Barttelot, and twenty-three days after the departure of Jameson, Stanley himself arrived at Banyala. This is how he described what he found:

"The life of misery which was related was increased by the misery which we saw. Pen cannot picture nor tongue relate the full horrors witnessed within that dreadful pest-hole. The nameless scourge of barbarians in the faces and bodies of many a hideous-looking human being, who, disfigured, bloated, marred, and scarred, came, impelled by curiosity, to hear and see us who had come from the forest land to the east, and who were reckless of the terror they inspired by the death embodied in them. There were six dead bodies lying unburied, and the smitten living, with their festers, lounged in front of us by the dozen. Others, worn to thin skin and staring bone from dysentery and fell anæmia and ulcers large as saucers, crawled about and

267

hollowly sounded their dismal welcome, a welcome to this charnel-yard. Weak, wearied, and jaded in body and mind, I scarcely know how I endured the first few hours. The ceaseless story of calamity vexed my ears. A deadly stench of disaster hung in the air, and the most repellent sights moved and surged before my dazed eyes. I heard of murder and death, of sickness and sorrow, anguish and grief, and wherever I looked the hollow eyes of dying men met mine with such trusting, pleading regard, such far-away yearning looks that it seemed to me if but one sob were uttered, my heart would break."

Bonny looked on dumbfounded.

"And you—you, are the only one left?" asked Stanley.

"The only one, sir. Barttelot's grave is but a few yards off."

Stanley writes a death-plaint on the Major.

"What, Barttelot! That tireless man with the ever-rushing pace, that jolly young soldier, with his dauntless bearing, whose soul was ever yearning for glory. A man so lavishly equipped with nature's advantages, to bow the knee thus to the grey craftiness at Stanley Falls! It was all an unsolved riddle to me. I would have wagered he would have seized that flowing grey beard of Tippu-Tib and pounded the face to pulp, even in the midst of his power, rather than to allow himself to be thus cajoled time and time again. The fervid vehemence of his promise not to wait a day after the fixed date yet

268

rings in my ears; I feel the strong grip, and see the resolute face, and I remember my glowing confidence in him."

Does not the leader really understand why things have gone so hopelessly awry?

CHAPTER TEN

ATTEMPT AT AN INTERPRETATION

THERE is a very remarkable tale by Joseph Conrad entitled *Heart of Darkness*. Reading and re-reading it, I continually had the impression that the writer, a man intimately acquainted with the tropics, must have had the tragedy of Yambuya in his mind—though he may not have been fully conscious of the fact. I cannot but feel that at some time or another in the course of his life he must have been decisively influenced by the sinister story of what happened there. For sinister, uncanny, was the fate of this Rear Column of the Emin Pasha Relief Expedition, which came under the spell of the "Heart of Darkness," the spell of a hitherto unknown and terrible world. Think of those "cheery young officers" suddenly removed from the comfortable and familiar life of the great cities of Europe into that sultry wilderness, into those regions of pullulating swamps, where men, animals, and plants are huddled together in wanton profusion; into that hothouse atmosphere of

270

luxuriant growth, into trackless wilds, set apart from the known world. Think of them surrounded by suspicious and treacherous blacks, and by Arabs wedded to cruel customs and privileges dating from centuries back. Day after day they were harassed by inexplicable hostilities, by the mutual enmities of the tribes, by the malice of Tippu-Tib, who was ostensibly their partner but was continually putting difficulties in their way. Bear in mind, too, how their energies were being sapped by the murderous climate; and, above all, that they were deprived of their leader, the man whom they had followed so enthusiastically into the wilds, Stanley the Rock-Breaker, the sole white man in the expedition intimately acquainted and competent to deal with the dangerous men and the still more dangerous natural conditions of Central Africa. Only when we have taken all these facts into consideration, can we begin to understand what sort of life they lived at Yambuya, and how inevitable was their disastrous fate.

Yet the weakness they showed seems almost incredible. Perhaps it would be better to say the softness, the loss of morale and of bodily energy. As one reads the story, one feels as if they had sunk deep down in a quagmire. They manifested strong but aimless and impotent desires. Whatever they did was futile, whatever they planned to do was ineffective. They suffered much from fever—the malignant fever of tropical Africa —so that often they were delirious day after day; and

271

when they had taken enough quinine to set them on their feet once more, their mental powers had been dulled, their memory had been disordered, their energies had been undermined. Anxiously they looked forward to the next paroxysms, and sometimes even doubted their personal identity. They felt unequal to the tasks that had been imposed upon them; and this, indeed, was the most disastrous feature of their condition, that it had come to seem to them that cause and effect were no longer interconnected as they had been in the existence they had previously known. The waters of forgetfulness were sucking them down—in a word, they lapsed into a condition of poisonous inertia both of mind and of body, lit up only from time to time by painful flashes of the remnants of egoism.

Yet all this is insufficient to account for their behaviour. "For some mysterious reason," writes Stanley, "they pinned their faith with the utmost tenacity to Tippu-Tib." It seems to me that here Stanley is deliberately refusing to face the truth. What can the "mysterious reason" have been other than that some definite lure drew them to Tippu-Tib ever and again? But what was the nature of this lure?

Nowhere does Stanley, who in his two volumes entitled *In Darkest Africa* writes with seeming bewilderment upon the subject, give the faintest hint that erotic influences may have been at work—obvious though the suggestion must be to any unprejudiced observer. Nor,

272

so far as I know, has anyone else hitherto attempted to explain the enigma of Yambuya in this way, though any other explanation leads us into a blind alley. We can sympathise with Stanley's attempts to save the honour of his officers by the assumption that they must have been affected with something like a periodic mental disorder—but we of a later generation have no need to find such excuses. Very little imagination is required to enable us to penetrate the veil of silence Stanley wrapped round these matters, to pierce through the discretion which really amounted to a deliberate assumption of ignorance. In his journal a few weeks later, coming back to the problem of Barttelot's death (apropos of an epidemic of smallpox, against which the Zanzibaris had been rendered proof by vaccination, but which was developing with terrible rapidity among the other natives now attached to the expedition), he writes: "Among the Manyuema were two insane women, or, rather, to be quite correct, two women subject to spasms of hysterical exaltation, possessed by 'devils,' according to their chiefs, who prevented sleep by their perpetual singing during the night. Probably some such mania for singing at untimely hours was the cause of the Major's death. If the poor Major had any ear for harmony, their unmelodious and excited madhouse uproar might well have exasperated him." This inference may seem as logical as it is simple—but it is better suited to explain the hap-

273

penings in a girls' boarding-school than those in the primeval forest at Aruwimi!

Since we have no documents, no reports, relating to what went on behind the scenes, we are left to speculation; but the recorded facts make it plain enough that moral decay and disorganisation set in at Yambuya after Stanley's departure. The cause, after all, is not far to seek! Tippu-Tib, the "uncrowned king" of those parts, must have made up his mind to employ methods of his own in order to undermine the morale of these new-comers from Europe, young fools as he must have regarded them. There can be no question that he had conceived a venomous hatred for Stanley. This was natural enough, seeing that Bula Matari was from his point of view a spoil-sport, interfering with "legitimate business," inasmuch as Stanley had drawn the attention of Europe to the tainted, the sanguinary sources of the Arab's wealth, and had established the power of the Congo Free State in regions where previously Tippu-Tib had been able to carry on his man-hunts without restraint. Nothing could be attempted against Stanley in person, who was too strong, too great a man, and fully able to take care of himself, so Tippu-Tib would set traps for Bula Matari's subordinates. In accordance with the ancient arts of his own country, we may well suppose that he inaugurated a brothel in the wilderness, at which he could stage the subtlest of temptations. A nod, a wave of the hand, and his underlings would do his will as if

they had been the jinn and the jinneeyeh, the slaves of
the lamp and the ring in the *Thousand and One Nights*.
Dancing-women from Araby, Negro belles from Somali-
land, slender black girls from the Upper Congo—these
attractions would suffice, to the accompaniment of bar-
baric and enervating strains of music and the weird folk-
songs of the primeval forest. The stimulating rhythms of
the wooden drums of the savages would inflame the blood
of these inexperienced Englishmen to madness, since
fear and voluptuous passion are so closely akin. Tippu-
Tib must have played the generous host, whose greatest
ambition it was to make his young friends from Europe
feel at home. He knew well enough that the sensual joys
they experienced at Stanley Falls would attract them
thither again and again. He knew how to dose his gifts,
how to increase the stimuli, how to reawaken dormant
passion with fresh promises. A master of all such arts,
how could he fail, the crafty and corrupt old man, to
work his will upon those youthful infidels, who looked
upon Africa as a sort of show-booth; how could he fail
to entangle them in his nets, and thus frustrate the
schemes of the dreaded Bula Matari? Had he not done
much harder things than that before? They were easily
limed! Very little trouble was required. Just as the old
Arab was greedy for gold and ivory, so did they find
sweet the stolen waters he gave them to drink, pleasant
the bread eaten in secret places. It had for them all the
charm of hashish, dulling their consciences, vice in un-

275

precedented forms, a paradise in which lust marched
shoulder to shoulder with death. He must have known
how to weld the aphrodisiac influences of the aroma of
flowers, the juices of plants, and the seductive spells of
the tropical night. In these respects, unlimited means
were at his disposal.

Obvious though this explanation of what happened
must seem, it was natural that Stanley should turn a
blind eye towards the matter. His assumed ignorance
was in keeping with his whole character. Whether in
private conversation he kept up the fiction, I do not
know. Probably not. He was well aware what sort of a
man Tippu-Tib was, and what kind of wiles were to be
expected from the Arab—every conceivable treachery,
all possible perfidy, the extremity of baseness and un-
conscientiousness. When the Arab showed this side to
him personally, he was indifferent, for experience had
hardened him. He cannot really have been very much
surprised to find that the men whom he had trusted had
been snared by the dangerous old intriguer. The fact
that he preserved so obstinate a silence concerning the
means by which his subordinates must have been led
astray was typically English, typically American, was
Stanley all over, bearing in mind the puritanism of the
'eighties—the puritanism which, in the English-speaking
countries of those days, grew rank, and became hypocrisy. As to Stanley's own erotic life, we know nothing. There is not a word about the matter in his diaries

276

or in his *Autobiography;* and not a word in anything written about him by others. His books describe him exclusively as a traveller and an explorer. He would have regarded it as obtrusive—nay, as unseemly—to acquaint the public with feelings and experiences which concerned himself alone. But when, as in this book of mine, an attempt is made to present in to-day's forum a historically notable figure, to describe a great man as he actually was and actually lived, the picture must deal with his whole being; for we, under stress of the curiosity and ruthlessness of a new era, want to see, to understand, to know, not only the extraneous aspects, but the inner life as well. What is a revelation worth if it does not reveal mysteries, if it does not enable us to plumb almost unfathomable depths?

It is hard to believe that a vigorous, and organically healthy man who spent ten or twelve years in the interior of Africa can have lived there the life of a Trappist monk. Certainly that is not what such men normally do. There are various indications (the Kalulu episode, for instance) which may incline us to suppose that Stanley—like many men who live at high tension, like many men who are ostensibly cold in the loneliness of their spirit, many men of action, many artists, many thinkers—was, now and again, at least, the subject of erotic inversion. Since this was certainly not a decisive trait in his make-up, it would be superfluous, almost undignified, to allude to the matter, were it not that in

England, above all during the later years of his life, evil rumours were attached to his name, especially in the way of accusations that he had treated the natives cruelly. But, except for occasional corporal punishment of the men he had hired (corporal punishment which he inflicted reluctantly, only when his patience had been strained to the uttermost, only when discipline could be maintained in no other way), there is absolutely no warrant for such accusations. There is not a shadow of ground for the belief that Stanley ever became afflicted by what has been termed "tropical frenzy"; that he ever manifested the sadism to which so many Europeans in out-of-the-way parts of Africa fall a prey, so that they degenerate into torturers and executioners as soon as they possess powers of life and death over their black-skinned fellows. (Consider, for instance, the imaginative descriptions in Stacpoole's Congo novel *The Pools of Silence*.) The man's whole story, the epitome of it here presented, suffices to prove the contrary; and no one has seriously and honestly endeavoured to put forward proof that his behaviour towards the blacks was anything but exemplary, a blending of comradeship and authority, of sympathy and educational endeavour. I think, therefore, that the evil repute to which I have referred can only have been the outcome of whispers concerning this particular form of sexual "misconduct," which to Stanley's prejudiced fellow-countrymen seemed repulsive and blameworthy—although (as is characteristic of

278

this particular form of hypocrisy) the charges were never explicitly made. Still, some reports of the kind, false, or true, or half-true, must have become current; but Stanley, a proud man, easily mortified, endowed with a high conception of individual freedom, finding the aspersions unendurable, may perhaps have actually repressed all memory of these experiences into the unconscious. In such respects he was wholly a product of his own time and of his own country. It must have been for this reason that he wrapped a veil of mystery round the disastrous strayings of his young officers, doing so in this case deliberately and consciously. Yet it must have been hard for him to refrain from throwing light upon the mystery. That he was able to refrain was one of the ways in which he showed his heroism.

CHAPTER ELEVEN

THE EMIN PASHA PUZZLE

SEPTEMBER was well on its way before the disastrous situation at Yambuya and Banyala had been reduced to something like order, so that the Rear Column was able to start on its journey, and it was not until three and a half months later that Stanley got back to Fort Bodo.

Only upon this third journey across the primeval forest did he fully grasp its magnitude and impressiveness; not until then did all its wonders reveal themselves to his eyes. A considerable section of his work *In Darkest Africa* is devoted exclusively, at this stage of affairs, to the Central African forest, which he no longer speaks of as a place of horror and torment.

"We have no time to examine the buds and the flowers or the fruit, and the many marvels of vegetation, or to regard the fine differences between bark and leaf in the various towering trees around us, or to compare the different exudations in the viscous or vitrified gums, or which drift in milky tears or amber globules

280

or opaline pastils, or to observe the industrious ants which ascend and descend the tree shafts, whose deep wrinkles of bark are as valleys and ridges to the insect armies, or to wait for the furious struggle which will shortly ensue between them and yonder army of red ants. Nor at this time do we care to probe into that mighty mass of dead tree, brown and porous as a sponge, for already it is a mere semblance of a prostrate log. Within, it is alive with minute tribes. It would charm an entomologist. Put your ear to it, and you hear a distinct murmurous hum. It is the stir and movement of insect life in many forms. . . . Lean but your hand on a tree, measure but your length on the ground, seat yourself on a fallen branch, and you will then understand what venom, fury, voracity, and activity breathe around you. Open your notebook, the page attracts a dozen butterflies, a honey-bee hovers over your hands; other forms of bees dash for your eyes; a wasp buzzes in your ear, a huge hornet menaces your feet, an army of pismires comes marching to your feet. Some are already crawling up, and will presently be digging their scissors-like mandibles in your neck. Woe! Woe!

"Imagine the whole of France and the Iberian Peninsula closely packed with trees varying from twenty to one hundred and eighty feet high, whose crowns of foliage interlace and prevent any view of sky and sun, and each tree from a few inches to four feet in diameter. Then, from tree to tree run cables from two inches to fifteen inches thick, up and down, in loops and festoons, and W's, and badly formed M's; fold them round the trees in great tight coils, until they have run up the entire height, like endless anacondas; let them flower and leaf luxuriantly and mix up above with the foliage of the trees to hide the sun; then from the highest branches let fall the ends of the cables reaching near to the ground by hundreds with frayed extremities, for these represent the air routes of the epiphytes; let slender cords hang down also, in tassels with open threadwork at the ends. Work others through and through these as confusedly as possible, and pending from branch to branch—with absolute disregard of material, and at every fork and at every horizontal branch blend cabbage-like lichens of the largest kind and broad spear-leafed plants—these would represent the elephant-eared plant—and orchids and clusters of vegetable marvels, and a drapery of delicate ferns which abound. Now cover tree, branch, twig and creeper with a thick moss like a green fur. Where the forest is compact as described above, we may not do more than cover the ground closely with a thick carpet of phrynia and amoma and dwarf bush; but if the lightning, as frequently happens, has severed the crown of a broad tree, and let in the sunlight, or split a giant down to its roots, or scorched it dead, or a tornado has been uprooting a few trees, then the race for air and light has caused a multitude of baby trees to rush upward, crowd-

282

ing, crushing, and treading upon and strangling one another, until the whole is one impervious bush.

"But the average forest is a mixture of these scenes. There will probably be groups of fifty trees standing like columns of a cathedral, grey and solemn in the twilight, and in the midst there will be a naked and gaunt patriarch, bleached white, and around it will have grown a young community; each young tree clambering upward becomes heir to the area of light and sunshine once occupied by the sire. The law of primogeniture reigns here also.

"There is also death from winds, sickness, decay, hereditary disease, and old age, and various accidents thinning the forest, removing the unfit, the weakly, the unadaptable, as among humanity. Let us suppose a tall chief among the giants, like an insolent son of Anak. By a head he lifts himself above his fellows—the monarch of all he surveys. But his pride attracts the lightning and he becomes shivered to the roots. He topples, declines, and wounds half a dozen other trees in his fall. That is why we see so many tumorous excrescences, great goitrous swellings, and deformed trunks. The parasites again have frequently been out-lived by the trees they had half strangled, and the deep marks of their forceful pressure may be traced up to the forks. Some have sickened by intense rivalry of other kinds, and have perished at an immature age; some have grown with a deep crook in their stems up a prostrate log which had fallen and

283

bruised them obliquely. Some have been injured by branches, fallen during a storm, and dwarfed untimely. Some have been gnawed by rodents, or have been sprained by elephants leaning on them to rub their prurient hides, and ants of all kinds have done infinite mischief. Some have been pecked at by birds, until we see ulcerous sores exuding great globules of gum, and frequently tall and short nomads have tried their axes, spears, and knives, on the trees, and hence we see that decay and death are busy here as with us.

"To complete the mental picture of this ruthless forest, the ground should be strewn thickly with half-formed humus of rotting twigs, leaves, branches; every few yards there should be a prostrate giant, a reeking compost of rotten fibres, and departed generations of insects, and colonies of ants, half filled with mosses and vines and shrouded by the leafage of a multitude of baby saplings, lengthy briars, and calamus in many fathom lengths, and every mile or so there should be muddy streams, stagnant creeks, and shallow pools, grown with duckweed, leaves of lotus and lilies, and a greyish-green scum composed of millions of finite growths."

No one will deny that this description is extraordinarily energetic and vivid. It has the charm and the inimitable truth of something actually experienced; it is the work of one who was in love with what he depicted; and the author to whom we owe it cannot be considered of little account as a literary artist. Only, perhaps, because such passages as the foregoing are buried amid a superfluity of repetitive detail, have they hitherto, as a rule, been disregarded. A careful selection from Stanley's writings would provide a series of descriptions of Nature that have never been surpassed.

The fort and its garrison were in good condition when he arrived; Nelson was fully restored to health, bountiful harvests had been garnered—maize, bananas, potatoes, beans, tobacco. Stairs' report was extremely encouraging; but not a word had come from Jephson, who had been left with the Pasha, nor from Emin himself. Well, there was nothing to be done but carry the loads on to the lake, a difficult job, since there were fifty-five more loads than porters. After some deliberation, it was decided to make double marches between Fort Bodo and the Ituri River on the edge of the plains, where Lieutenant Stairs and the officers and sick would be left at the well-supplied clearing of Kandekore, and thence Stanley would march to the Nyanza to search for Emin Pasha and Mr. Mounteney Jephson. Volunteers were called for the double duty, and the necessary fifty-five were soon forthcoming at the promise of extra reward for each camp made by them twice over.

By the time they were assembled at Kandekore, Stanley had grown anxious, owing to the delay and the lack of news from Jephson and Emin. Summoning Stairs

285

and Parke, he addressed them as follows: "It is now January 10th [1889]; I promised to be on the Nyanza again, even if I went as far as Yambuya, by the 16th; I have six days before me. You see how I am pulled this way and that way. If I could trust you to obey me, obey every word literally, that you would not swerve one iota from the path laid down, I could leave you with confidence, and find out what is the matter with Jephson and the Pasha."

"I don't see why you should doubt us. I am sure we have always tried to do our very best to please and satisfy you," replied Stairs.

"That is strictly true, and I am most grateful to you for it. But the case of Yambuya seems to be repeated. Our friend Jephson is absent, perhaps dead from fever or from some accident; but why do we not hear from the Pasha? We cannot sit down to let the mystery unfold itself, and I can do nothing towards penetrating it with one hundred and twenty-four men who require a long rest to recover from their fatigues and sicknesses. Therefore I am compelled to trust to you and the Doctor, that you will stay here until I know what has happened, whether for one month or for two months. . . . Gentlemen, the causes of failure in this world are that men are unable to see the thing that lies ready to their hands. They ignore their work and forget their tasks in an attempt to do what is not wanted. . . . All I ask of you is to stay here and look

286

after the camp alertly, and I want the Doctor to attend
to those sick men and cure them, not to stint medicines,
but nurse them with good food from morning until
night.... Are you ambitious of distinction? Here is
your chance, seize it. Your task is clear before you and
you are required to save these men, who will be the
means of taking you home, and of your receiving the
esteem of all who shall hear of your deeds."

Thereupon Stanley, the indefatigable, set forth with
the ammunition destined for the Pasha. This was on
January 11th, and by the 16th he was within a day's
march from the lake. There, at 5 p.m., he met two
Wahuma messengers with letters from Kavalli. "As I
read them, a creeping feeling came over me, which was
complete mental paralysis for the time, and deadened
all sensation except that of unmitigated surprise."

In the first letter, from Duffle, under date September 2, 1888, the Pasha congratulated Stanley (very
much in advance of time, and obviously on the strength
of a false report) upon the latter's return to the lake.
Then, in vague terms, Emin went on to refer to matters
of which Jephson "who has been of good help to me
under very trying circumstances," would give a fuller
account. He added: "In the case of your coming, you will
greatly oblige me by taking measures for the safety of
my little girl, about whom I feel most anxious. Should
you, however, decide not to come, I can only wish you
a good and safe return to your country, and at the same

287

time I may be permitted to request you to tender my cordial thanks to your officers and your people, and my cordial acknowledgment to those kind-hearted benefactors in England by whose generosity the expedition was started." Did the Pasha really believe that Stanley would return without seeing him again, and without having accomplished his mission?

In the second letter, from the same place, under date November 6, 1888, Emin explained that he had for some time been a prisoner.

In the third letter, even shorter, from Tunguru, under date December 21, 1888, Emin confirmed the information given in the previous letter, and added, enigmatically: "Everyone is now fully decided to leave the country for finding shelter somewhere. Nobody thinks, however, of going to Egypt, except, perhaps, a few officers and men. I am nevertheless not without hope of better days; but I join my entreaties with those of Mr. Jephson, asking you to say where you are [once more!], namely at Kavalli, and to send only word of your arrival as quickly as you can."

Jephson wrote much more explicitly: "On August 18th a rebellion broke out here, and the Pasha and I were made prisoners. The Pasha is a complete prisoner, but I am allowed to go about the station, though my movements are watched. The rebellion has been got up by some half-dozen officers and clerks, chiefly Egyptians, and gradually others have joined. . . . The two prime

288

promoters were Egyptians, who, we heard afterwards, had gone and complained to you at Nsabe. One was the Pasha's adjutant, Abdul Vaal Effendi, who was formerly concerned in Arabi's rebellion; the other was Achmet Effendi Mahmoud, a one-eyed clerk. These two and some others, when the Pasha and I were on our way to Rejaf, went about and told the people they had seen you, and that you were only an adventurer, and had not come from Egypt; that the letters you had brought from the Khedive and Nubar Pasha were forgeries; that it was untrue that Khartoum had fallen, and that the Pasha and you had made a plot to take them, their wives, and children out of the country and hand them over as slaves to the English. Such words, in an ignorant and fanatical country like this, acted like fire among the people, the result being a general rebellion, in which we were made prisoners.". . . The Pasha was deposed. Those officers who were suspected of being friendly to him were removed from their posts, and those friendly to the rebels were put in their places. It was decided to take the Pasha away as a prisoner to Rejaf, and some of the worst rebels were even for putting him in irons, but the officers were afraid to carry these plans into execution, as the soldiers said they would never permit anyone to lay a hand on him. Plans were also made to entrap Stanley on his return and strip him of all he had.

Then, in this letter of Jephson's under date November 7, 1888, came even more startling news: "We were informed that the Mahdi's people had arrived at Lado with three steamers and nine sandals and nuggars, and had established themselves on the site of the old station. Omar Sali, their general, sent down three peacock dervishes with a letter to the Pasha demanding the instant surrender of the country. The rebel officers seized them and put them in prison, and decided on war. After a few days the Donagla attacked and captured Rejaf, killing five officers and numbers of soldiers, and taking many women and children prisoners, and all the stores and ammunition in the station were lost. The result was a general stampede of people from the neighbouring stations, who fled with their women and children, abandoning almost everything. The Pasha reckons that the Donagla number about 1,500."

Now, the rank and file of Emin's men, being very much afraid of the Mahdist fanatics, murmured against their officers, who were themselves greatly alarmed at the disasters they had conjured up. At length Emin's forces came to look upon Stanley as a rescuer whose advent was eagerly desired, and Jephson was given full liberty of action. But obviously he had lost his nerve, for in his last letter, dated Tunguru, December 18, 1888, he described the situation as desperate, and warned Stanley against leaving Kavalli and coming to Emin unless with a very strong force.

Stanley found it difficult to make head or tail of this warning. Where was he to get a "very strong force"?

290

Where could he get allies? Where could he find trustworthy friends? However, with the calm usual to him
in dangerous situations, he made a plan of campaign,
giving clear directions to Jephson, and hoping to ensure
the rescue of the Pasha. He made his dispositions with
as much care as if he had a force of a million men under
his command. All the same, his letter to Jephson, dated
at Kavalli on January 18, 1889, was somewhat acrimoniously worded. "Your missives contradict one another. I
have read them half a dozen times over, but I fail to
grasp the situation thoroughly, because in some important details one letter seems to contradict the other.
In one you say the Pasha is a close prisoner, while you
are allowed a certain amount of liberty. In the other you
say you will come to me as soon as you hear of my arrival here, and you say, 'I trust the Pasha will be able
to accompany me.' Being prisoners, I fail to see how
you can leave Tunguru at all. All this is not very clear
to us who are fresh from the bush."—"Fresh from the
bush"—that means unconcerned about petty things. The
fact was that, after his experience at Yambuya, Stanley
was disinclined to trust any one, and was especially suspicious of this well-intentioned young Jephson who had
paid £1,000 in order to come to Central Africa. Stormily
he wrote: "I could save a dozen pashas if they were
willing to be saved. I would go on my knees to implore
the Pasha to be sensible in his own case." Again: "Let
me repeat that I have read your letters half a dozen

291

times, and my opinion of you varies with each reading. Sometimes I fancy you are half Mahdist or Arabist, and then Eminist. I shall be wiser when I see you! Now, don't you be perverse but obey; and let my order to you be as a frontlet between the eyes, and all, with God's gracious help, will end well."

The words of a confident commander! One who amid grave troubles can write with such assurance must be a born leader. He asks the Pasha for "a definite answer to the question, if you propose to accept our escort and assistance to reach Zanzibar, or if Signor Casati proposes to do so, or whether there are any officers or men disposed to accept of our safe conduct to the sea. . . . If at the end of twenty days, no news has been heard from you or Mr. Jephson, I cannot hold myself responsible for what may happen." From a note appended to this letter on page 199 of the second volume of *In Darkest Africa*, we learn that Emin was nettled by the tone of Stanley's communication: "I have read this letter scores of times, yet I fail to see how an officially worded letter, which, as suggested by Mr. Jephson, might have fallen into the rebel officers' hands, could have wounded the most delicate susceptibilities. Yet I was informed that the Pasha was very much offended at it. Nothing was further from my mind than to offend a friend, my sole object being to obtain a definite answer to the question, 'Will you stay here, or accompany

292

me?' " How, in fact, was it possible to deal satisfactorily with so touchy a creature as Emin?

On the second day after reaching Kavalli, Stanley sent thirty riflemen to the lake-shore, conveying his replies to Emin Pasha and to Jephson. The tedium of awaiting their rejoinders was relieved by a little of the customary fighting with the savages, after which Stanley moved back to the plateau. There Jephson found him on February 6th, and at length Stanley received a full verbal report of what had been going on during his absence—a report which did not show Emin, the Mudir of Equatoria, in a very good light. Emin's written answer to Stanley, brought by Jephson, was curt, noncommittal, and gloomy. Jephson, summing up his opinion of the man with whom he had been living for nine months, said: "Sentiment is the Pasha's worst enemy. No one keeps Emin Pasha back but Emin Pasha himself." But during this and subsequent conversations, it became plain to Stanley that Jephson had become "a pronounced Eminist." For instance: "Well, you know, the poor, dear Pasha! He is a dear old fellow, you know. 'Pon my word, I can't help but sympathise with the Pasha, he is such a dear good man," etc., etc. This was intermingled with the most crushing criticism of Emin's administration of the province. Extremely English, such a mingling of contempt with good-natured regard. Of the Egyptians, Jephson had nothing but evil to say. They were "unmitigated scoundrels, depraved

293

fellows, treacherous dogs, unscrupulously vile, animals with foxy natures." The Sudanese were "brutishly stupid." One chief clerk had falsified accounts at the Khartoum arsenal and had had fifteen hundred stripes with the kurbash; another had been detected making huge profits by adulterating the gunpowder with charcoal. A major had been convicted of trading in government stores; others had been sent to the Siberia of the Equator as convicts, guilty of various felonies, arson, murder, etc. If all these tales were true, obviously no one but such a man as Gordon could have handled a gang of ruffians of the kind. One would surely think that nobody endowed with a modicum of self-respect would hesitate to leave such a command when he could honourably do so; but Emin, for inexplicable reasons, clung to his governorship of Equatoria to the last possible moment. He would not face the facts, was perpetually self-deceived. When his officers begged his pardon for the offences committed against him, he was reduced almost to tears —though behind his back they made mock of him. He was glad to be able to play the pasha once more, and nothing gave him greater pleasure than to forgive penitent sinners.—This was what Stanley gathered from Jephson's conversations and from his written report.

"But," writes Stanley, "while we were discussing the probable decisions of the Pasha and awaiting the arrival of Stairs' column, events unknown to us were occurring which decided the matter for us as well as

294

for Emin." Jephson had gone back to the lake, and, under date February 15, 1889, reported to Stanley (still on the plateau) that he had met the Pasha, who had called a meeting of the officers, and decided to start the next day for Kavalli, taking two days on the road. "The Pasha will come to see you, will perhaps stay a few days in your camp, and then return and bring up his daughter and the rest of his loads, which amount to about two hundred, consisting of millet, salt, sesame, etc. The officers will only bring twenty loads, as they are merely coming up to talk to you about bringing up their troops and goods. The clerks bring up all their loads and remain with us." The officers were Casati, a Greek named Marco, Vita the apothecary, and several others.

Stanley was thunderstruck. "The Pasha, two hundred loads! Casati, who has lost everything, eighty loads! Vita, the apothecary, forty loads! Marco, the Greek, sixty loads! That is to say, three hundred and eighty loads for four persons! Well, if I gave a promise, it must be kept, I suppose."

Two or three days later, Emin arrived at Kavalli with a large escort, coming in grand style, as governor. "He was accompanied by his daughter, a little girl of six years old, named Ferida, the offspring of an Abyssinian woman. She is extremely pretty, with large, beautiful black eyes. . . . The Pasha informs me that another mail arrived from Wadelai on the 25th, and that an official letter from the rebel officers announced that he was deposed from his position as chief commander of the troops, and that he and Casati were sentenced to death by court-martial! ... This is quite in the Jack Cade style."

Wishing to pay the deposed governor due honour, Stanley now appointed the Pasha, "with his own consent, and indeed, on his own proposal," naturalist and meteorologist to the expedition. In these capacities he was in his proper element, devoting himself to scientific studies with fanatical zeal, and apparently forgetting all his troubles. He had become the typical German scientist, shot birds and stuffed them, collected insects, and so on. Stanley found this more than a little trying. (Stanley's religious predilections must not be forgotten.) "I have attempted to discover during our daily chats whether Emin was Christian or Moslem, Jew or pagan, and I rather suspect that he is nothing more than a materialist. Who can say why votaries of science, though eminently kindly in their social relations, are so angular of character? In my analyses of the scientific nature, I am constrained to associate with it, as compared with that of men who are more Christians than scientists, a certain hardness or rather indelicacy of feeling. They strike me as being somewhat unsympathetic, and capable of only cold friendship, coolly indifferent to the warmer human feelings. I may best express what I mean by saying I think that they are

296

more apt to feel affection for one's bleached skull and frame of unsightly bones, than for what is divine within a man. If one talks about the inner beauty, which to some of us is the only beauty worth knowing, they are apt to yawn, and they return an apologetic and compassionate smile. They seem to wish you to infer that they have explored the body through and through and that it is waste of time to discuss what only exists in the imagination. . . . We have some dwarfs in the camp. The Pasha wished to measure their skulls; I devoted my observations to their inner nature. He proceeded to fold his tape round the circumference of the chest. I wished to study the face. The Pasha wondered at the feel of the body. I marvelled at the quick play of the feelings as revealed in lightning movements of the facial muscles. The Pasha admired the breadth of the frontal bone. I studied the tones of the voice, and watched how beautifully a slight flash of the eye coincided with the slightest twitch of a lip. The Pasha might know to a grain what the body of the pigmy weighed, but I only cared to know what the inner capacity was. This is the reason why the Pasha and I differ about the characters of his men. He knows their names, their families, their tribes, their customs; and, little as I have been with them, I think I know their natures."

Is not Stanley deceiving himself? Readers of his books may well doubt if he had gone very far in an understanding of the natures of the Africans. However that may be, Emin and he were absolute antitheses.

One of the Pasha's subordinates, a man named Shukri Agha, the commandant of a station, was ordered to go to Wadelai to get together those who wished to march with Stanley to the coast. The station was to be abandoned, and Shukri Agha was to be back in ten days. He had solemnly promised to return in that time. Emin had said that Shukri Agha would certainly keep his promise. The Egyptian, however, obviously did not know the meaning of the word "obey," and no further news of him was heard for some time. On March 26, 1889, therefore, Stanley summoned his own officers, Stairs, Nelson, Jephson, and Parke, put the whole situation before them, and said: "We believed when we volunteered for this work that we should be met with open arms. We were received with indifference, so that we came to doubt whether any of Emin Pasha's people wished to depart. I ask you, then, whether you think we shall be wise in extending the time of delay beyond the date already fixed, that is to say April 10th?"

The officers, one after another, replied in the negative.

Emin, who was present, was startled. Stanley said: "There you have your answer, Pasha. Whatever happens we march on April 10th."

Emin inquired whether Stanley and the other officers could conscientiously acquit him of having aban-

298

doned his people, supposing he were to join the march if they had not arrived by the specified date. Stanley and his men replied that unquestionably they could do so.

Emin, however, was not convinced, and Stanley's resoluteness got on his nerves. Still, the unruly men under his command were informed that the expedition would set forth on April 10th for Zanzibar, and not a day later.

On the last day of March, the Pasha came to Stanley's tent to say that Captain Casati was not well pleased at the idea of Emin's leaving, and thought it was his duty to stay.

"Stay where, Pasha?"

"With my people."

"What people, please?"

"Why, with my soldiers."

"With the soldiers whose prisoner you were? With the soldiers who had threatened to take you in irons strapped on your bedstead to Khartoum? And I am sure you know as well as I do what that means."

"That is true. You must not think that I am about to change my mind. As I said to you, I leave with you on April 10th. That is settled. I wish, however, you would see Casati about this and talk to him."

"I should be most happy to do so, but my French is wretched, and his is still worse."

299

"Oh, if you will send a boy to call me, I will come and be your interpreter."

Casati was a queer character, a sort of reflexion of Emin Pasha. He was extremely loth to quit Equatoria. There he was somebody; there he could do what he pleased. If he went back to Europe he would become a man of no account. The curious thing was that Emin, when in Casati's company, felt that it would be wrong for him to leave, and Casati did all he could to make his chief's conscience uneasy. He took a sort of malicious delight in giving pin-pricks. For instance:

"The governor of a fort should never surrender his charge."

"I quite agree with you," said Stanley, who was present on this occasion, "if his troops remain faithful to him; but if his troops arrest him, haul down the flag, and open the gates, what can the poor governor do?"

"A captain of a warship should fight his guns to the last."

"Quite so, but if the crew seize the captain and put him into the hold in irons and haul down the flag, what then?"

"No, I don't agree with you," said Casati emphatically. "The Pasha should remain with his people."

Emin grew more and more uneasy, and became the centre from which uneasiness, dissatisfaction, purposelessness radiated. Stanley had continually to intervene, trying to set things right. There were strange incidents.

300

Casati had adopted a little Sudanese girl, who had become dear to him in his loneliness. It is not clear whether she was his own child. Emin deplored Casati's "morbid attachment to his servants, male and female." One of Emin's soldiers suddenly laid claim to the little girl, and threatened Casati's life when the latter would not give her up. The Pasha was afraid to exercise his authority for the settlement of this dispute, and his vacillation made matters worse.

Another case was that of an Egyptian engineer and his pretty young wife, who had become Ferida's nurse, and formed part of the Pasha's establishment. Probably incited by some of Emin's other servants, this woman refused to live any more with her husband, who thereupon complained stormily to Stanley.

"Really, my friend Mohammed," said Stanley, "I have no authority to settle such delicate questions. Have you been to the Pasha? Have you asked him to exercise his authority? Seeing that she is a nurse in his household, he is the person you should apply to; not me."

However, Stanley spoke about the matter to Emin, whose authority proved ineffective. Everyone knew his weakness, and that whoever had last had his ear would seem to him right. There were dramatic scenes in Stanley's tent. The wife accused the husband of having treated her brutally; she said she hated him, and would never have anything to do with him again. The husband breathed threats of vengeance; the Pasha urged con-

301

ciliation. It would be too long a story to tell in all its details, how Stanley stiffened the back of Emin, who was afraid of Mohammed's wrath; how Stanley compelled the angry Egyptian to recognise his duties to the Pasha; and how he induced the disobedient wife (to whose charms, as his description shows, he was by no means blind) to return to her husband. In part he got his way by cajolery, and in part by permitting the husband to use mitigated force. The story is brightly told, and shows the writer's knowledge of Moslem human nature. But, successful though he was in this and similar instances, he found it impossible to establish a satisfactory and permanent understanding with Emin. The Pasha did not understand him! To Emin, the Englishman was a stranger being than any African savage, than any pigmy of the primeval forest. In short, Emin hated Stanley, and yet had to do Stanley's will.

A few words must be said about the ivory, of which Emin was supposed to have collected so great a store, and which the Relief Expedition was going to carry back to the coast. Here another disappointment awaited Stanley. In all, Emin brought along only sixty-five small tusks. There were a few very big ones, each weighing one and a half cwt., but these had to be left behind, being too heavy for the porters. (Why they were not carried by the beasts of burden is not explained.) It does not appear that Stanley said anything to the Pasha

302

about the alleged vast store of ivory. Was he ashamed of his own false expectations? Was he afraid of putting Emin to shame? Certainly the dread of arousing Emin's susceptibilities must have been continually present. As late as five days before that fixed for the start, he was still hesitating as to whether he would or would not accompany Stanley. The letters from the rebels at Wade-lai had scared him; the duplicity of the Egyptians in the camp made him hopelessly perplexed.

Stanley gave up the attempt to unravel the man's fluctuating motives, and decided to cut the tangle. After a conversation with Emin in which he had put the plain alternatives once more, "I rose and sounded the signal for a general muster under arms. . . . Within five minutes the companies were under arms and stood attentive along three sides of the great square. The Pasha, seeing that I was in earnest, came out, and begged me to listen to one word.

" 'Certainly, what is it?' I asked.

" 'Only tell me what I have to do now.'

" 'It is too late, Pasha, to adopt the pacific course I suggested to you. The alarm is general now, and therefore I propose to discover for myself this danger and face it here. Sound the signal, please, for muster of your Arabs before me.'

" 'Very good,' replied the Pasha, and gave the order to his trumpeter.

"We waited ten minutes in silence. Then, perceiving

303

that not much attention was paid to the signal, I requested Mr. Jephson to take No. 1 Company, arm the men with clubs and sticks, and drive every Egyptian and Sudanese into the square, without regard to rank, search every house, and track out every male therein."

The scene which followed was delightful.

"When the line was satisfactory, I stepped up to them and informed them that I heard they wished to fight, that they were eager to try what kind of men the Zanzibaris were. They had seen how well my men could work; it would be a pity if they were not able to see how well they could fight!

"The Vakeel [lieutenant-governor] replied: 'But we do not wish to fight.'

" 'Then what is this I hear, that one of you is as good as ten of my men, of rifles being stolen, of plots and counterplots each day that you have been here, of your resolve not to follow the Pasha after making us build your houses and collect food for you, and carrying hundreds of loads the last two months up this mountain from the lake, and last night three of our houses were entered, and you laid your hands upon our weapons. Speak, and say what it all means.'

" 'Oh, Pasha, no one of us wishes to fight. Let the thieves, if found, die.'

" 'If found! Will any thief confess his theft and deliver himself to be shot? Will you, who are all of one mind, betray one another and submit yourselves

304

to punishment? Do you intend to follow your Pasha?'

" 'We all do,' they answered.

" 'Very well, then, those who intend following the Pasha form rank on that other side, like soldiers, each in his place.'

"At once there was a general quick movement in regular order; they then turned about and faced me again.

" 'So! Is there none of you desirous of staying in this fair land with Selim Bey [the ringleader of the disobedient], where you will be able to make these natives do your work for you, cook for you and feed you?'

" 'None, not one. *La il Allah il Allah!*'

" 'Why, Pasha, you have been misinformed, surely; these people vow they are all faithful. There is not a traitor here.'

" 'I don't see my servants and orderlies here,' replied the Pasha.

" 'Oh, Lieutenant Stairs, please take a party and rouse every man out. On the least resistance, you know what to do.'

" 'Right, sir.' "

Lieutenant Stairs took his company, gave his orders, and in a few minutes the Pasha's servants were brought into the square. They were deprived of their rifles and accoutrements.

" 'Now, Pasha, please ask them severally before me what they intend doing.'

"Upon the Pasha asking them, they all replied they were willing to follow their master to the end of the world, excepting one Seroor.

"The Pasha, pointing out Seroor, said, 'That is the chief conspirator in my household.'

" 'Oh, it will take only one cartridge to settle his business.'

" 'But I hope, for God's sake, that you will try him first and not take my word for it.'

" 'Undoubtedly, my dear Pasha, we invariably give such people a fair trial.'

"Seroor was placed under guard with three others whom the Pasha pointed out.

" 'Now, Pasha, this business having been satisfactorily ended, will you be good enough to tell these officers that the tricks of Wadelai must absolutely cease here, and that in future they are under my command?' "

Emin had no choice but to comply. The Egyptians were amazed at this other white man who took so strong a line with their soft and pusillanimous chief. A new tone!

"Poor Pasha!" writes Stanley, in comment on these incidents. "It was as clear as the noonday sun why 10,000 followers had dwindled in number to Bilal the solitary one!"

The next day he writes: "Poor Casati is not on

speaking terms with the Pasha, because of his judgment against him in the matter of the little black girl the other day; and I suppose the Pasha will not be on speaking terms with me because of the shock of yesterday. The march will do them all good. When the Pasha is in the presence of Ruwenzori—the Mountains of the Moon—he will recover tone."

At 7.30 a.m. on the appointed day, the column streamed out of camp, led by No. 1 Company, then followed by the Pasha and his people, with their allotted number of carriers. Stanley gives the total number as 1,510, there being 230 belonging to his own expedition, 130 Manyuema, 350 plateau natives; 200 from Kávalli; 600, the Pasha and his people. Three days after the start, Stanley was taken violently ill with gastritis, requiring morphia for the relief of the pain from which he suffered. The expedition had to be halted for a time, and with the leader thus incapacitated, disorder again became rife.

There were frequent desertions from among the Egyptians and the Sudanese. On April 13th, twenty-two left in a body, with several rifles belonging to Stanley's expedition. Stanley summoned Stairs to his sick-bed.

"Pick out forty good men, march to the Nyanza. You will find the rendezvous of these fellows at the Lake Shore. Be wary, and let your capture of them be thorough and sudden. By taking our rifles they have made themselves liable."

Four days later, Lieutenant Stairs returned, having made an excellent haul of carefully guarded prisoners, among whom was Rehan, the ringleader. A court-martial was held, and Rehan was sentenced to be hanged. Stanley said: "Now I will give you one more chance for life. Look around at those men with whom you have eaten and drunk; if there is any one of them who will plead for you, your life is spared. What say you, Sudanese and Zanzibaris? Shall this man have life or death?"

"Death," came from every voice unanimously.

"Then let him depart to God!"

Sick though Stanley was, it was useless to entrust such matters to Emin to handle. He saw nothing, understood nothing, regarding himself as one of the victims of this Bula Matari, who was not only a rock-breaker, but had himself a heart of stone. The Pasha was, as it were, hypnotised by Stanley, and yet resented his position. He was as sulky as a spoiled child, and found his only relaxation in shooting and stuffing birds.

Stanley shows no inclination to depreciate his companion. He says, indeed, that the latter had not the "fine military figure" he had been led to expect by what he heard in Cairo; but still Emin had "a peculiar greatness" of his own. Perplexity, mingled with disappointment, characterise what Stanley writes of the

308

Pasha. Never, he says, had he met anyone like Emin, though he had perhaps read of such characters. Emin was neat in his person, stiffly polite in his manners, a good conversationalist, an able medical practitioner, a gentleman through and through. Not a Gordon by any means, although Gordon was his ideal. "Even though we admired him, we always felt there was something inexplicable in him." The actual details given by Stanley do not arouse an impression of greatness, or explain why anyone should have admired Emin Pasha. He tells us that one of Emin's officials and an Egyptian officer came to talk to him about the Pasha, and, to his great indignation, immediately began to abuse their chief, every word they uttered being inspired by the utmost contempt. Stanley studied Emin's character most carefully, without ever being able to come to a clear judgment concerning the man. All that we get from his descriptions is a picture rather than an understanding. We see the melancholy shape of the head, the instinctive way in which the Pasha lifts his hand, the seriousness of his expression, the sorrowful look in his eyes, the resigned shrug of the shoulders which seems to say: "Why should force be used on me, who am an enemy of force?" We have here the portrait rather of a dreamy man of science than of one to whom the destiny of his fellows and the governance of provinces should have been entrusted. One who can only read large print when the paper is a couple of inches from his eyes is

309

incapable of studying the faces of those with whom he has to deal, incapable of discovering whether his subordinates are loyal or false.

Emin was not one of the arrogant and pretentious Germans of whom we often read and whom we sometimes encounter; he was a modest man. For this reason he was liked by Gordon. Stanley tells of the Pasha's relations with that master of men.

"In the course of his promotions, Emin shows he is ambitious. He wants seeds for the fields; he applies to Gordon for them, and Gordon's reply is: 'I don't want you for a gardener; I sent you to govern. If you don't like it, go away.' A proud young Englishman would have taken him at his word, descended the Nile, and parted from Gordon sulkily. Emin sent an apology, and wrote: 'Very good, sir.' Later Emin wanted a photographic apparatus, and was admonished: 'I sent you to the Equatorial Provinces as governor, not as photographer.' Emin says in reply: 'Very well, sir; I thank you, sir. I will do my duty.' Nor does he bother the Governor-General with complaints that he never gets his mails in due time, or of the provisions supplied him. What a valuable man he was! He showed consideration and patience, and Gordon appreciated this."

The real problem was whether Emin, who seemed so much like Christian's neighbour Pliable, had any grit in him at all. This was the nut which Stanley was vainly endeavouring to crack. He felt that a European

310

who came in close contact with the Egyptians must
either develop into a dictator or else degenerate, becoming like those he was professing to rule. Long, long
ago Emperor Hadrian had written of the Egyptians that
they were frivolous and untrustworthy, fluttering at
every wave and rumour, and were the most fickle, un-
stable, and criminal race in existence. Stanley endorsed
this opinion. "Our camp bred rumours as the ground
bred flies; the least trifle caused them to flutter like a
brood from under the mother bird. A report from Wadelai made them run gadding from one circle to another,
from hut to hut, from the highest to the lowest, emu-
lating the cackle of many hens." Each day they found
some new enthusiasm, some new falsehood, some new
god. Misrepresentation was second nature to them.
Order, they detested. How could Emin Pasha possibly
have been content to live so long in such an atmosphere?
Having been content, was it not inevitable that he had
been infected with the disease he was fain to hide?
Stanley, the moralist, the puritan, was continually turning this question over in his mind. Another thing which
perturbed him was the way in which Emin, the governor
of Equatoria, had winked at rapine, at crime and murder, which were perpetually going on within his domain.
Had his tolerance been due simply to contemptible
weakness, or to cowardice, or to mere apathy? Subsequently Stanley came into possession of documents
which showed clearly that the rebel officers at Wadelai

311

had wanted to entrap him and hand him over to the Mahdi. Had the Pasha been aware of this? Stanley could never discover, but weakness was to him the root of all evil; it revolted him, made him feel positively ill. That Stanley was able, without once betraying his feelings, without once losing self-control, to associate with Emin for months on the most cordial terms, manifests a power of inner discipline, a degree of moral self-control, which cannot be too highly esteemed. There are few men of action who, out of consideration for a dreamer, for a slave of imagination, would thus have mastered their natural impulses, and have shown themselves more inclined to self-criticism than to criticism of so impracticable a companion. A dictator, a conquistador, who is none the less moderate and kindly, is so rare a being that, when discovered, he is entitled to be put upon a pedestal.

Emin Pasha had had a remarkable career. Born in 1840, as son of a Jewish merchant in a small way of business at Oppeln in Silesia, he studied medicine, and when four-and-twenty years of age was appointed a quarantine surgeon in Albania. Four years later he removed to Scutari, where he became involved in a love affair with the wife of the governor, Ismail Hakki Pasha, who must have been a complaisant husband, for Dr. Schnitzer (as Emin still called himself) accompanied Ismail to posts in various parts of the Near East; Constantinople, Trebizond, Janina, Tripoli, and Yemen. In

312

1878, Hakki Pasha died. Emin wound up his chief's affairs, and returned to his homeland, to Neisse, taking the wife and children with him. Soon, however, wanting to be quit of these ties, he left them there, and took no further thought for them. We next hear of him at Trieste, then in Cairo, Khartoum, Unyora, Uganda, and upon the lower Bahr el Jebel, where he studied some hindrances to the flow of the Nile. Thence he went to the Albert Nyanza; a year later he was in the country of the Makrakra; and the year after that, among the Latuku and the Obbo. In 1882, he was back in Khartoum. In 1883, there came letters penned by him in Mombuttu Land; and in 1887, he became attached to the service of General Gordon. No doubt he told Stanley about all these wanderings and vicissitudes, in the evenings over the campfire or in the tent, during the march to the Indian Ocean, which occupied nearly eight months. He abandoned the reserve which he had at first shown towards Stanley. I think indeed, although Stanley does not say as much, that it must have tickled Emin's vanity to parade the wealth of his experiences in conversation with a man who had become famous as an explorer, while concealing how futile this life of his had really been, how barren, how unhappy. What did Stanley think of the restless, self-complacent German? Did he regard Emin as a comparatively unsuccessful brother; as a counterpart or a caricature of himself; as a seeker without a goal; as a man infirm of purpose, who never-

313

theless longed to do great deeds; as a coward running away from his own shadow; as a venturesome gamester, eager for offices and dignities; as a scientist to whom research was more important than anything else in the world; or as one to whom science was only the pretext for adventures? We shall never know, for Stanley did not choose to reveal his thoughts in this matter.

Beneath the splendid mountain of Ruwenzori, travelling (while still weak) in a hide hammock borne by two men, Stanley sketched the route they were to follow. The caravan made its way by Utinda, Mboga, Kiryama, Awamba, Bakikundi, Ugarama, Bukoko, Banzombe, Mtarega, and Rusesse to the Albert Edward Nyanza; thence through Kitete, Kibwiga, Katara, Wamaganga, Nyamatoso, Kassussu, and Namianja to the Alexandra Nile. This was in the country of the Wahuma, a branch of the Bantu stock, whom Stanley speaks of as the most interesting people, next to the pigmies, in all Central Africa. (As a matter of fact, says Stanley, "Bantu," though used by scientists as a racial term, is merely a Central African word for "man"!) "The Wahuma are the exact opposites of the dwarfs. The latter are undersized nomads, adapted by their habits to forest life; the former are tall, finely formed men, with almost European features, adapted by immemorial custom and second nature to life in pastoral lands only. . . . They are descendants of the Semitic tribes or communities which migrated from Asia across the Red Sea and settled on the coast and in the uplands of Abyssinia, once known as Ethiopia. From this great centre more than a third of the inhabitants of inner Africa have had their origin." The amount of intermixture of Negro blood varies much from region to region, but the Wahuma are a comparatively pure Semitic stock.

In Ankori, Captain Casati fell sick. One day, being extremely weak, he lay out in the broiling sunshine without his sun-helmet to protect his head, and nearly died of sun-stroke. The young pigmy damsel who had been with the expedition for more than a year began to show symptoms of chronic ill-health, and was left behind with the chief of Kirurumo. It was plain that these creatures of the forest could not endure transplantation into the open grasslands. "The little thing," writes Stanley, "had performed devoted service to Surgeon Parke, who had quite won her heart with those soft, gentle tones of his that made everybody smile on the Doctor. She used to be the guardian of his tent, and whenever the Doctor had to absent himself for his duties, she crouched at the door, faithful as a spaniel, and would permit no intruder to approach the doorway. . . . On the road she carried the Doctor's satchel, and on nearing the resting-place she was as industrious as a bee in collecting fuel and in preparing him a cup of tea, which, after patient teaching, she had learned to be necessary for his welfare. Kibbo Bora, a headman of the Manyuema, lost his wife at the Hot Springs, and so great was his grief that he had to be restrained lest he should commit suicide. Sitting apart in the gorge of Mtagata, he howled his laments during twenty-four hours, and his followers formed a chorus to respond to his mournful cries. None of us had much sleep that night, and thus we became involuntary partakers of his woe. It was several days before the poor fellow recovered from the shock."

The march continued by way of Kafurro, Kavari, along Lake Urigi, through Ngoti and Amranda, to Mackay's mission station on the Victoria Nyanza. The two missionaries, Mackay and Deakes, gave them a warm welcome; provided them with "a sumptuous dinner: roast beef, roast fowl, stews, rice and curry, plum pudding, and a bottle of medical wine. And, as the custom is in civilised lands, speeches terminated the banquet. It fell to my share to propose the health of Emin Pasha." On they went through Ikoma, Seke, Sinyanga, Muhalala, Mpwapwa, Ungerengeri, to Msua, where, on the Kingani River, they met Major Wissmann, and by him and Lieutenant Schmidt were conducted to Bagamoyo on the Indian Ocean. There Emin Pasha had a serious accident, as strange as everything connected with the life of this enigmatic being.

It was on the afternoon of December 3, 1889, at

four o'clock, that the column entered the town. "Close at hand was the softly undulating Indian Sea, one great expanse of purified blue. 'There, Pasha,' I said. 'We are at home!' "

"Yes, thank God," Emin replied.

"At this instant," continues Stanley, "the battery thundered a salute in the Pasha's honour, and announced to the warships at anchor that Emin, the Governor of Equatoria, had arrived at Bagamoyo. . . . The people were conducted to huts ready constructed near the beach, and as the carriers dropped their loads and the long train of hammocks deposited their grievous burdens of sick men and women and poor children, for the last time, on the ground, they, like myself, must have felt profound relief, and understood to the full what this arrival by the shore of the sea meant. . . . We were congratulated by the Banian and Hindu citizens, and by many a brave German officer who had shared the fatigues and dangers of the arduous campaign which Wissmann was prosecuting with such well-deserved success against the Arab malcontents of German East Africa. . . . We dismounted at the door of the mess-house of the German officers, and were conducted upstairs to a long and broad veranda about forty-five by twenty-five feet, which had been converted into a palmy bower, gaily decorated with palm branches and German flags. Several round tables were spread, and on a wide buffet was arranged a sumptuous lunch, of which our appetites enabled us to

317

partake fearlessly; but dubious of the effects of champagne after such long abstinence, I diluted it largely with Sauerbrunn water. The Pasha was never gayer than on this afternoon when, surrounded by his friends and countrymen, he replied to their thousand eager questions respecting the life he had endured during his long exile in Africa. . . . At 7.30 p. m. there was a banquet. . . . We assembled in the palmy bower, thirty-four persons all told." There were present the captains of the German and the English warships, the padres from the missions, the officials of the German East Africa Company, the imperial commissary's staff, all assembled to greet Stanley and his companions as well as Emin Pasha. "The band of the 'Schwalbe' was in attendance to give éclat to what was a very superb affair for Bagamoyo."

The guests having assembled, Major Wissmann led the way to the long banqueting-hall, into which the central room of the house had been converted on the occasion. "While we were feasting within, the Zanzibaris—tireless creatures—were celebrating the close of a troublous period in a street just below the veranda, with animal energy, vented in active dance and hearty chorus." Stanley, though it all "appeared wonderful" to him, felt ill at ease; and his discomfort was intensified when a congratulatory telegram from Emperor William II was read, and when Wissmann proposed the health of the guests, which was drunk amid acclamations. Stanley replied drily, after his fashion, ending with the remark: "Emin is here, Casati is here, I and my friends are all here; wherefore we confess that we have a perfect and wholesome joy, in knowing that, for a season at least, the daily march and its fatigues are at an end."

Next came Emin's speech, "delivered," says Stanley, "with finished elocution—clear, distinct, and grammatical—and in a deep, resonant voice, so that it took the company with an agreeable surprise." Thereafter, the formalities being over, Emin looked supremely gay and happy, wandering from one end of the table to the other, exchanging cheerful remarks with various members of the company. After a time he disappeared, while Stanley was absorbed in listening to Wissmann's account of the events of the East Coast War. "Presently Sali, my boy-steward, came and whispered in my ear that the Pasha had fallen down, which I took to mean 'stumbled over a chair'; but, perceiving that I did not accept it as a serious incident, he added, 'He has fallen over the veranda wall into the street, and is dangerously hurt.'" Stanley hastened to the place where the accident had happened. There were two little pools of blood on the ground, but Emin had already been removed to the German hospital. In the banqueting-hall the news of the accident was kept from most of the guests, for it would have been a pity to interrupt the merry-making. Stanley, however, went at once to the hospital, and, at the door, met a German officer who, with uplifted hands, revealed the impressions gathered from his view of the unfortunate man. "Guided upstairs, I was shown to a bed surrounded by an anxious-looking group. On obtaining a view, I saw the Pasha's form half undressed extended on the bed, wet bandages passed over the right side of the head and the right eye. A corner of the wetted lint was lifted up, and I saw that the right eye was closed by a great lump formed by swollen tissues, and discovered that the lint was crimson with blood oozing from the ear. No one was able to give an exact account of how the accident happened, but the general impression seemed to be that the Pasha, who was half blind, and had been so for the last two years, had moved somewhat too brusquely towards the veranda, or balcony wall, of that 'palmy bower' wherein we had lunched, to look at the happy natives dancing in the moonlight, and, misjudging its height, had leaned over too suddenly and too far, and, unable to recover his balance, had toppled over. . . . He fell into the street some eighteen feet below. Had not a zinc shed, five feet below the balcony which shaded the sidewalk, broken the fall, the accident would no doubt have been fatal."

Two German naval surgeons, called in consultation next morning, decided that there had been a fracture of the base of the skull, and that the condition was dangerous, but not hopeless. In fact, he recovered—to be murdered not very long afterwards in another African journey.

In Stanley's view, the banquet, the champagne, the

exciting speeches, the sudden inroad of civilisation, were mainly responsible for the disaster. He writes bitterly: "To one like me, what are banquets? A crust of bread, a chop, and a cup of tea are a feast to one who, for the best part of twenty-three years, has not had the satisfaction of eating a shilling's worth of food a day. Receptions! They are the very honours I would wish to fly from, as I profess myself slow of speech, and nature has not fitted me with a disposition to enjoy them. Medals? I cannot wear them; the pleasure of looking at them is even denied me by my continual absence. What then? Nothing. No honour or reward, however great, can be equal to that subtle satisfaction that a man feels when he can point to his work and say, 'See, now, the task I promised you to perform with all loyalty and honesty, with might and main, to the utmost of my ability, and God willing, is to-day finished.' "

Here, in German East Africa, upon soil which had become German, he suddenly felt himself to be an Englishman, an Englishman whose national rights had been infringed; and what he took most amiss in Emin (for the very reason that he had long foreseen it) was the Pasha's determination to enter the German service. Before reaching Bagamoyo, when Emin himself had, perhaps, not yet entertained this design, Stanley said to him: "Within a short time, Pasha, you will be among your countrymen; but while you glow with pride and

321

pleasure at being once more among them, do not forget
that they were English people who first heard your cries
in the days of gloom; that it was English money which
enabled these young English gentlemen to rescue you
from Khartoum."

"Never; have no fear of that," replied the Pasha.

Yet he did forget. When it was an accomplished
fact, all that Stanley wrote was: "That he has ultimately
elected to serve Germany in preference to England appears perfectly natural, and yet the mere announcement
surprised some of his warmest and most disinterested
friends, among whom we may number ourselves." In the
end, it came to light that Emin, at the very time when
he was negotiating with the German Government, with
a view to entering its service, had replied to a cable
from the Khedive offering him a post in Cairo: "Hearty
thanks for your kind offer."—A man with no stability!

After Emin had parted from Stanley, the Pasha
gave vent to all the spleen, all the suppressed jealousy,
which had so long animated him in secret towards this
domineering Englishman who had violated his personality. It was as if he had at length been able to
throw down a burden. Perhaps the fall from the balcony
was symbolical in the psycho-analytical sense—self-
inflicted injury as a method of retaliation, such as is
sometimes practised by children. When, having crossed
to Zanzibar, Stanley sent his boy-steward Sali to Bagamoyo for news of the Pasha's health, the lad returned

322

"protesting that he had been threatened with a short shrift if he ever visited Bagamoyo again; and never message nor note did I receive from Emin, the late Governor of Equatoria."

That was Emin Pasha's gratitude!

CHAPTER TWELVE

UPSHOT

———————

"Now and then, athwart the memory, will glide spectres
of men cowering in the rainy gloom, shivering with cold,
gaunt and sad-eyed through hunger, disappearing in the
midst of the unknown; we shall hear the moans of dying
men, see the stark forms of the dead, and shrink again
with the hopelessness of our state. Then, like gleams of
fair morning, will rise to view the prospects of the grassland, the vistas of green bossy hills, the whirling swathes
of young grass waltzing merrily with the gale, the flying
lines of boscage darkening the hollows, the receding view
of uplifting and subsiding land-waves lengthening to the
distance where the mountains loom in faint image
through the undefined blue. Thought will wing itself
lighter than a swift, and soar in aerial flight over sere
plain, blue water, vivid green land, and silver lake, and
sail along the lengthy line of colossal mountain shoulders
turned towards the Semliki; and around the congregation
of white heads set in glory far above the Afric world,

and listening to the dripping waters as they tumble down around the winding curves of Ruwenzori, in sheaves of silver arrows, and speed through the impending rain-clouds, and the floating globes of white mist over unexplored abysses; through the eternal haze of Usangora, and up with a joyous leap into the cool atmosphere over Ankori and Karagwe, and straight away over three hundred leagues of pastoral plains and thin thorn forest, back again to marvel at the delightful azure of the Indian Ocean."

A rural elegy; a song of farewell.

Now comes a very different picture: "The fashionables of Cairo, staring at me every time I went out to take the air, made me uncommonly shy; they made me feel as if something must be radically wrong about me; and I was too disconcerted to pair with any of them, all at once. They had been sunning without interruption in the full blaze of social life, and I was too fresh from my three years' meditations in the wilds. If any of the hundreds I met chanced to think kindly of me at this period, it was certainly not because of any merit of mine, but because of their innate benevolence and amiable considerateness. I am inclined to think, however, that I made more enemies than friends, for it could scarcely be otherwise in an irreflective world. . . . Indeed, no African traveller ought to be judged during the first year of his return. . . . His nerves are not uniformly strung, his mind harks back to the strange scenes he has just left,

325

and cannot be focussed upon that which interests
Society. . . . A thousand scenes floated promiscuously
through my head, but when one came to my pen-point
it was a farrago of nonsense, incoherent, yet confusedly
intense. . . . My thoughts massed themselves into a huge
organ like that at the Crystal Palace, from which a master hand could invoke Handel's *Messiah* or Wagner's
Walküre, but which to me would only give deep dis-
cords."

Audiences of the Khedive and of King Leopold;
political conversations with one notable and another;
schemes for the suppression of the slave-trade; negotiations about African affairs; the fixing of the boundaries
of the Congo Free State; the colonisation of the regions
round Lake Albert; the gathering and transport of rubber; the building of saw-mills; the hasty, far too hasty,
writing of *In Darkest Africa;* lectures, receptions—how
infinitely tiresome it all was!

In the *Autobiography* he gives an amusing account
of a meeting with Gladstone, at which the "Grand Old
Man," quaint and obstinate as ever, would not, as
Stanley wished, discuss the slave-trade, but took exception to some of the geographical names chosen by the
explorer.

"When I came to Ruwenzori his eyes caught a
glimpse of two isolated peaks.

326

" 'Excuse me one minute,' said he; 'what are those two mountains called?'

" 'Those, sir,' I answered, 'are the Gordon Bennett and the Mackinnon peaks.'

" 'Who called them by those absurd names?' he asked, with the corrugation of a frown on his brow.

" 'I called them, sir.'

" 'By what right,' he demanded.

" 'By the right of first discovery, and those two gentlemen were the patrons of the expedition.'

" 'How can you say that when Herodotus spoke of them two thousand six hundred years ago and called them Crophi and Mophi? It is intolerable that classic names like these should be displaced by modern names.'

" 'I humbly beg your pardon, Mr. Gladstone, but Crophi and Mophi, if they ever existed at all, were situated over a thousand miles to the northward. Herodotus simply wrote from hearsay and—'

" 'Oh, I cannot stand that.'

" 'Well, Mr. Gladstone,' said I, 'will you assist me in this project of a railway to Uganda, for the suppression of the slave-trade, if I can arrange that "Crophi" and "Mophi" shall be substituted for "Gordon Bennett" and "Mackinnon"?'

" 'Oh, that will not do; that is flat bribery and corruption.' And smiling, he rose to his feet, buttoning his coat lest his virtue might yield to the temptation.

" 'Alas!' said I to myself, 'when England is ruled

327

by old men and children! My slave-trade discourse must be deferred, I see.' "

Like poisoned arrows from an ambush, the old accusations were still being fired at him. The most absurd of them was that on this Emin Pasha Relief Expedition he had deliberately employed slaves. He felt that it was beneath his dignity to defend himself, and yet to remain silent might imply an admission that the charge was true. A man in such circumstances cannot silence calumny, either by trying to cleanse himself of it or by contemptuously ignoring it. "Throw plenty of mud," says the old adage, "and some of it will stick." This charge that he had employed slaves, rankled. Continued ill-health was superadded to mental distress. "Stanley," writes his wife, "was continually being attacked by fever, and by internal pains, which came without warning, and with such intensity that breathing was impeded. . . . During the malarial attacks, the shivering that preceded the hot stage was so violent that the bed he lay on would shake, and the glasses on the table vibrate and ring. 'Africa is in me,' he would say when the fever raged."

In July, 1890, he had married Miss Dorothy Tennant. Stanley writes: "During my long bachelorhood, I have often wished that I had but one tiny child to love, but now, unexpectedly, as it seems to me, I possess a wife, my own wife!" The marriage appears to have been a very happy one. Lady Stanley (who remarried a few

328

years after Stanley's death) survived her first husband
by twenty-two years.

Soon after his marriage, Stanley stood for North
Lambeth as a Liberal Unionist. One gathers that his wife
and his friends had advised this step as the only possible
means of keeping him from returning to Africa (should
we not say "returning home to Africa"?). At the first
attempt he was defeated by a narrow majority, but was
elected three years later. During these three years of
probation, and subsequently, he travelled widely, sometimes alone, sometimes with his wife: to Switzerland, the
United States, Australia, New Zealand, Tasmania, etc.
In October, 1897, he went to South Africa in order to be
present at the opening of the Bulawayo railway. Meanwhile he had been given honorary degrees by the univer-
sities of Oxford, Cambridge, and Halle, and had been
made an honorary member of the most noted geographical societies of Europe. He read numerous scientific
works, wrote monographs, delivered speeches, sketched
a plan for the Uganda railway, and suffered the fate of
all who are growing old, in that death began to snatch
away his friends. Mackinnon died; Parke died; Alexander Bruce, Livingstone's son-in-law, died; Samuel
Butler died.

He felt out of his element in parliament. "I have,
as an M.P., less influence than the man in the street.
On questions concerning Africa, Dilke, or some other
wholly unacquainted with Africa, would be called upon

329

to speak before me. I have far less influence than any writer in a daily newspaper; for he can make his living presence in the world felt, and, possibly, have some influence for good; whereas I, in common with other respectable fellows, am but a dumb dog. . . . I am glad at the prospect of retiring, and being quit of it all." In November and December, 1898, he was on the look-out for a country house, visiting fifty-seven before he made his choice. He decided upon Furze Hill, at Pirbright, less than thirty miles from London, a fine estate, not very large, "just a house, gardens, a few fields, a wood, and a quiet lake, fed by a little stream."

His wife writes: "He took an ever-increasing delight in Furze Hill. He planned walks, threw bridges across streams, planted trees, built a little farm from his own designs, after reading every recent book on farm building, and in a very short time transformed the place." A strange evening, this, to an adventurous life. Bula Matari in Lilliput! The lake was called Stanley Pool; the little wood, the Aruwimi Forest; the stream was called the Congo. "To the fields," writes Dorothy Stanley, "I gave such African names as Unyamwezi, Mazamboni, Katunzi, Luwamberri, etc. One side of Stanley Pool is Umfwa; on the other, Kinchassa and Calino Point." In this year 1899, when Stanley settled at Furze Hill, he was made a G.C.B. What can such an honour have meant to him? Anyhow, the recognition came too late.

330

At the end of the *Autobiography* are published some "Thoughts from Notebooks." I quote the following:

"When a man returns home and finds for the moment nothing to struggle against, the vast resolve which has sustained him through a long and a difficult enterprise dies away, burning as it sinks in the heart; and thus the greatest successes are often accompanied by a peculiar melancholy."

"Civilisation never looks more lovely than when surrounded by barbarism; and yet, strange to say, barbarism never looks so inviting to me as when I am surrounded by civilization."

"It was owing to repeated attacks of the public and the Press that I lost the elastic hope of my youth, the hope and belief that toil, generosity, devotion to duty, righteous doing, would receive recognition at the hands of my fellow-creatures who had been more happily born, more fortunately endowed, more honoured by circumstances and fate than I. It required much control of natural waywardness to reform the shattered aspirations, for it seemed as though the years of patient watchfulness, the long periods of frugality, the painstaking self-teaching in lessons of manliness, had ended disastrously in failure. For what was my reward? Resolute devotion to an ideal of duty, framed after much self-exhortation to uprightness of conduct, and righteous dealing with my fellow-creatures, had terminated by my being proclaimed to all the world, first as a forger, and then as

331

a buccaneer, an adventurer, a fraud, an impostor. . . .
Spears in Africa were hurtful things, and so was the
calumny of the Press here; but I went on and did my
work, the work I was sent into the world to do. . . . A
man must not swerve from his path because of the bark-
ings of dogs."

Three glimpses of the character of Henry Morton
Stanley, to round off the story of his life. What they
especially disclose to us is that he was sore at heart
during these closing ten years, despite honourable recognition, domestic happiness, the affection of his wife, and
the company of a little son whom he adopted when he
stood almost at the edge of the tomb.

This shadow which could not be lifted from
Stanley's mind in the declining years was like the
shadow which lies across a wide landscape at sunset—
the outcome of great actions which were setting like the
sun. There is a rhythm of events, thanks to which a man,
having completed what he set out to do, lingers amid
the gestures of activity; he finds it hard to realise that
his day is over; in fantasy he still pursues the round of
active movement. He cannot accept repose; he does not
know that he is dreaming; the harmony formed by doing
and being eludes him. Need we be surprised, then, if
the world of things, of trodden pathways, of resolves, of
purposes, of external hardships, of triumphs, fades; if
he himself becomes no more than a surviving vestige
of his great deeds, the mere skeleton of that which he still

332

believes himself to be? Nineteen men out of twenty
(most of them, it is true, lesser men than this one, less
heroic, less conspicuous as examples) find themselves in
the same situation during the last phase of their career.
It is the tragedy of a lost balance, the fruit of a will
that is too strong for the personality to sustain it.

"Africa is in me." A profound saying, perhaps the
profoundest ever uttered by Stanley. We are told that in
the evenings, beside the fire in his library, he would describe his experiences in the African forest so vividly
that his hearers held their breath. "Never shall I forget
one late afternoon when Stanley, in the gathering darkness, told us the story of Gordon," wrote the American
novelist, Richard Harding Davis, to Lady Stanley.

It is Dorothy Stanley who records the following:
"A short time after my marriage, I went to tea with a
dear old friend. After talking of many things, my friend
suddenly put her hand impressively on mine and said,
'Would you mind my asking you a question, for somehow I can't help feeling—well—just a little troubled.
It may, in some mysterious way, have been deemed expedient; but why, oh why, did your husband order a
little black baby to be flung into the Congo?' The dear
good lady had tears in her eyes, as she adjured me to
explain! Indignation at first made me draw away from
her, but then the ridiculous absurdity of her story struck
me so forcibly that I began to laugh, and the more I
laughed the more pained and bewildered was my friend.

333

'You believe that story?' I asked. 'You could believe it?' 'Well,' she replied, 'I was told it, as a fact.' When I repeated it to Stanley, he smiled and threw out his hand. 'There, you see now why I am silent and reserved. Would you have me reply to such a charge?' And then he told me the story of the little black baby in Central Africa."

Let me give this story, and a second story about black babies. The first explains the innocent happenings that gave rise to the legend which had come to the old lady's ears. The second is a moving tale, the stuff out of which impressive myths grow.

The former is given in Stanley's own words: "As the expedition advanced, we generally found villages abandoned, scouts having warned the natives of our approach. The villagers, of course, were not very far off, and, as soon as the expedition had passed, they stole back to their huts and plantations. On one occasion, so great had been their haste, a black baby a few months old was left on the ground forgotten. They brought the little thing to me; it was just a gobbet of fat, with large innocent eyes. Holding the baby, I turned to my officers and said in chaff: 'Well, boys, what shall we do with it?' 'Oh, sir,' one wag cried, with a merry twinkle in his eye, 'throw it into the Congo!' Whereupon they all took up the chorus, 'Throw it, throw it, throw it into the Congo!' We were in high boyish spirits that day! I should rather have liked to take the baby on with me, and would have done so, had I thought it was abandoned; but I felt the mother was not far off, and might even then be watching us with beating heart, from behind a tree. So I ordered a fire to be kindled, as the infant was small and chilly, and I had a sort of cradle-nest scooped out of the earth before the fire, so that the little creature could be warm, sheltered, and in no danger of rolling in. I lined the concavity with cotton cloth as a gift to the mother, and when we quitted that encampment the baby was sleeping as snugly as if with its mother beside it, and I left them a good notion for cradles!"

The other story is told by Lady Stanley: "Many children were born during the march of the Emin Relief Expedition; at one time there were over forty babies in camp! The African mothers knew well that their little ones' safety lay with 'Bwana Kuba,' the 'Great Master.' When the expedition emerged from the forest, a report got about that the expedition was shortly to encounter a tribe of cannibals. That night Stanley retired to rest early, and soon fell asleep, for he was tired out. In the middle of the night he was awakened by a vague plaint, the cry, as he thought, of some wild animal, the wail was taken up by others, and soon the air was filled with cat-like miaouls. Much puzzled, Stanley stood up, and then he heard slappings and howlings. Thereupon he rose and strode out, to find forty or so infants, carefully rolled up and laid round his tent by the anxious mothers. Bula Matari, they said to themselves, would

335

never allow the dreadful cannibals to eat their little ones, so they agreed that the night nursery must be as close as possible to the Great Master's tent. This, however, had to be forbidden in future, as it made rest impossible."

Yes, Africa was in him, the huge forests, the numberless lakes, the mighty rivers and their cataracts, the gloomy morasses, the confused jungle, the fabulous beauty of the flowers, the majestic, snow-capped mountains, the vast plains of the grassland, the fever-stricken coast, the abundance of wild life, lions and snakes, elephants and gorillas, antelopes and giraffes (although, strangely enough, he writes little of the fauna, his thoughts being too anthropomorphic) and of the varied races of men who inhabit the wondrous continent, the thousands upon thousands of tribes, from the finely made Masai and Bantu to the misshapen pigmies, the dialects he had mastered, ranging from Swahili to Nyam-Nyam, the music of the native instruments, the horns and the drums—this was the world he carried with him in his mind, the world to which he really belonged. Europe-America was a heavy burden to him. He had come to recognise, prophetically as it were, the vanity, the falseness of that civilisation which for most of his youth and his manhood had seemed ideal to him; had grown aware that it was ripening towards decay. This warfare in his mind between his love of an ideal civilisation and his loathing of civilisation as it actually was,

HENRY M. STANLEY

rent his whole being in sunder, and he could only find rest from the unceasing inward conflict in a life of perpetual action.

In truth he was a stranger in Africa and a stranger in Europe-America. His life might well be entitled "The Life of a Stranger." Maybe his fellow-countrymen felt this. The feeling found expression after his death, when the Dean of Westminster refused to allow Stanley to be buried in Westminster Abbey. Lady Stanley, therefore, had her husband's body interred in the village churchyard at Pirbright, and had Dartmoor searched to find a suitable monolith for a tombstone. It weighed six tons, and bore the inscription "Henry Morton Stanley—Bula Matari—1841 to 1904—Africa."

It was on May 5, 1904, that he died, early in the morning; not at Furze Hill, but in London. When the hour sounded from Big Ben, Stanley opened his eyes and said: "What is that?" His wife told him that it was four o'clock striking. "Four o'clock?" he repeated slowly: "How strange! So that is Time! Strange!" A little later, when he was offered drink, he gently pushed away the cup and uttered his last word: "Enough."

BIBLIOGRAPHY

I. WORKS BY HENRY MORTON STANLEY

How I Found Livingstone. Sampson Low, London, 1872.

Coomassie and Magdala. Sampson Low, London, 1874.

Through the Dark Continent, 2 vols. Sampson Low, London, 1878.

The Congo and the Founding of its Free State, 2 vols. Sampson Low, London, 1885.

In Darkest Africa, 2 vols. Sampson Low, London, 1890.

My•Early Travels and Adventures, 2 vols. Sampson Low, London, 1895.

Autobiography, edited by his wife, Dorothy Stanley. Sampson Low, London, 109.

II. OTHER WORKS

Livingstone, David. *Missionary Travels and Researches in South Africa.* Murray, London, 1857.

Baker, Samuel White. *The Albert Nyanza,* 2 vols. Macmillan, London, 1866.

Marston, E. *After Work.* Heinemann, London, 1904.

Article on "Emin Pasha" in *Allgemeine Deutsche Biographie.*

INDEX

341

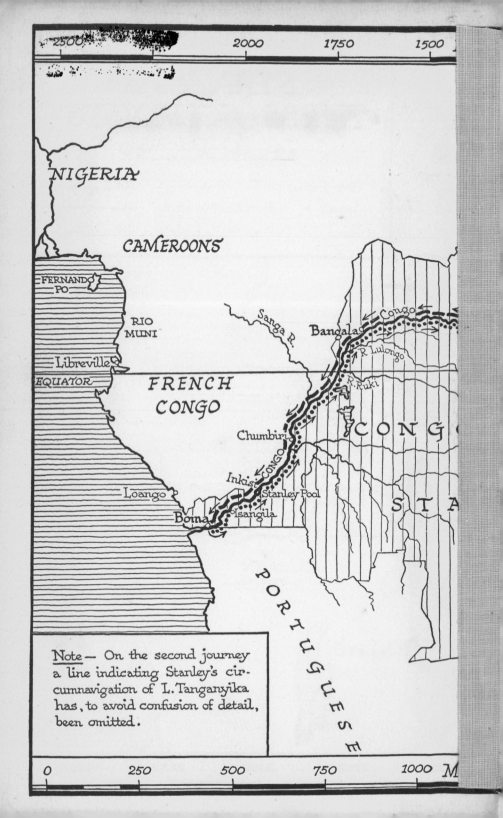

2300 2000 1750 1500

NIGERIA

CAMEROONS

FERNANDO
PO

RIO
MUNI

Libreville

EQUATOR

Loango

Boma

FRENCH
CONGO

Sanga R.

Bangalas

Chumbiri

Inkisi

Isangila

Stanley Pool

CONGO

R. Lulongo

R. Ruki

CONGO

STA

PORTUGUESE

Note — On the second journey
a line indicating Stanley's cir-
cumnavigation of L. Tanganyika
has, to avoid confusion of detail,
been omitted.

0   250   500   750   1000 M